"Reading this book is like spending five years studying at the knee of a wise partner at a successful consulting firm. Whether you own an IT services business or aspire to, this book delivers essential information to build your practice and your career."

—Paul Glen, author, *Healing Client Relationships* and *Leading Geeks: How to Manage and Lead People Who Deliver Technology*

"Running a successful IT services firm requires the unique insights and business fundamentals presented in this excellent consulting reference."

—Rudolf Melik, president and CEO, Tenrox, author, *Professional Services Automation*

"An in-depth and in-detail look at the world of IT consulting. Helpful information and advice, concisely presented and deeply valuable. Just the tool you need to build your IT consultancy!"

—Tim Sosbe, editorial director, *IT Contractor* magazine

"Rick's done it again! Just the right book at just the right time! Written by someone who's lived it and truly knows what it takes to build an IT consulting practice. Is your IT business facing new challenges? Want to grow your IT company? Thinking about starting your own IT consulting practice? Don't take another step without first buying this resource!"

—Elaine Biech, author, *The Business of Consulting* and *The Consultant's Quick Start Guide*

"*Building the IT Consulting Practice* is a great response for anyone starting, thinking of starting, or growing an IT consulting business. Companies from small regional to large global organizations will benefit from Rick's practical advice on all aspects of running an IT professional services business. The book is packed with specific suggestions and best practices for running a successful IT firm, and the distinctions that can make or break your success. The in-depth interviews provide insights and best practices from some of the most recognized IT consulting firms around."

—Suzanne Saxe, president, Advance Consulting Inc. and author, *The Consultative Approach*

Building the IT Consulting Practice

Rick Freedman

JOSSEY-BASS/PFEIFFER
A Wiley Imprint
www.pfeiffer.com

Published by Jossey-Bass/Pfeiffer
A Wiley Imprint
989 Market Street, San Francisco, CA 94103-1741 www.pfeiffer.com

Readers should be aware that Internet websites offered as citations and/or sources for further information may have changed or disappeared between when this was written and when it is read.

Jossey-Bass also publishes its books in a variety of electronic formats. Some content that appears in print may not be available in electronic books.

Acquiring Editor: Matthew Davis
Director of Development: Kathleen Dolan Davies
Developmental Editor: Susan Rachmeler
Editor: Rebecca Taff
Senior Production Editor: Dawn Kilgore
Manufacturing Supervisor: Becky Carreño
Illustrations: Lotus Art

ISBN: 0-7879-5515-9

Library of Congress Cataloging-in-Publication Data

Freedman, Rick.
Building the IT consulting practice / Rick Freedman.
p. cm.
Includes bibliographical references and index.
ISBN 0-7879-5515-9 (alk. paper)
1. Information resources management. 2. Information consultants. I. Title.
T58.64 .F73 2002
658.4'038—dc21
2002007170

Printing 10 9 8 7 6 5 4 3 2 1

For Leila

It has never been my object to record my dreams,
just the determination to realize them.

Man Ray, artist and photographer, 1890–1976

And for Terri

Let us be grateful to those who make us happy;
They are the gardeners who make our souls blossom.

Marcel Proust, French novelist, 1871-1922

CONTENTS

ACKNOWLEDGMENTS

Every book is a collaboration. I'd like to thank the following people for their invaluable contributions:

- Sharon Hemeon at Intel Solution Services. Trust and collaboration always get the best results, and learning is always a two-way exchange. Also Rick Echevarria, Charlie Emde, Mike Lischke, and Paul Edgecombe at Intel Solution Services for inviting me into their world.
- Tish Gill and Jonathan Heng at Compaq for allowing me to coach their team.
- Jim Clark and Barbara Dabbs at Swish Consulting for showing me that playing with TinkerToys is a valid consulting experience.
- Gayle Jones for giving me the chance to teach the great students at Johnson County Community College and the Center for Business and Technology.
- Paul Baldwin at TechRepublic for the opportunity to talk to the wide community of IT professionals.
- Faruk Capan and the team at InTouch Solutions.
- Atul Singh and the team at Teva NeuroScience.
- Tim Trabon, David Windhausen, and the team at Trabon Solutions.
- Larry Tanning and the team at Tanning Technology.
- Jeff Vilmek at Microsoft for his help.
- Ken Taormina at KPMG for taking the time.
- Andrew Bibby and David LaBar at Razorfish for their patience and cooperation.
- Malcolm Frank and Veronica Zanaletto at NerveWire for the kind assistance.

The field of professional services, once neglected and under-analyzed, has in the last decade attracted the attention of superb analysts and thinkers. A work like mine could not exist without the prior thought and contribution of the following authors:

- David Maister, the master;
- Elaine Biech, the mentor;
- Andrew Sobel, the philosopher; and
- Russ Dawson, the polymath.

Plus my friends:

- Matt Holt; I'll meet you at Nathan's!
- Paul Glen at C2 Consulting, the healer;
- Ron Bendian, the builder;
- The team at Jossey-Bass/Pfeiffer: Kathleen Dolan Davies, Susan Rachmeler, Dawn Kilgore, Samya Sattar, and Jin Im.

As always: Leila, Danny, Dalia, Shawn, Josh, Jeremy, Abby, Ellie, Katie, Mikey, Patrick, Joey, Emily, Miles, Dinah, Buddy.

PREFACE

Why do we need a book on building an IT consulting firm? The gurus of the professional services business, such as David Maister, Andrew Sobel, Mark C. Scott, and Russ Dawson, have done an excellent job of presenting the fundamental disciplines and philosophies of firm management. Any entrepreneur or manager in the IT consulting business who has not read and absorbed the works of these experts is missing an important piece of his or her business education. The IT consulting business has much in common with the law firms, accounting firms, and management consulting firms that these authors examine. We all bill our clients for furnishing specialized expertise. We all need to attract and retain the skilled subject-matter experts who provide these services. We all need to develop repeatable and consistent processes for delivering what is essentially a customized service, different in each engagement.

Still, there is a gap. The IT consulting practice has many elements that make it unique. From the extraordinary speed of technological change, to the singular personal characteristics of the individuals drawn to our business, to the intangible nature of the benefits we provide, the IT services business has enough distinctive traits to make an examination of the challenges of building and growing an IT consulting practice worthwhile.

The decade of the 1990s turned the IT services landscape upside down. The giant mainframe-focused firms have morphed into eBusiness partners. Due to increased scrutiny by the SEC and other regulatory agencies, many of the "Big Five" accountancies have divested themselves of their consulting practices to avoid any appearance of conflict of interest. So Ernst and Young's IT services organization has merged with Cap Gemini, and Andersen Consulting is now Accenture, a standalone entity about to make an initial public offering (IPO) of its stock. Many of the upstart PC-focused resellers, who seemed poised to challenge the big players due to their intimate knowledge of the new tools of corporate computing—the PC and the network—have instead gone away or been absorbed by other players, as illustrated by the recent acquisition of Entex by Siemens. The hordes of mid-size shops have not gone away, but there are now far more web-design boutiques than COBOL programming shops. The Internet boom of the late 1990s spawned a number of IT consulting firms that attempted to overthrow the rules of the consulting business, a handful to great success, but the majority to spectacular failure.

KEY ELEMENTS OF THE IT CONSULTING PRACTICE

With all of this change, what are the fundamental elements of the IT consulting practice? What questions and issues does the entrepreneur or manager need to answer and confront, whether she's starting up a web boutique or accepting a promotion to regional manager of a Big Five firm?

IT services firms have some unique concerns. The accelerating rate of change in both the content and the process of IT consulting is one of those concerns. As the technology changes, and entire new industry segments and areas of expertise pop up and become mainstream overnight, the managers of IT service firms face several decisions. Is this a technology with staying power that will have a lasting impact on our business, or is it a momentary fad that will fade? Should I be investing resources in developing these capabilities, or should I stick to my current portfolio of offerings? What are the competitive implications of standing pat or of making the investment? How will I keep my staff current while still trying to utilize their time to generate billable revenues? This last point is especially challenging and is often a pivot point of significant dispute in the services business. Many IT consultants take to contracting specifically because they relish the opportunity to learn new technologies and test their mettle against new challenges. On the other hand, the firm manager has business results to deliver and must weigh any new technical direction against the desires of the marketplace and the potential for profit. At this axis, many retention and consultant satisfaction problems emerge.

The recruiting, retention, and management of talented IT technical staff is one of the most challenging issues that firm managers must face. Without resorting to the stereotypical language of geeks and nerds, it's nonetheless an accepted fact that IT technologists are a unique breed with special management needs. Watts Humphrey, one of the gurus of technical management, in his landmark book *Managing Technical People,*[1] makes a simple but vital comment when he says, "Engineers share a basic drive to accomplish something they can point to as their own unique achievement. The best engineers and scientists don't work for a company, university, or laboratory; they work for themselves." And Richard Florida, founder and director of Carnegie Mellon University's Industry Center and a leading researcher of the needs of high-tech workers, recently told *Contract Professional* magazine[2] that

> "Creative high-tech talent is part of a global class that comes in all nationalities, ethnicities, genders, and sexuality. Creative, talented people want creative, funky neighborhoods. They want brew pubs and outdoor cafes. They want places to bike, rollerblade, walk the dog, play with their kids. They want vibrant neighborhoods for everyday living. They want visual and auditory energy. They want a lively music scene. They want to see people having fun, to see visual evidence that this is a city they can have a blast in."

These quality-of-life issues are critical to the IT services manager today in a way they never were before. Add to these special needs the requirement for training, for ever-evolving technical challenges, and for participatory management styles, and it's clear that the human asset component of IT professional services is enough to tax the management skills of the world's best and brightest leaders. We'll spend a significant amount of time on these unique challenges in this book.

The intangible nature of the business benefits our services create for clients is another factor in this complicated mix. Services, whether IT related or not, are by their nature ambiguous and hard to measure. How can a layman judge whether he's received the best value for dollars spent on legal, accounting, or medical services, when it's the layman's very lack of expertise that compels him to seek out professional assistance in the first place? At least with those services, however, we can tell by the outcome whether the services were delivered with quality. Did we win the court case, survive the audit, or make it through that bout with pneumonia? While we may not be in the best position to judge whether we received the optimum care and value, we can at least tell whether we succeeded or failed. In IT, the measurement of benefits has been a subject of controversy, and even ridicule.

Nobel Prize winning economist Robert Solow has stated with scorn that computers show up everywhere but in the productivity statistics.[3] The respected British business publication *The Economist* has stated that "Organizations would have done better to have invested that same capital [that was spent on IT] in almost any other part of their business."[4] With all this skepticism about the advantages of IT to the business, IT firms have an additional burden that other professionals do not; not only must we deliver quality services, we must also justify their benefit and assist our clients in devising measurements and benchmarks to prove that these services have a meaningful impact.

Entrepreneurs, managers, and consultants who wish to build a practice around the delivery of IT services must develop strong, competitive strategies for the basic components of management, sales, and delivery that any professional services firm must address, and they must deal with the added complexity of the elements we've just outlined. Why would anyone take on this enormous and difficult undertaking? Because, as Watts Humphrey stated, we want something we can point to with pride, and, despite the ambiguity of measuring IT benefits, we know that by delivering quality IT services we can make a difference and have an impact.

The first twenty years of my IT career were spent learning the hard lessons that only the competitive marketplace can teach. My humble attempt to codify and structure those lessons led to the publication of my first book, *The IT Consultant.* Since then, as a consultant and advisor to IT services firms, I've had the unique opportunity to peek into the practices of IT consulting companies around the globe. I've seen the consulting business from both sides, as client and practitioner, an experience that taught me some valuable lessons about the consultant-to-client relationship.

As a client, I've seen the good, bad, and ugly of IT services firms, and I've learned how important a robust methodology, solid individual skills, and an enduring client focus are. As a client, I want to know that my consulting partner has a proven process that fosters success, and that the firm approaches all elements of the relationship with professionalism. I want to see a roster of reference sites that indicates that my consulting partner leaves every engagement with a satisfied customer, after delivering an IT solution that provides quantifiable business results. I want a lot more than just a bunch of good technicians; I want a qualified partner and an entire experience that assures me that I'll achieve the results I expect.

As both a consultant and a manager of consulting firms, I've experienced first-hand the difficulties of running an IT services firm. Clients become more sophisticated and demanding every day. The technology changes so quickly that just keeping pace is a full-time job. The difficulty of attracting, recruiting, and retaining the skilled practitioners you need to deliver services is a constant challenge. Building sales teams that can engage with the client in a consultative manner, articulate the benefits of the technology, and sell your approach and your organization in the face of extreme competition is another management ordeal. Utilization, billing rates, training, leverage, consultant development, vendor relationships—all of these elements conspire to make managing an IT services firm one of the hardest jobs I've ever tackled.

PRINCIPLES FOR IT CONSULTING

As an advisor to consulting firms, I've had the opportunity to walk into IT consultancies with robust methodologies and also to work with those that, due to lack of process and methodology, invent every solution and every engagement anew and make up their project process as they go along. I've spent the last few years working with both established firms and startups as they struggle to develop processes that guarantee quality and strategies that ensure marketplace acceptance. Most importantly, I've seen both the IT landscape and the consulting business go through revolution after revolution, each more dislocating and unpredictable than the last. Through all of these changes, I've learned a few simple principles that will form the basis of this book.

The first principle is that consulting businesses have the same fundamental concerns as any other business. They must deliver with quality those products and services that the marketplace values. They must make the best use of scarce resources. They must turn a profit. These concepts may seem fundamental, but some of the recent boom-and-bust flameouts in the eConsultancy sector of our business indicate that, obvious or not, some of these principles were disrespected, and those guilty of ignoring them have paid the price. In order to ensure that we have a common understanding of the fundamental underpinnings of the IT consulting business, I'll begin this book with a section on the foundation disciplines and practices that managers and entrepreneurs must understand in order to build and sustain a practice.

It's not contradictory to also state that consulting is different from other businesses. Unlike the production line or the retail shop, our product is new every time, because every consultant, every engagement, every client relationship, and every business situation is unique. This element of the consulting profession makes the work of the consulting manager highly complex. We must build and enforce a method of practice, without which we would face anarchy. At the same time we must be flexible enough to adapt to the differing circumstances of each new project. The development of a flexible yet disciplined engagement process is no trivial task. My work as an advisor to IT services firms has taught me that no off-the-shelf methodology can solve this problem, since every firm has a different culture, a different management team with different needs, a different target market, and a different need for both rigor and adaptability in its processes. Those firms that have developed robust methodologies often use them to differentiate themselves in the marketplace, but, as the newly deceased eConsultancies of the world can testify, they're no guarantee.

We also need to make some fundamental decisions about the practice structure we'll employ and the target market we'll attack. Will we focus on "break/fix" services, outsourcing, tech-for-hire "body shop" work, project ownership, or strategic consulting—or will we follow the new "agency" model that integrates branding, marketing, and design advice with technology expertise? Will we focus on a vertical marketplace, such as health-care or financial services, or will we target a broad horizontal marketplace? Will we build our practice based on an efficiency model, doing the same kind of engagement over and over until we develop best practices that allow us to implement quickly and economically, or will we build an expertise practice, in which we apply our special knowledge to tough business problems and develop innovative solutions? Each of these decisions will have profound and enduring implications for the success of our endeavors.

We also must judge and appraise our teams not only on their subject-matter skills, but also on their human interaction capabilities, their advisory skills, their professionalism, and their maturity. The individual consultant, after all, is the product, and as such must incorporate the values and techniques the firm preaches and markets. The challenge of finding, recruiting, training, and retaining the mature and professional practitioners we need is one of the defining characteristics of the IT services business.

WHO SHOULD READ THIS BOOK?

This book will be of interest, I believe, to both practicing consultants and their managers. Consultants need to understand the business issues and competitive pressures that face the firm every day, so they can understand how their personal efforts and achievements add (or detract) from the goals and objectives of the firm.

They need to have a grasp of the wide range of decisions, from target market to sales approach to technical specialization that their management teams grapple with. I'm a strong believer in "open-book management," but opening the books is meaningless if team members don't have the basic business understanding to interpret what they're seeing.

For entrepreneurs and managers in the IT services business, I hope to lay out a clear framework for understanding the decision points they need to address and the decision criteria they need to consider in order to make the choices that will guide them to a prosperous future. From the challenges of recruiting, to the trials of competitive selling, to the difficulty of delivering quality services, I hope to relate my experience and my observations in a way that consulting managers can use as a touchstone in their own struggles to build a successful firm.

Finally, clients of the consulting firm will benefit, I hope, from understanding the fundamental concerns that both practitioners and managers must confront every day. I hope that those IT managers and other potential customers of IT services will gain some valuable insight into our business from this work and that that knowledge will empower them to make better purchasing and partnering decisions.

I hope I've illustrated that building and sustaining an IT consulting practice is a complex and challenging mission, requiring serious strategic planning and rigorous decision making. I also hope to make clear throughout this book my belief that it can be an extraordinarily rewarding undertaking as well, both financially and personally. Some of the most creative, motivated, skilled, and dedicated individuals I've met have been the consultants and entrepreneurs I've advised and partnered with in this business. I hope to offer here a set of guidelines, based on the lessons I've learned and the hard knocks I've experienced, to those who decide to build IT service firms that guide clients to sustainable competitive advantage through IT.

End Notes

1. Humphrey, W. *Managing Technical People,* Reading, MA: Addison-Wesley, 1997.
2. Teuke, M.R. What's Hot about Hotspots? *Contract Professional,* May 2001.
3. Solow, R. Review of *Manufacturing Matters* by Cohen and Zysman. *New York Review of Books,* July 12, 1987.
4. IT Investment. *The Economist,* August 24, 1991.

chapter ONE

What Is the IT Consulting Business?

THE SIZE AND SHAPE OF THE BUSINESS

In 1943, Thomas Watson, Sr., the patriarch of the International Business Machines Corporation, made one of the most wrongheaded predictions in business history. "I think there is a world market," said Mr. Watson, "for maybe five computers."[1] As with all unprecedented developments, the computer's path to value and profit was not obvious. It took Watson's son, Thomas Watson, Jr., to see the potential of the computer as a business device, and, over his father's vigorous opposition, to transform the former Computing-Tabulating-Recording Company into IBM, the giant that stood astride the computing universe for decades.

Now, half a century later, what is the state of the information technology industry, especially the services portion in which we are interested? According to a report by the respected investment analysis firm Cherry Tree & Company, the IT industry accounted for 13 percent of the total U.S. gross domestic product in 1996.[2] That percentage translated to about a trillion dollars in revenue that year, and that amount has grown significantly since then. Information technology today is a larger industry than healthcare in the United States. That's a far cry from Mr. Watson's five computers!

Of course, for those of us in the IT services industry, it's great that the use of computer hardware and software is huge and growing. Rather than looking at the entire IT universe, however, it will be more instructive for us to take a targeted peek at the results in the services segment. IT services, according to the Cherry Tree report, generated $545 billion in 1996, and made up 7 percent of the total domestic product that year. Cherry Tree dissected our industry a bit further by categorizing the types of services that IT firms provide, as follows:

- Project based services such as IT consulting, systems integration, and project management;
- Operations management services such as IT hardware and software management, and business process management (for example, call center operation), network management, and IT staffing and recruiting services;
- Maintenance services such as hardware repair and maintenance and software maintenance;
- Support and training services for IT personnel and end users; and
- Business process utility services, such as credit card processing, payroll services, and order fulfillment.

If we examine this report further, we can get a flavor for the size and scope of these IT service business segments. Looking only at publicly traded companies, Cherry Tree represents the 1996 earnings for these segments in Table 1.1.

Table 1.1. IT Service Business Segment Earnings

Sectors	# of Firms	Revenues (Millions)	Market Value (Millions)
Project-Based (Project Mgmt. & System Integration)	26	$5,618	$20,829
Project-Based (Software & Installation)	15	15,436	63,573
Operations Management (Hardware & Software Mgmt.)	11	26,238	33,698
Operations Management (Staffers)	16	16,555	12,713
Support & Training	4	591	3,678
Business Process Utilities	12	17,718	59,463
Other	3	19,840	34,666
Totals	87	101,996	228,619

Source: "IT Services: Emerging Investment Sector" by Cherry Tree & Company © 1998. Used by permission.

As a great number of firms are privately held, it seems clear that these numbers are but a fraction of the total activity in our field. The $21 billion generated in the project-based segment was earned by just forty-one firms! Anyone in this business knows that there are hundreds and perhaps thousands of smaller, local firms that offer these services, whose revenues didn't make it to this analysis. Nonetheless, these numbers are impressive. It should be clear that, with over $100 billion dollars of revenue, and with over $228 billion in market value, the IT services business is healthy and displays the revenue potential to attract ambitious entrepreneurs.

One interesting statistic that emerges from Cherry Tree's findings is their contention that 79 percent of all IT services are performed by *internal* IT organizations.[3] As most IT services firms have discovered, the internal IT team is often our most potent competitor! The flip side to this statistic is the clear message that, as more companies accept the concept of IT as a utility rather than a core competency, there is a tremendous potential for growth in our business. Growth in the IT services sector averaged 12 percent through 2001, as compared to average GDP growth of about 5 percent. Interestingly, this figure works out to account for almost 20 percent of all economic growth in the United States during that period. As evidenced by the major economic dislocations caused by the downturn in technology spending in late 2000 and early 2001, IT has become the main engine of growth in the U.S. economy. When IT sneezes, the overall economy catches pneumonia.

If we look at the individual segments a bit more closely, we can see that certain components of the IT services business have even brighter growth prospects. According to this report, the consulting and project segments of the business will sustain growth of over 14.5 percent, and Internet/intranet services will grow at over 100 percent. While the bursting of the Internet bubble will likely put a crimp in these projections, it's nonetheless clear that there is real opportunity here for those who can come to market with a competitive advantage.

These types of aggregate financial projections are interesting for the investor and industry commentator, but what do they tell those of us who need to build and run IT services firms? There are, in fact, other reports and surveys that may be better able to help us gain the knowledge and make the critical decisions that will determine our success in the marketplace. Rather than looking at these collective industry numbers, let's now examine a report that takes a more close-up look at the IT services activity in a particular region.

THE RANGE OF SERVICE POSSIBILITIES

In 1999, the Information Technology Association of America commissioned Purdue University and the consulting firm of Sina & Royce to perform a survey of IT consulting firms in the Chicago area.[4] This survey was done to fill a gap in the publicly available information about the IT services business. As we saw in the Cherry Tree report, the performance of the large firms are all on the record. These firms are publicly traded and so must report to the SEC and the investment community regularly. Their business strategies, their successes, and their challenges are regularly scrutinized by the business press. The next tier of firms—from the "two guys in a garage" programming shops to the vertically focused middle-market firms—are much less visible. What are their strategies for differentiating themselves? How do they go to market? How do they turn a profit? Are there any discernable trends or traits that can help us understand these mid-market players?

The ITAA study set out to examine middle-tier IT services firms in the Chicago metropolitan area. Chicago was selected as a representative city. By searching the web, and sorting through associations, mailing lists, and the Yellow Pages, the survey team was able to identify 430 firms in the Chicago metropolitan area that fit their definition of an IT services firm. The study team gathered extensive market evidence about middle-tier IT consulting firms, asking questions about sales and marketing effectiveness, about recruiting and retaining talented IT teams, and about the services and products they sell. Additionally, they conducted in-depth interviews with executives of fifty-five of these firms. The study team then analyzed the results of these surveys and interviews and prepared some overall findings about firm performance, sales effectiveness, services development, employee dynamics, and future directions.

This study produced some very illuminating results. The team's definition of what constitutes an IT services firm was itself interesting. The team determined that any professional services firm that expressed an "interest in IT as part of its service delivery" model was an IT services firm! This broad criterion illustrates the difficulty of deciding exactly who fits in our industry. The criterion for firm size was similarly broad—any firm with more than twenty and fewer than one thousand consultants was included. The study team also devised a scheme for segmenting the firms it surveyed. Rather than grouping firms by the type of technology they address or the markets they target, they categorized them by their size and by the maturity of their delivery processes. They formulated three categories: *small practitioners, boutique specialists,* and *emerging expansionists.* In the small practitioners category they put firms with an average workforce of about thirty consultants. These firms, they found, typically had informal and flexible project processes and competed based on their customer intimacy. Boutique specialist firms were found to compete based on deep, single-technology expertise, to be more likely to have some established standards and processes, and typically had about seventy consultants delivering services to clients. Finally, the emerging expansionists were typically multi-location shops running multiple lines of practice, and they had developed beyond process toward structured methodologies. They usually had more than one hundred consultants on staff.

Once we go beyond these surface categories, however, the picture becomes more complex. The firms surveyed displayed many different organizational models. Some were wholly owned subsidiaries of larger consulting firms. Some were publicly traded entities. Some were partnerships. Many were privately held corporations. When asked how they developed new business, some replied that that was the responsibility of the partners. Some had a "rainmaker" model, in which specific partners or executives focused exclusively on business development. Some had dedicated sales teams. Some relied on alliances with vendors to generate new business. Many used combinations of these business generation models.

The complexity extended beyond the organizational issues. When polled about specific problems and concerns, the responses indicated that these firms were struggling to construct winning business models. Only 60 percent said that they were effective at generating growth in their businesses. Less than 15 percent rated themselves "excellent" at marketing, and only 23 percent said they were meeting their marketing objectives. Only a third of respondents said their sales efforts were as good as their competitors were, and 20 percent still used price as their main differentiator in the sales cycle. Seventy-one percent said that their use of alliances and partnerships to drive sales needed to improve. Half said they couldn't recruit the technical staff they needed, and 45 percent said once they recruited them they couldn't keep them. Forty percent said that they had doubts about the profitability of their relationships with some of their clients, and the same number expressed concerns about the profit potential of one of their lines of business.

The results of this survey illustrate some of the key concepts we'll explore in this book. The IT consulting firm is different from other professional services firms.

The structure, organization, and processes in the legal profession, the medical office, or the accounting firm are fairly well-established. Not so in IT consulting. The simple act of finding and hiring staff offers challenges in our business that have no corollary in these other types of professional firms. Methods for marketing and delivering our services are still being defined. Management practices are being invented as we go along, and many managers aren't clear about the measurements that should be applied. In short, this survey, and my experience working with IT services firms, indicate that there are still a lot of open questions about the most effective ways to build and sustain an IT consulting firm.

Based on my experience and a careful review of analysis regarding the IT services business, I would segment our business into three categories:

- Outsourced IT Services;
- Consulting and System Integration; and
- Custom Application Development.

These categories are not the only dividing lines in the IT services business, of course. Like the larger professional service firm universe in which they live, IT services firms are positioned all along a spectrum from the large global firms that provide a complete range of services to clients across industries and regions, to the small local technical specialists providing highly targeted services to a specific industry. There's an old adage in the professional services industry, "Big firms like to work with big firms." This is true not only because of the perceived cultural fit between large corporate entities, but also because there is a clear economy of scale in working with a firm that can create and implement global IT strategies appropriate to a global enterprise. These economies of scale accrue mostly on the client side, however, as the global enterprise still must be serviced from local offices, with the accompanying costs and resource utilization. Still, despite the lack of compelling economies of scale for the service firm, the marketing message of working with one firm globally for all your IT service needs, the so-called "one-stop shop" approach, with the reduction in management bandwidth for the client that this implies, creates a distinct competitive advantage that small firms struggle to overcome. This is one reason why many smaller firms decide that, even though the Fortune 500 is "where the money is," the costs of competing in these firms make them an unattractive target.

At the other end of the spectrum are the local boutique shops that specialize in one particular business model, technology, or industry. Specialists by business model include those firms that have decided that their best competitive advantage lies in offering hardware maintenance contracts, for instance, or website development. These firms attempt to build a defensible competitive niche by focusing on a piece of their clients' overall IT needs and striving to fill those needs at the best value. Technology specialists focus on a particular technical area, from database design to customer relationship management software implementation, and develop depth of experience and expertise in that area in order to compete. Vertical industry specialists target a specific industry, from healthcare to restaurant management, and continuously improve their expertise in the application of IT to that industry's needs, building superior domain expertise as their competitive advantage. Obviously, many winning business models in IT services are a hybrid of these approaches, such as the Microsoft-focused healthcare application development house. I present this spectrum as a model to help guide our conversation.

So we've seen that there is a wide range of possible business models in the IT services industry and just as broad a variety of sizes and market focuses. Now that we've named and defined the business models that make up our industry, let's go back to our original intent. How does knowing these categories help the entrepreneur and manager build an IT consulting practice? Obviously, the firm leaders need to make decisions about where their core competencies lie, and where they wish to compete.

Outsourced IT Services

The Outsourcing Institute, a trade association that focuses on providing information and an online community for those in the outsourcing sector, publishes an annual industry overview entitled "The Outsourcing Index."[5] The Outsourcing Institute collaborates with Dun & Bradstreet to measure and evaluate the current state of the industry and to project future directions and trends in the growth of the outsourcing market. The most recent Outsourcing Index contains some illuminating data about corporate acceptance of IT outsourcing and the challenges and opportunities facing those of us who decide to target this marketplace. For firms in the IT consulting industry, one statistic stands out: over 20 percent of all outsourcing dollars are spent on IT outsourcing. In an overall outsourcing market that has expanded from $150 billion in 1997 to almost $400 billion in 2001, 20 percent represents a huge opportunity. Another important finding of the Outsourcing Institute's Index is that of those firms that are not currently outsourcing IT functions, over 18 percent are actively considering it. This augurs well for continued growth in this marketplace, even in the tough economic times that IT is experiencing after the bursting of the Internet bubble.

Before we dig deeper into the current state and future potential of the IT outsourcing business, let's define this business in a bit more detail. In a landmark study entitled "Information Systems Outsourcing: Myths, Metaphors, and Realities,"[6] the authors performed a rigorous academic study of IT outsourcing by reviewing and analyzing a representative sample of outsourcing deals in various industries and came to some interesting conclusions. For background, they divided IT outsourcing into three categories:

- *Body Shop:* using contract IT personnel to meet short-term demands;
- *Project Management:* outsourcing specific projects to external IT providers and transferring the responsibility for the outcome of the project to the outsourced provider; and
- *Total Outsourcing:* putting the external vendor in total charge of a significant piece of IT work. This includes total data center outsourcing and the associated hardware and software support.

To these categories, devised in the early 1990s, we should add some newer categories:

- *Application and Infrastructure Outsourcing:* services that utilize the standard protocols and interfaces of the Internet to contractually hand off responsibility for deploying and managing applications or IT infrastructure to an external provider; and
- *Selective Outsourcing:* in which IT departments divide their IT services into those that they determine can be outsourced and those they wish to retain in-house. Examples of this are the outsourcing of desktop support, network management, or IT help desk services. In the ever-evolving jargon of the outsourcing business, this is sometimes referred to as "out-tasking."

Across the spectrum of IT outsourcing business models, from body shop to ASP, the underlying business logic is the same. The argument is that IT outsourcers can reduce costs because IT is a commodity, a utility that is subject to economies of scale. From the economies of recruiting, retaining, and developing multiple IT resources in a body shop environment, to the economies of serving generic business applications to multiple clients from one IT infrastructure, the concept of deriving economies and so delivering IT services to clients more cost-effectively is the central driver of the outsourced model. This underlying model has undergone extreme change in the last few years, as the advent of the Internet and its standardized protocols and interfaces has created new opportunities to "virtualize" the IT department.

According to the 1993 IT outsourcing study, organizations surveyed decided to outsource their IT functions primarily for cost reasons. Some of the momentum that has driven the outsourcing industry in the past decade can be attributed to the claims for cost/benefits that have been publicized in this study and other publications. Consider, for instance, just a couple of the many results quoted in this study:

- American Standard Corporation claimed to have saved 40 percent of their overall IT costs by outsourcing their data operations; and
- Hibernia National Bank projected savings of up to $100 million from their outsourcing arrangement with IBM.[7]

Another factor cited in the drive toward outsourcing is the desire to gain access to IT skills, talent, and expertise that may be difficult to obtain in the job market. As stated by Kathy Hudson, Eastman Kodak's former CIO, who is credited with starting the IT outsourcing trend with Kodak's landmark deal with IBM, DEC, and BusinessLand, "If you're a really good technical person, do you think you'll have a better career at a photography company or a computer company?"[8] This access to the best talent in the IT talent pool is one of the key sales messages of the outsourcers. I've been along on many outsourcing sales calls in which the primary message was "We can offer technicians a better career path, more development, more diversity of assignments, so we get the best and the brightest." As the IT shortage of the late 1990s is replaced by an IT glut, as seems to be happening, this argument may lose some of its impact.

As we've noted, the Outsourcing Index report for 2000 shows some impressive growth, growing from $290 billion to over $340 billion in total revenue in the most recent year alone. Of course, this represents all outsourcing, not just IT, but even our 20 percent slice ain't peanuts. Our percentage is even larger when you consider that this report separates customer service and grants it an additional 7 percent of the market, and some component of that is related to IT help desks and call centers. The Outsourcing Institute projected an 18 percent growth rate for IT outsourcing in 2001. Their report found that 29 percent of companies with revenues over $10 million outsource some of their functions, as do 36 percent of larger companies with revenues over $50 million. It's also interesting to note that, according to the OI report, 10 percent of all outsourcing expenditures are occurring overseas, often in international departments of U.S. companies. This is another indication of growth potential in the outsourcing market.

We've noted a couple of reasons why businesses might decide to consider outsourcing. Let's look at the entire list presented by the Outsourcing Institute, to get a more complete picture of the outsourcing decision process. According to the OI, the top ten reasons that companies outsource are as follows:

1. Reduce and control operating costs;
2. Improve company focus;
3. Access to world-class capabilities;
4. Free resources for other purposes;
5. Resources not available internally;
6. Accelerate reengineering benefits;
7. Function difficult to manage or out of control;
8. Share risks;
9. Make capital funds available; and
10. Cash infusion.

Apart from the oft-repeated claims of reduced costs and access to enhanced capabilities, many companies are now looking at outsourcing as a way to improve company focus, often articulated as the desire to "stick to our knitting" and focus on the core competencies that provide competitive advantage and allow other providers to take care of non-core functions. This indicates that some clients are beginning to see outsourcing as a strategic, as opposed to a purely tactical, decision. By considering core competency and "unique value proposition" issues, clients are acknowledging that, as the outsourcers have often claimed, there are certain functions within IT that are more of a utility than a real competitive competency. This acknowledgement is an important step in the migration of outsourcing to a higher perception of added value. This migration requires us, as IT service providers, to migrate from the "body shop" mode of merely bringing commodity services to the table. We're now expected to have a strategic value conversation with our prospects, rather than an "I have great engineers cheap!" conversation.

Another important element outsourcers should notice about this list are the references to risk and manageability. As noted in items 7 and 8 of the above list, many clients want to outsource their most difficult and intractable functions to external suppliers, and they expect those providers to take on the risks associated with managing those challenging tasks. IT services firms that decide to enter the outsourcing arena must recognize that, because clients want to get rid of the headaches and negative exposure associated with problem functions, outsourcers must have a solid, disciplined approach to risk management. In short, we must make sure, with every engagement we undertake, that we understand how much risk the client is trying to shift to us and match that to profits and benefits of the relationship, in order to calculate the amount of risk we're willing to take on. I've seen many outsourcing arrangements turn into strained marriages, with tense meetings across the table every day, as the outsourcing service provider realizes the true extent of the problems and risks that have been shifted to them, and the client realizes that just dropping a function into an outsourcer's lap does not automatically solve longstanding manageability problems.

It's important to note some of the downside arguments, to balance the rosy growth and customer acceptance scenarios we've discussed so far. The evolution of the outsourcing business from the pure commodity supplier of IT "bodies" to the provider of strategic infrastructure and application services has not been without its casualties. The rise and fall of the application service provider (ASP) marketplace provides a persuasive case study of the hazards of the outsourced IT services market. In 1999, IT analyst IDC predicted a worldwide ASP market worth $16 billion in 2002, and Forrester, another respected IT analysis firm, expected $21 billion by 2001. Dataquest forecast that the worldwide ASP market would reach $22.7 billion by 2003. In reality, the total ASP market accounted for a comparatively paltry $300 million in 1999, and by 2000 some of the largest entrants, such as the SAP/Intel joint venture Pandesic, were calling it quits, and others, such as USInternetworking, were losing hundreds of millions of dollars. IDC has since scaled its 2002 revenue estimate for the ASP industry back to $2.4 billion. The Gartner Group has predicted that of the five hundred ASPs spun up in the last few years, only about sixty will remain by 2002. According to some Silicon Valley wise guys, the acronym "ASP" now stands for "Anyone Still Paying?"

From the beginning, there were doubters of the ASP gospel, citing the difficulty of the "one-app-fits-all" idea and the challenge of differentiating an "apps-on-tap" business. Security concerns, the need for customized applications, and the difficulty of making a profit in an expensive, service-intensive business—all of these factors bolstered ASP nonbelievers. The demise of their dot.com customers was another confirmation of the ASPs' vulnerability. Many ASPs saw huge revenue projections dissipate as their startup clients ran out of money and blew away. Pandesic, in its swan song, hit on the crux of the ASPs' difficulties; they cited "slower than anticipated market acceptance" and "no path to profitability." That deadly combination, combined with the gloomy environment that followed the bursting of the Internet bubble, has created an aura of skepticism around the ASP concept.

Still, many investors, analysts, and entrepreneurs believe that, as in many areas of the Internet, some unique and valuable companies will eventually crawl from the wreckage of the ASP market. In a perceptive report published by investment analysis firm Cherry Tree,[9] the lessons learned from the ASP rookie years are clearly stated: "Today, the proposition of merely offering hosted applications does not pull much weight with customers, analysts, or investors." The report goes on to state that "The companies that are building sustainable ASP business models are offering far more than hosted applications. Additional value-added components need to be offered in order to build long-term, strategic relationships with customers."

It's clear that there are no slam-dunks in the complex enterprise of outsourcing. I can attest from personal experience managing outsourced service relationships that they are very intimate, in that the client lets you into the inner workings of their business, and that intimacy can quickly lead to extreme strain if expectations are not met or unforeseen issues arise. Although there are clearly tremendous opportunities in this market space, there are also significant risks and uncertainties, as the demise of highly funded, "can't miss" ventures like Pandesic illustrate.[10]

Consulting and System Integration

The outsourcing business, as we've just explored, is all about economies of scale and process improvement, about streamlining and optimizing back-office functions and applying proven practices to operational activities. The consulting business, even though it's often lumped in with outsourcing as an IT service, couldn't be more different. Outsourcing is about doing repetitive and similar work more efficiently, while consulting is about seeing the unique and different circumstances and opportunities within each client. World class outsourcers try to see the similarities in every organization's IT structure so that they can gain economies and efficiencies through combining them, as in the ASP model, or in applying consistent processes to them. Consultants try to understand the differences in personality, culture, and corporate mission so that they can develop customized solutions that fit not only the technical needs of the client, but the cultural and organizational needs as well. Consulting and system integration are project-based disciplines, judged on the classic project metrics of scope, schedule, and budget, while outsourcing is an operational activity, judged by adherence to service levels and to ongoing economic efficiencies. Clearly these two IT services are distinctly different businesses, and the entrepreneur or manager responsible for growing these businesses must apply different skills and techniques, must build different types of teams with different skills, and must approach his or her marketplace and client in a different manner.

The IT consulting marketplace has a broad spectrum of competitors, from the single practitioner in a specialized niche to the giant global providers. We all have in common the need to develop trust relationships with our clients and the requirement to offer some specialized knowledge or experience that the client values. The best firms are masters of relationship marketing, building their firms not through mass marketing or advertising but one client at a time, through the famous "four Rs": *relationship, reputation, reference,* and *referral.* The consulting business as a whole, not just the IT component, has become the innovation and creativity engine for many firms. From the design of the corporate identity and logo, to the marketing campaigns and promotional programs, to competitive analysis and positioning, and including internal and external communications, press relations, and, most importantly, strategic direction, many firms have delegated these responsibilities to their outside advisors rather than keeping them in-house. Many companies have discovered that partnering with specialists in the consulting world allows them to stick to their operational competencies. They can contract with the best and brightest minds in the marketplace to do the project-oriented work they need and then send the experts home when the project is done. This cycle of divesting inside expertise to rely on outside consultants is self-perpetuating, as the most talented people gravitate to the consulting firms, where they can experience multiple challenges in multiple industries throughout their careers, rather than being "stuck" in a single position for life. The consulting firm has become the employer of choice, as they are best suited for the mobility demands and the need for new challenges that motivate the modern workforce. This virtuous cycle also positions consulting firms to offer the best rewards and career opportunities to the talented practitioners, whether they're straight from the MBA program or from the ranks of experienced experts. As Tom Peters has said, "The professional services firms [PSFs] perform intellectually based services, own little in the way of hard assets, and deposit billions of dollars on the bottom line. Life in a PSF is about as far a cry from Dilbert Drones in DrearyVille as one can imagine."[11]

The same self-perpetuating virtuous cycle has played out in the world of IT consulting. Because the technology changes so quickly and impacts competitiveness so directly, many companies become extremely reliant on outside experts and advisors to keep them current with the latest operating system, network architecture, or business application. These advisors and their firms, in turn, become much more attractive to the IT professionals, who are driven as much by challenge and stimulation as they are by compensation and security. Because of the gravity they exert on the best minds and the intelligence and knowledge they gain from being engaged on the most challenging projects, the IT consulting firms become the repository of knowledge and experience that then are applied to other challenges and strategic opportunities.

What does all this have to do with building an IT consulting firm? Entrepreneurs who want to play in this arena of the IT services marketplace need to understand that this is a business driven by talent and knowledge, by experience and expertise. In a nutshell, true IT consulting firms must do three things extraordinarily well in order to rise to the top of this segment:

1. They must attract, hire, develop, and retain the best, most talented, and most productive consultants;
2. They must gather and manage the knowledge of these consultants and experts; and
3. They must develop lasting trust relationships with their clients.

These imperatives are easier said than done. Identifying, attracting, developing, and retaining talented practitioners, while a bit easier now that the Internet boom has gone bust, is still an extraordinarily challenging thing to do, for a couple of reasons. Unlike the "body-shop" type of IT services firm, consulting firms need to hire not just for technical expertise, but also for the less tangible, and less measurable, attributes of advisory skills, project skills, business context skills, and customer relationship skills. The immature, incommunicative or unpresentable technician who may be acceptable in a back-office outsourcing deal or a body-on-site engagement will never do in a consulting role. Finding, screening, and developing these unique individuals can become a consuming occupation for managers of consulting firms, and entrepreneurs considering this field must take this responsibility seriously. Many consulting firms have been sunk by their naïve belief that having the best technical talent is enough. In the one-on-one relationship-oriented world of professional consulting, it is not. Add to this the constant requirements to keep current on dynamically changing technology and to learn and understand new business applications of that technology, and the demands of building a consulting workforce loom large.

As the hype around the "knowledge management" buzzword should indicate, gaining control and ownership over the knowledge and expertise that reside in your consultants' heads is another huge challenge. Knowledge, previously considered a totally human attribute, has now become a commodity that supposedly can be captured, codified, and reused, rather than needing to be reinvented or ferreted out each time it's needed. I say "supposedly" because, despite all the hype, not many organizations have been successful at transferring their consultants' unique and specialized knowledge, experience, and understanding into any type of accessible system. Undeniably, the payoff is potentially great; not needing to reinvent the proposal, the scope of work, the methodology, or the technical delivery details for each engagement should present enormous opportunities for efficiencies and economies that could change the way professional services are delivered. Moving from concept to execution, however, is the rub. How do you take human experience and knowledge and turn that into retrievable data? How do you motivate individuals to share their "secret sauce," the unique insights and experiences that make them valuable and irreplaceable? What type of system do you develop that understands what knowledge you're hoping to access and aids you in finding it? The race is on to answer these questions, and some firms have made great progress. To be competitive, entrepreneurs and managers must grapple with these questions.

Finally, the development of trust relationships is a talent that goes far beyond expertise or technical savvy. It encompasses human characteristics such as maturity, empathy, and simple likability. Creating the type of culture that enables, encourages, and rewards these behaviors and attributes is also part of the challenge of creating a consulting practice. Clients want to work with, and develop relationships with, folks they like and trust. The attributes of empathy, integrity, and honesty are not taught in any technical certification class; yet without them even the best technician will never add to the value of a consulting practice. Maturity and business sense develop over time and can be aided with thoughtful mentoring and coaching. The role of coach, in fact, is one of the most important roles an entrepreneur or manager in a consulting practice can play, as everyone, from the sales team to the consultant and including the accounting clerk and the person on the support desk, adds or detracts from the client's experience with the firm.

Custom Application Development

The application development market is another huge segment, with entrants from small web boutiques developing websites and eCommerce applications for local businesses all the way to the huge development teams at EDS, IBM, and their Big Five compatriots. According to the 1997 U.S. Economic Census, custom software development was a $38 billion industry, with over 31,000 firms participating.[12] The growth rate for the application development industry from 1997 through 2001 was a robust 12.8 percent, indicating that more and more companies are deciding to dispense with the expense and management overhead associated with running an in-house development function and are instead engaging outside application development shops when they need a new application. Only the largest or most specialized enterprises maintain an in-house programming capability today, as the cost-effectiveness of outside development has been proven to the satisfaction of most IT managers.

Application development is close to consulting on the IT services spectrum. Both require an intimate understanding of the client's business and culture, and both rely on trust relationships. They both are project-oriented disciplines that can only succeed if they adhere closely to the fundamentals of scope, budget, and schedule. They both benefit tremendously from the reuse of established knowledge. In the software world, entire programming languages and techniques have been developed specifically to encourage the reuse of functions and modules that have already been developed. Both are dependent on the talents of a team of specialists and on the team's ability to achieve results together.

There are some major differences as well. In many consulting engagements, the outcome is a strategic plan, a training program, a technology roadmap, or an even less tangible result such as good advice. In the world of application development, however, intangible deliverables are not acceptable—the client engages software developers to create an application for a specific use, to deliver specific functionality at a specific time for a specific cost. Robust project, quality, and risk management are important in the world of consulting and system integration; in the application development world, they are life and death issues. Although I'm a vigorous advocate of project disciplines in every IT services business, I must admit that I've seen successful consulting or system integration firms that rely on the technical expertise of their engineers and apply project management only in the most rudimentary form. They are successful because their technicians are so strong technically, so experienced and so dedicated that, even in the absence of robust project controls, they do what it takes to deliver a result.

This phenomenon does not exist in the world of application development. The demands for complexity, interoperability, and system interdependence just do not allow for ad hoc methods. Entrepreneurs considering entry into the world of application development must have a deep understanding of, or even a reverence for project discipline, for structured programming methods, and for the associated disciplines of risk management and quality control. As the Software Engineering Institute has noted, trying to build a software development capability before project management disciplines are in place is an exercise doomed to fail.[13]

The Software Engineering Institute is a good place to start our exploration of software development disciplines. The Software Engineering Institute is a federally funded project, sponsored by the Department of Defense and hosted by Carnegie Mellon University in Pittsburgh, Pennsylvania. The SEI's mission, according to their website,[14] is to make software engineering more like other types of engineering: manageable, predictable, and subject to a set of practices and methods that allow software to be developed better, faster, and cheaper. The practical outcome of their work has been a series of techniques and methods that any IT organization can follow to ensure that it is applying the best and latest practices to the development of software. From an appraisal process that helps managers understand their current capabilities, to a detailed improvement plan, and including a set of step-by-step actions that firms can take to ensure that the quality of their software deliverables meet the highest standards, the SEI has delivered a roadmap for every software entrepreneur to follow. For those firms that decide to make application development their core offering, ignoring these models would be like ignoring the rules of physics when designing a spacecraft.

As an advisor, I'm always amazed to find that firms decide to take on a complex and competitive marketplace such as application development and then, either through lack of homework or sheer arrogance, believe they can disregard the established principles of good practice. I've encountered numerous firms that decided to get into the application development business either because the founder was a programmer who enjoyed developing software and thought she was good at it or because, after a perfunctory review, the entrepreneur decided that application development is "where the money is." These eager entrepreneurs then often go out and hire a bunch of "whiz kids" who know how to program, and then, after floundering for a few months, they call and ask my advice. After some questions about the factors that drove them to tackle the application development market, I'll ask about project management methodologies. "Are you following the PMI Body of Knowledge?" "Have you applied the SEI maturity models?" As you can probably guess, the response is typically a blank stare, or a response like the following: "I've got some really smart kids. My lead programmer, my neighbor's kid, built a website in high school that won a prize at the technology fair!"

Tremendous effort and study have gone into analyzing and systematizing the factors that lead to success in IT system and software development, and then those findings are consistently ignored by the managers and practitioners in the field. The number of books, studies, and models created, tested, and validated by organizations such as the Association for Computing Machinery, the SEI, the Institute for Software Testing, and many others is huge and growing, and the quality of their research is superior. Yet IT professionals, both inside companies as IT departments and as outside contractors, continue to cling to the old, unstructured and undisciplined methods. It's as if doctors could choose to ignore medical advances and decide instead to wave a chicken over a patient because it was just too much trouble to actually perform surgery. IT firms, over and over, ignore the tremendous advances in development theory and instead decide to run projects by the seat of their pants, simply because applying the project management and engineering disciplines is just too complicated. In the world of application development, this undisciplined approach is worse than immature—it's tantamount to malpractice. It's also damaging to our industry, as the general perception that both custom and off-the-shelf software is of inferior quality to other manufactured goods is widespread and has substantial basis in fact. So for entrepreneurs who are considering entering this marketplace, or for those who are currently competing in this market and want to grow their firms, my first advice is to study the established disciplines and apply them. They are proven, they work, and they are an absolute prerequisite to continued success.

Every element of these disciplines illustrates another set of implications for the entrepreneur entering the software business. The ability to develop a clear, unambiguous, and mutually accepted scope of work, at a detailed functional level, is an absolute prerequisite to building an application development practice. The implications of this imperative are deep, as it becomes clear that simply hiring good Java programmers won't cut it. Someone from the firm, either the programmers themselves or some representative from sales, management, or consulting, must be prepared to have a strategic conversation with the client to elicit the business needs driving the project. Someone must be able to uncover the needs of the users who'll sit in front of the screens or read the reports generated by the system under development. Study after study, from the Standish Group's CHAOS studies[15] to the project best practices work done by Dr. Bill Hetzel of the University of North Carolina[16] emphatically cites scope and requirements management as a critical success factor. The ability to dissect a scope into its component parts, so that a project plan and an estimated schedule can be developed, is another critical skill in this business. Philip Metzger, expert on application development and author of *Managing a Programming Project,* points out that poor planning is the source of problems in software development more often than any other problem.[17] This is not a skill that is inherent in talented programmers, pointing again to the need for IT services managers to recruit and hire for a mature set of skills and to create an atmosphere within the firm that encourages and enforces these techniques.

Other elements of the software disciplines, such as risk management and quality control, also illustrate interesting dilemmas when we examine them a bit. In my experience, both risk and quality turn out to have emotional baggage wrapped around them that make them more challenging then they might appear at first glance. Why are software engineers reluctant to talk about risk? First, the risk management disciplines are intimidating—they often look like calculus, with coefficients and probability calculations. Most importantly, the mention of risk often invokes an emotional reaction from software developers: "You mean you don't trust me to get this done?" Immature programmers are especially prone to this and will often respond to any attempts to apply discipline by bristling at the idea that you lack faith in their innate genius. Also, sales folks hate to mention risk because they think it will scare away the prospect. Efforts at testing and other quality control techniques often evoke the same response. It's our responsibility as managers of the development function to educate not just our clients, but also our teams, on the importance of risk and quality management and to assure them that these disciplines are not meant to impugn their talents or abilities.

Change control, another critical element of development discipline, can often get a negative reaction from the client. "Why are you so bureaucratic?" is a classic client response to a structured change management discipline, and so the temptation is to drop the discipline so as to appear "customer-focused." The problem, of course, is that unmanaged changes threaten the client as well as the IT services provider, and so we're not doing the client a favor by dropping them. Instead, we are probably putting their project at risk. This is another example of the fact that these disciplines require an education and reassurance effort, and it goes to illustrate that just pulling a methodology out of a book (or a Capability Maturity Model) is not enough. Entrepreneurs and managers need to evangelize, support, educate, train, and hire with these methods in mind in order to build a team that lives the discipline and so protects the firm, the clients, and the project at hand. These disciplines apply at all stages of the software development lifecycle. From the development of a project statement, to the creation of a scope of work document, and through the design, coding, testing, and quality assurance stages of a project, there are well-defined and well-understood standards and principles that have been proven to produce superior results. Now the question is simply: Do we have the self-control to apply them?

For entrepreneurs and managers considering an application development practice, the need to build an atmosphere, a team, and a methodology around these standard practices is the critical success factor. We'll discuss a lot of other factors that also influence success as we go further in developing a firm-building process.

COMMON ELEMENTS

This extended exercise in reviewing the segments of the IT services business will, I hope, lay the groundwork for much of our discussion to follow. As I've said, the IT services business is very different from other professional services businesses like accounting or law. While these types of firms may have specialties, the underlying activities they perform are basically similar. In our business, although we may call it all "IT Consulting," I hope this chapter has demonstrated that we are in fact discussing a group of fundamentally different businesses. There are, however, some common elements, and in the next chapter, we'll look at these components that IT services firms have in common, and we'll develop some general principles that apply to all firms providing IT services.

End Notes

1. As quoted on the IBM website, www-1.ibm.com/ibm/history.
2. Cherry Tree & Co., "IT Services", May 1998.
3. ibid.
4. "The 1999 Chicago IT Consulting Trends Study." Sina & Royce, Inc., in conjunction with Purdue University; commissioned by The Information Technology Association of America, www.itaa.org/itserv/chicago.ppt.
5. *The 2000 Outsourcing Index.* The Outsourcing Institute and Dun & Bradstreet, www.outsourcing.com.
6. Lacity, M., & Hirscheim, R. *Information Systems Outsourcing: Myths, Metaphors, and Realities.* Chichester, England: John Wiley & Sons, 1993.
7. ibid, p. 15.
8. ibid, p. 21.
9. Cherry Tree & Co. *Second-Generation ASPs.* September 2000.
10. This discussion of the ASP marketplace is based on an article by the author entitled "Has the ASP market gone vertical?" www.techrepublic.com, July 17, 2001. Used by permission. All rights reserved.
11. Peters, T. *The Professional Service Firm 50.* New York: Borzoi Books, 1999.

12. U.S. Census Bureau. *1997 Economic Census, Summary Statistics.* December 20, 1999.
13. Burlton, R. Managing a RAD Project: Critical Factors for Success. *American Programmer,* December 1992.
14. www.sei.cmu.edu/sei-home.html.
15. The Standish Group. *CHAOS 2001.* www.standish.com.
16. Hetzel, B. *Making Software Measurement Work: Building an Effective Measurement Program.* New York: John Wiley & Sons, 1993.
17. Metzger, P. *Managing a Programming Project.* Englewood Cliffs, NJ: Prentice Hall, 1981.

The Structure of the Practice

chapter TWO

The skills required to manage, sell, and deliver a custom programming project are as different from those needed to provide an outsourcing deal as accounting is from law. Yet custom programming and outsourcing are both considered IT services. The IT consulting business encompasses many different business models, yet there are elements that all IT services firms have in common. Obviously, all IT services firms need managers who understand professional services, need sales talent that can sell those services, and need delivery teams that can provide valuable services to clients. Let's explore these common components, make some general observations, and see whether or not there are any universal rules or techniques we can apply whether we're building an ASP or a software development firm.

We've seen so far that analysts and commentators on the IT services business have found an astounding variety of business models. The ways in which these firms are structured also is highly diverse. From sole proprietors to partnerships, and from private corporations to publicly traded companies, IT consulting firms run the gamut of organizational structures. I've observed, in my work with IT service firms, that, alas, the organization of the firm often impedes rather than cultivates success. Let's explore some of the different management structures that IT firms might have in place and review some of the choices that managers and entrepreneurs make when building a practice. To set the foundation for our discussion about practice management structure, let's first review the basic possibilities. I won't talk about the legal or accounting reasons why an entrepreneur would choose a partnership over a corporation. Every entrepreneur must consult with professionals in law and accountancy before making those decisions. I'm more interested in the ways in which these decisions affect the ability of the firm to compete and to deliver great client service.

SOLE PROPRIETOR

The sole proprietor model is still quite prevalent in our business, and, with the increasing acceptability and availability of free-agent consultants who can be brought in and rolled out of projects as needed, this can be an effective model. In a recent interview I did with Elaine Biech, author of *The Business of Consulting,* Elaine described her progression from sole proprietor to manager and back to solo consultant:

> "I started out as a one-person shop, and within a very short period of time I found a project that was too big for me to deliver alone, so I brought in another consultant to help, and then the two of us found other projects that were too big for us, so my business began to grow. It grew to twenty employees, and I wasn't liking what I was doing, administering the business rather than working with clients. I decided to bring the organization down, so I worked with the staff, helped them start their own consulting businesses. My practice now is me and one support person, and I work with about thirty-five subcontractors. This works better for me—I make more money, have more time, and work fewer hours. This way of working isn't just better for you and me, it's better for the client. When I size up a consulting project and say, for instance, I need a good training designer, or I need someone who understands ISO 9000, or an expert in staffing and recruiting, I go out and recruit the best people, they deliver quality work, and when the job is done they're done. What was happening before was that I'd get these specialists on staff, and when we didn't have a project in their specialty we'd put them on something else that they may not have been suited for, and it wasn't good for them and wasn't the best fit for the client."[1]

Biech highlights the important decisions that many consultants confront when deciding whether to grow their firms or to remain sole proprietors: Am I interested in the administrative and human issues that firm managers must deal with? Is it best for the client to bring in experts as needed, or is a team of employees more likely to deliver consistent quality? Will I get the personal client interaction and technical challenge I crave if I decide to grow my firm? Many consultants (myself among them) decide that, as sole proprietors, we can have the control, freedom, and client contact we want without the administrative headaches for which we have no desire.

The tradeoff between the use of "free agents" and quality delivery is a tricky decision point. Many firms will follow Biech's model of creating a core team and then augmenting that team with subject-matter experts from the ranks of the free agents as required by the project. Other firms insist that this mode of staffing opens the firm up for major quality issues, as temporary staffers who have no affiliation with the firm are less likely to deliver the level of quality and consistency of service that the firm requires to build a reputation and a reference base. There's no easy answer to this dilemma. I've personally experienced quality issues that have arisen as a result of taking the free agent model too far. As a manager of a regional consulting team, I've brought in technicians from a consulting brokerage house, only to find that they lacked the commitment and connection to the firm's culture that make for a consistent team. Biech's model of identifying a roster of freelancers who can be called in for specific types of projects seems to be a happy medium between staffing permanent positions and using technical staffing agencies to buy "bodies."

Many IT consulting firms are based around the talents and drive of a founding entrepreneur, often a talented consultant or technician who starts the practice as a sole proprietor. The successful sole proprietor often owes his or her success to relationship skills and "bedside manner," as well as technical and business talents. Successful sole proprietors have often spent years struggling to build a business from scratch and have learned lessons of professionalism, relationship building, and personal marketing that are hard to hire or train for. In my consulting engagements, I often see entrepreneurs who have been successful as sole proprietors struggle with the migration from a business model in which every decision and task comes from them to a delegated model in which the power to decide and to act is dispersed throughout the organization. Rather than moving to a CEO role, in which they focus on strategic vision and executive-level relationship building, they attempt to remain in the midst of every engagement and every project.

This leads to many kinds of counterproductive behavior, in which the founder may, for instance, walk into a project meeting and, without having been involved in the stream of decisions and events that led the team to their current situation, make pronouncements or give instructions that undermine the team's direction and confuse the troops. I've seen some founders with this problem of "letting go" focusing on the color of the stationery while the competition vaults ahead with bold strategic moves. As is obvious to anyone who has watched the high-tech industry, people like Larry Ellison and Bill Gates are the exception, and many founding entrepreneurs find that the skills needed to fuel a startup enterprise are not the same skills as those necessary for growth. The growth path from sole proprietor to practice manager or CEO is fraught with tangles, and many decide to stay solo—or take the plunge into growth and then go back to a smaller model, as Elaine Biech described.

PARTNERSHIP

For those that do intend to grow, the partnership model is often a natural progression from the sole proprietor shop. Partnerships are an accepted model in the professional services world, used by law firms, accountancies, and architectural firms, as well as many of the major consulting firms. The partnership offers some distinct advantages in the professional services world. Partnerships present a natural and organic growth model. From the sole proprietor to the partnership is an accepted growth sequence, as the solo consultant partners with a colleague to offer additional services or bring new clients under one umbrella. Typically, these partners have complementary skills and, in the best partnerships, also fill some of the gaps in experience or technique for each other, to present a more rounded and complete set of offerings. Each partner can then build a team around himself, often with either technical or industry specializations. From the ranks of these teams, new partners can rise, and they can build teams around themselves in turn.

This model provides the benefit of presenting a clear career path and goal for team members, as the best firms dangle the benefits of partnership, such as enhanced compensation and access to plum assignments, as a carrot to motivate the staff to achieve. Every carrot has a stick, however, and many partnerships follow an "up or out" promotion philosophy, in which those staffers who are not deemed to be "partner material" are encouraged to move on to another firm. While this was the rule in years past, and is still in practice in the large consulting and law firms, many firms have now developed alternate career paths for those talented technicians who lack the skill or desire to move up to partner level. Every IT consulting firm I've managed or advised had some team members who were outstanding technical contributors, yet had no interest in the "rainmaking" or management duties that come with partnership. Throwing these valuable contributors overboard simply because they'd never be partners has finally been recognized as a gross disservice to both the firm and the individual. Creating alternate technical paths, such as subject-matter expert (or even "guru," a designation used by one of my clients), gives these team members a respectable growth path and short-circuits the old "up or out" mentality.

Many firms remain as small partnerships, with a couple of partners balancing sales and delivery management between them, as an example. I've seen many partnerships in which one partner was the rainmaker, responsible for business development, sales, marketing, and vendor relationships, while the other managed the consulting staff and acted as a senior project executive and quality control manager. I've worked with many other partnerships with different permutations and combinations of roles, based on the skills and desires of the partners.

Partnerships, while having some real advantages, also have their complications. Partner compensation is typically a sticky issue, as those partners with sales responsibilities can often expect a different compensation plan than those who focus on administrative or public relations duties. Seniority can also be a complicating factor in compensation programs, and many firms have "senior partner" and "junior partner" designations. As the firm grows, compensation programs can become complex and unwieldy. Partner responsibilities can be another source of contention, as partners vie for the juicy assignments and the most prestigious clients.

Another issue that IT consulting entrepreneurs must consider is accountability. In many firms, attaining partnership is like attaining a sinecure, a ceremonial position that requires no contribution. The "special projects" partner is an example of this type of position. Some firms are bringing creative thinking to the issue of partners "retired in place." In a recent interview I did with Ken Taormina,[2] a senior vice president at KPMG, he described an inventive way for senior or less active partners to add value to the firm. As Ken described it:

> "We have a quality management organization of very experienced partners who have been doing this a long time and know practice management inside and out. These quality management partners are

> totally independent. These people report up to our CEO. They meet with the client, they meet with our team, they go through a very specific questionnaire with the client and with the team on how they're doing things. Then they review all their work papers, the schedule, the charging on the contract, making sure we have good integrity, that the products and the deliverables are on time and what the client wants. Then they put together an independent report that gives the project a red, a yellow, or a green. We use very senior and experienced partners; what happens is a lot of them have retired and just work half-time because they love doing it. They get to travel and it's worked out very well. It's dramatically reduced our write-offs."

In summary, the best partnerships are ones in which the skills and temperaments of the partners are complementary and the division of duties is clear. Those partnerships that I have observed in which both partners try to take on all roles, or in which the partners are both technicians or both from the sales side of the house, are less successful. As outlined in David Maister's landmark book, *Managing the Professional Service Firm* (1993), the activities that partners pursue have a direct and substantial impact on the success of the firm. Maister outlines six key performance indicators for partners, as follows:

1. Profitability of work supervised;
2. Client satisfaction on work supervised;
3. Coaching on work supervised;
4. Contributions to practice development;
5. Contributions to success of others; and
6. Personal growth (career strategy).

Clearly, the first three metrics apply not only to partners, but to any manager of professionals, and they highlight the manager's responsibilities to the firm, the client, and the team. An important point to emphasize is the need for partners to act as managers and coaches, and so build the firm's current profitability and long-term strength, rather than as "super-consultants" who are mostly focused on generating their own billable hours. Managers and entrepreneurs in IT services who decide that a partnership organizational structure is a good fit for their needs must implement an appraisal system that sets concrete goals for the metrics described above and that rigorously and honestly assesses achievement against these goals.

CORPORATION

The corporate structure, common in the industrial world, is also widespread in the consulting business. Many of the small consulting companies I work with have chosen this structure. As I stated at the beginning, I'm not going to go through the typical "should I incorporate" material that is the stuff of myriad consulting books; see Elaine Biech's excellent *The Consultant's Legal Guide* (2000) for a thorough treatment of that aspect. My interest is in the effect that these choices have on your ability to build a successful firm.

As we saw in the ITAA Chicago IT Services survey, many of the firms included were either privately held corporations or branches of large national corporations. The survey offers no evidence that these structures inherently bring any positive or negative impact to success in themselves. As in any enterprise, there are legal reasons why it make sense to incorporate and so limit liability and create an ongoing permanent legal entity. I've worked with many IT service companies that are organized under a corporate structure, and it's my observation that this structure has some obvious advantages and disadvantages.

On the plus side, the corporate structure creates a clear line of decision-making power. Partners are often seen as equal in status and decision power, and the process of making difficult or controversial decisions can often become deadlocked. While the corporate structure doesn't grant immunity from this type of stalemate, at the end of the day it's clear that the CEO, and ultimately the chairman of the board, can end the debate and make a decision. This clarity of decision power and ability to cut off debate and move forward can be a real advantage in a dynamic market, where "analysis paralysis" can be a real hazard to the health and longevity of the firm.

As any of us who have worked in large corporations can attest, however, the "big company" mentality can sometimes have the opposite effect, providing a secure hiding place for those whose fondest wish is never to have to make a decision or be held accountable for anything. My experience at some of the national consulting firms that I've advised has been of extraordinary risk aversion, vacillation, and lack of accountability. Remote management, removed from the details of daily project work and local client interaction, can often make decisions that don't reflect the reality "on the ground" locally. The very clarity of decision power described above can often manifest itself as the kind of autocratic, hierarchical management style that is anathema to most talented IT practitioners. It's important, whether the firm is managed as a partnership or as a corporation, that Maister's six key performance activities, noted above, be enforced.

The corporate structure, while not inherently positive or negative, is reliant on the culture and atmosphere inculcated by the firm's leaders. While it's my belief that the partnership structure is a more natural and organic model for the professional services firm, I want to emphasize that the determination of corporate structure is one that should be taken under advisement from professional legal, accounting, and tax experts.

ELEMENTS IN COMMON

Of course, no matter whether a firm is a partnership or a multi-location corporation, there are certain elements that every firm needs. Every firm needs management, a sales function, and the talented individuals or teams that actually deliver the services to the clients. All firms need administrative staff to manage the time tracking that is the lifeblood of any professional services firm, and most IT firms also have a customer service organization, to provide after-sale support to clients using highly complex and customized solutions. Just enumerating these functions doesn't help the IT manager or entrepreneur much, so let's look at each function in turn. I'll recount some of the most successful, and some of the less successful, strategies I've encountered in these areas in my consulting work with IT service firms.

In Figure 2.1, I've depicted the functional organization chart of a fictional IT services company. Partnership, corporation, or sole proprietor, these are the functions that I believe the firm must take responsibility for. This doesn't mean that each of these functions will have a full-time individual assigned to it. In many cases multiple functions are owned by one individual; in other circumstances one function could be shared by many team members. The point of the graphic is to illustrate one possible way the firm could be organized, out of many possible configurations.

Figure 2.1.
A Typical Organizational Structure for an IT Services Company

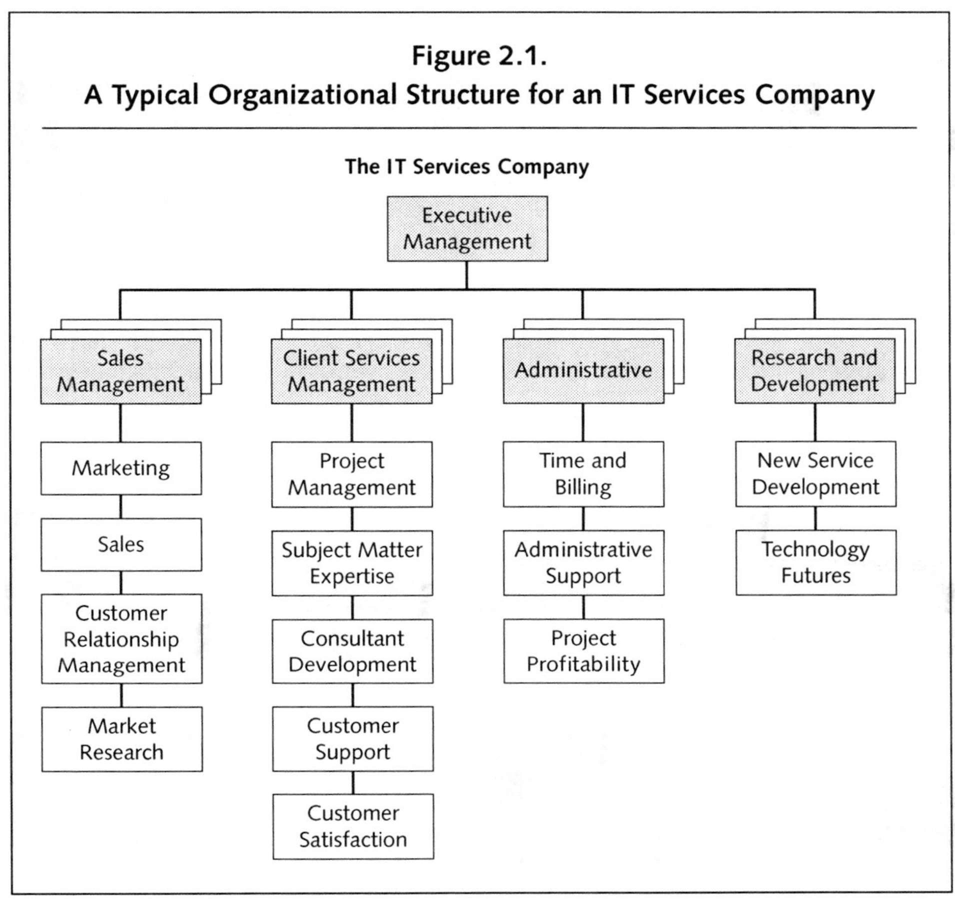

Management

Amidst all the hype that emerged from the Internet bubble of the late 1990s, one element of truth also surfaced: Managing talented technical teams in the 21st Century requires new skills and a new attitude. It's become axiomatic that IT technicians won't be receptive to the autocratic, hierarchical management environments that were the style of the day from the 1950s through the 1980s. So before we enter into a discussion about the fiduciary and executive responsibilities of IT service firm managers, it's critical to talk about tone and culture.

Over the last few years, a new literature has emerged that analyzes the changes in organizational culture and management techniques that have swept the corporate world. Works such as *Practice What You Preach* by David Maister (2001), *The Service Profit Chain* by Heskett, Sasser, and Schlesinger (1997), and *Corporate Culture and Performance* by Kotter and Heskett (1992) advance the proposition that profitability and growth are symptoms of a specific type of culture. The central premise of these works is the idea that, by fostering communication, teamwork, participation, and respect, organizations can build high-achievement cultures that naturally lead to enhanced financial results and client and staff satisfaction. Maister, for example, coaches managers that, above and beyond the standard management skills of organizing, planning, and executing, they must master communication and listening skills, must articulate a compelling vision, must be even-tempered and enthusiastic, must show sensitivity to human issues, and must be thoughtful, sincere, and even noble! Maister further states, "Development of people precedes and has a greater priority than profits" and "If you have the right client base, the right people with the right attitudes, the money will follow." Finally, he states, "The nicer you can make it at work for people, the better it will be for your profits!"[3] Quite a far trip from the remote, autocratic, and high-handed "board room" manager or the tough-guy foreman of the industrial age! I'm not disputing Maister's concepts. In fact, I wholeheartedly endorse them. There is no doubt in my mind, from my experience as both a manager and an advisor in IT services firms, that, in our organizations, the right mix of freedom, participation, recognition, development, and technical challenge is the central success factor.

In our industry, managers have a complex of challenges in the creation of an achievement-oriented culture. It's widely acknowledged, even before this latest crop of books, that engineers, technicians, and programmers need to be handled differently than other employees for a variety of reasons. In the 1980s a series of books emerged that offered insight into the unique characteristics of engineers and software developers. Books like Fred Brooks' *The Mythical Man-Month,*[4] Tom DeMarco's *Peopleware,*[5] and Watts Humphrey's *Managing for Innovation*[6] started to develop a theory of technical management that was based on the proposition that, as Watts Humphrey states:

> "In striving for superior performance [from technical people], you need to combine many elements:

- A challenging and worthy goal;
- Talented, motivated, and capable people;
- The training and support to enable the work to be properly done;
- A manager with the drive and vision to make it happen;
- A leader who understands and cares about his or her followers."[7]

Watts Humphrey, through his work with the Software Engineering Institute at Carnegie Mellon University, has made an important contribution to the IT field by spearheading the development of models that outline superior management practices for technical teams. These models, known as the Capability Maturity Models, assemble "best practices" and findings from across the IT field in a rigorous set of documents and processes that help managers assess their own maturity in managing technicians and then improve their results by applying proven techniques. The People Capability Maturity Model (P-CMM)[8] should be a fundamental part of the learning process for any manager wishing to be effective while working with technical people. As the authors of the P-CMM state, "When members of the workforce are essentially interchangeable, organizations focus more on managing workforce costs than on increasing workforce performance. It is tragic when this old labor relations model is carried over into high technology, because it was based on jobs that were never so knowledge intense."[9]

These theories about the special needs of technicians are obviously critically important to any entrepreneur or manager in the IT services business. Our ability to provide an environment that attracts, retains, and motivates the human resources upon whom we base our business will define our success. The creation of a culture that offers challenging goals, motivated people, visionary leadership, and a supportive atmosphere where people can grow and develop is easier said than done, however. Figuring out how to deliver on this vision will be one of our central themes throughout this book. At this point, suffice to say that constructing this setting is the central role of IT management.

It is not the only role, however. As critical as tone and culture are, they can never outweigh the business fundamentals, as many of the eConsultancies learned to their dismay. Collaborative, fun, and visionary environments are important, but firms that cannot develop lasting customer relationships or deliver profitable results won't be around to sit on those beanbag chairs or play at those foosball tables for long. Understanding and managing the financial aspects of the firm are clearly key responsibilities of firm management. Every type of business has its key performance indicators, and in professional services it is the capacity of the firm to generate billable revenue, sometimes called "fee capacity."[10] This number, the product of the number of billable professionals, their utilization rate, and their average hourly rate is the theoretical maximum the firm can generate with its current staffing base. It gives managers an important window into the firm's performance at a glance. The management of this metric, as well as the underlying factors of which it is composed, is the "hygiene" of the firm, the basic financial discipline that positions the firm to succeed or fail, to thrive or wither.

While I agree with the concept, put forth in the books by Maister and Heskitt that I cited above, that profitability is a symptom of doing the right things, that doesn't mean that managers can take their eyes off the ball and just hope that profits will accrue. Profitable firms are built on profitable clients and profitable engagements, and on avoiding those clients and engagements that don't allow one to make a profit. Many of the struggling IT services firms I've met in my consulting career couldn't answer the following questions:

- Which clients and engagements were your most profitable?
- Which were your least profitable?
- What aspects of these projects caused them to be more or less profitable?
- How do you set profit expectations for engagements and clients before you accept them?
- How do you control the costs of delivering projects?
- How do you appropriately maximize the fees and profits on a particular engagement?

These elementary questions should be the center of any IT services manager's financial oversight techniques, yet many managers don't approach their engagements with these questions in mind and don't review their prior engagements in light of these criteria. We'll talk further about the techniques and tools that IT services managers must apply so they can answer these questions and so they can use the answers to better run their firms.

Delivery Organization

Many IT services firms, especially in the early days of their development, adopt an "everyone does everything" approach to internal organization. I've worked with many firms in which the same individuals are expected to manage customer relationships, manage projects, manage deliverables such as custom software modules or website content, and also keep an eye peeled for the next sales opportunity within each client. When I was a consultant working for one of the large IT consultancies, it was accepted that part of my job was to keep the customer relationship cozy and productive and to also be alert for chances to expand our depth within the account. While I am a strong believer in the concept that every team member has sales responsibilities, this is not the same as having undifferentiated roles within the organization.

It is not contradictory to say that IT services firms need delivery organizations that are discrete and separate from the sales function, while still maintaining the philosophy that "everyone sells." Part of this theory is based simply on my experience; the firms that I've worked with who follow the undifferentiated "everyone does everything" approach for very long after their infancy always seem to end up in trouble. The client becomes confused about the roles of those firm representatives who are servicing their account. Are they consultants, focused on the client's best interest and bringing meaningful expertise to the table without a selfish agenda? Or are they sales reps, looking for the main chance to integrate themselves into the client's operation? This confusion can quickly dilute the credibility of the consultant in the client's eyes and cast a taint of suspicion over every finding and recommendation the consultant puts forward. It's also an impossible juggling act for the consultants themselves, as they try to walk the wire of sales and delivery roles without upsetting the client or letting their position in the account be corrupted by a self-serving agenda.

As firms grow, most are wise enough to create a separate services or delivery organization. What do these departments need to look like? What are the skills and talents that they require? What is their appropriate role in the other functions of the firm such as sales and profitability management? Clearly, those responsible for managing the delivery team need all of the human relationship skills we discussed in the previous section, and then some. While the firm's executive management needs to create an atmosphere and culture of participation, respect, and creativity, those tasked with managing the technical team on a daily basis must promote and advance that culture on a day-to-day, face-to-face basis. Mission statements or corporate visions won't cut it here—these managers must prove every day that they understand the technology, that they believe and live the values and culture that talented technologists expect, and that they are committed to challenging and developing their team. We've devoted a later chapter to organizational culture to allow us to probe these issues fully.

As we discussed previously, managers must also look beyond cultural issues to the basic financial performance issues as well. Service managers, whether partners, entrepreneurs, or hired managers, own the profitability of their projects and clients, and they also own the management of team productivity. From the profitability of a particular project, to the lifetime financial value of each client, to the ability of individual consultants to maximize their fees, productivity, client value, and personal achievement—all of these responsibilities fall on the services manager.

Sales Organization

Many IT firms have struggled with making the transition from a product focus to a services focus. From the large manufacturers like IBM and HP to the small PC resellers such as Computerland (later Vanstar) and BusinessLand (which became Entex), the IT business has seen a change from a product-centric business model to a model that emphasizes services and solutions. In this transition, the key difficulty, in my experience, is migrating the mindset of the sales team.

Marketing and selling services is very different from selling products. Product marketing is all about the product and the firm that's selling it. The product company spends its time and marketing energy convincing prospects that their product is better, cheaper, faster, new, and improved. Services marketing is all about the client and his or her special needs and circumstances. Service sales teams need to spend more time listening than talking or touting—and must listen with great effectiveness. When selling products, the sales cycle culminates when you make the sale. Sure, there may be an ongoing relationship, but once the product is sold, that relationship is usually with a service technician or a customer support center. In services, the relationship begins when you close the deal. That's when your team invades the client's world, uncovering secrets, needs, and expectations, and proceeds to either create a lifelong partnership or an adversarial and dissatisfying relationship. Product selling is transaction-oriented, while services selling is relationship-oriented. Product businesses sell based on the "four Ps": *product, price, place,* and *promotion,* while service businesses sell based on the "four Rs": *relationship, referral, reference,* and *reputation. Products are tangible* and are built to specific functional specifications that either fit the customer's needs, or don't. *Services are intangible, come into existence as they are delivered, and are experienced rather than owned.* This litany of differences boils down to one essential fact: The sales skills required to sell services are vastly different from those needed to sell products.

Services sales teams must be prepared to make the intangible tangible, to make the non-existent exist in the client's mind, and to unearth and document the client's needs, desires, concerns, and expectations as well as their functional requirements. They require interviewing and facilitation skills, as the IT services sales cycle rarely consists of a meeting with a purchasing or procurement agent, and more likely includes a series of meetings and interviews of escalating specificity with numerous representatives, in various functional roles, from within the client organization. Information technology services sales teams must, of course, have business context skills, as they must be able to articulate for the client not only the technical options available, but their implications and consequences for each particular client. Although they needn't be deep technical experts, they must have sufficient technical familiarity to explain in business terms the firm's offerings, specialties, and core competencies.

In short, they must be consultants to their clients. In fact, in my experience many of the best sales professionals in the IT services business are former consultants. The skill set required to prepare for the sales call, to educate the client on the alternatives and their implications, to deal with questions and concerns, and to present an overall air of sympathy and empathy is similar between salesperson and consultant. The best model for the professional services salesperson is as a consultative advisor rather than an old-fashioned "closer." It's this difference in role that, in my experience, has tripped up many of the product firms that try to migrate to a services model. I've seen the same problem in product firm after product firm, as they try to transition to a services-based business model. From the top of the organization down through middle management and to the actual sales team itself, everyone insists on applying a product-based "closing" sales model to a business where it is inappropriate at best, and downright counterproductive at worst. I once had a vice president at a consulting firm tell me, in my role as a consulting services manager, "Selling is the art of getting people to do things they don't want to do." This line illustrates for me in the clearest possible terms the sharp difference in mentality between the old sales methods and the new, consultative ones. In product sales, we want the sale. In professional services we want clients who need our services, who understand the value we can bring, who are a good cultural and philosophical fit, and who are prepared to collaborate and engage as partners and build ongoing relationships. Entrepreneurs and managers building sales teams in the IT services world must understand and embrace the difference.

PUTTING IT ALL TOGETHER

Looking at a hypothetical organization chart is one thing; building and running a business is quite another. Any experienced entrepreneur knows that the daily firefighting and crisis management that commands the attention of the manager every day quickly sends planning and corporate culture issues to the back burner. I wanted, therefore, to close this chapter with some real-world advice from my experience building, running, and growing IT services firms.

Many firms are started and managed by former consultants who've decided to move past the sole practitioner model and to affiliate with a like-minded partner or hire a team of talented technicians. Whether sole proprietors, partners, or corporate officers, firm managers must resist the temptation to "stay in the game," to keep on doing the same things they were doing before they started to build a firm. The temptation to remain focused on consulting, delivering technical services, and generating billable revenue is one of the most destructive impulses for budding entrepreneurs in this business. That's what they've done to become successful, that's their comfort zone, and that's where their interests and desires lie. Entrepreneurs and managers must accept that they now have different responsibilities, and they must focus on activities such as networking, rainmaking, building firm credibility and exposure, developing talent, and planning for the future, and they must manage as well the more mundane tasks of financial management. Senior partners may have the highest personal fee potential, but their firm-building potential is far greater, as is their potential to develop lasting relationships with clients and to develop lasting careers for their teams through personal coaching and mentoring. The satisfaction that we used to gain from getting our hands dirty building a server, designing a network, or creating an application must now be derived from these more strategic, and ultimately more fulfilling and profitable, pursuits.

Interview with Ken Taormina

It's useful to talk theoretically about the options and alternatives that IT service firm managers can consider when organizing their firms, but it's also valuable to take a look at a real-world example. KPMG Consulting is a firm that employs over 10,000 professionals, generates over $2 billion in annual revenue, and operates in seventeen countries around the world. Although they are one of the global powerhouses of the industry, they're also one of the few old-line firms that has gained a reputation as a leader in the eBusiness world.

In this interview we chat with Ken Taormina, senior vice president at KPMG Consulting, Inc. Ken leads the Industrial, Automotive and Transportation Group within Consumer and Industrial Markets for KPMG. Ken's been at Oracle, Raytheon, and GE earlier in his career, and he's also worked as an independent consultant, so he has a wide range of experience, from the client side to the independent contractor side, and now as the vice president of a large firm. I chatted with Ken about the processes and practices at KPMG.

Rick: Ken, thanks for agreeing to chat with us regarding KPMG and your approach to the consulting process. Let's start by walking through your role at the firm and your day-to-day activity at KPMG.

Ken: Sure. I run the industrial, automotive, and transportation practice areas. I'm responsible for all the business we do, regardless of the type of solution, within that industry segment. I also, because of my past background with Oracle, run the Oracle practices for all of consumer industrial markets. I run our JD Edwards practices and SAP for industrial, automotive, and transportation industry clients. That gives you a thumbnail.

Rick: It sounds like KPMG is organized around vertical markets, but it also sounds like you've got some focuses like Oracle that are on specific technical practice areas. Help me understand organizationally how you're divided up and focused.

Ken: I think this makes us think about how clients approach the marketplace. We found, four or five years ago, the best way to attack the marketplace from a business standpoint is not by a geographic approach, which a lot of consulting companies were doing at the time, but to break it down into things that would make you much more intimate and closely tied to your client and their problems.

So we broke ourselves into about five industry segments, lines of businesses. We had communications and content, which is telecommunications and the entertainment industry. We had consumer industrial markets, which include sub-segments—I'm a segment leader—such as industrial, automotive, and transportation; chemical and energy; consumer and retail. And then we have our public sector, which is broken down into Department of Defense; federal, state, and local governments; higher education; and healthcare providers, like hospitals. And then we have financial services, which is broken down into retail and wholesale banking, and insurance and service companies. The last group is high technology manufacturing, which tends to consist of smaller, NASDAQ-listed types of companies. That was the way we decided to go to market as a way of growing our business. Everybody that worked in each one of those verticals and in those segments would come out of that industry; we would hire out of those industries, we would not hire all our people out of consulting companies. Probably around 35 percent of our people come from consulting companies. The rest come with specific industry knowledge. The other thing we did, we had solutions that cut across the verticals, and there is usually a solution leader in each one of those areas and specific practices to focus for that solution in that industry. So if we're going after Oracle work in industrial, automotive, or transportation, we have people who are really more attuned to what you would be using Oracle for in those industries, versus generic Oracle people.

Rick: So it's not just a subject-matter expert, but a subject-matter expert who also has some business context around that.

Ken: Exactly. And that started leading to very explosive growth. It hit on a nerve with our clients. That's something that they wanted, that showed up consistently in our surveys of clients. Our people liked it because they felt they had a home and they could become really good at an industry. They could go into an industry and be successful because they had industry knowledge. They weren't generic consultants. They felt they could add real value when they went on the job. Also it helped us have fewer people on an engagement to be successful, to keep our costs in line.

Rick: If we look at the engagement process with a client as a lifecycle, starting from the sales cycle and rolling all the way through to the deliverables and the satisfied customer, help me understand how KPMG approaches that lifecycle. Do you have a separate sales organization that's responsible for sales, or do you believe that consultants sell consulting, or is it a partnership?

Ken: A type of a partnership. The way we're organized is that we have over two hundred salespeople broken out by vertical and by segment. For example, in my organization, I have a national sales team that supports me. I have three sales directors: east, west, and central. The director really is a player/coach for all of their sales folks. We break our accounts into named accounts, key targets, and targets. A named account is a big company like Boeing or GE. We'll have a dedicated partner on that team, and the dedicated partner will have a team around him or her and will manage all the engagements that come out of that client relationship. He or she will be responsible to deliver that work and have long-term customer intimacy and become a trusted advisor for that client. The salesforce is oriented to help develop key targeted accounts in the named accounts, penetrating them, and when they become a named account, to farm the account with the partner and to build the relationship. Partners have to engage with the client, manage the deliverables, and ensure the quality of the delivery. If partners are trying to sell also, they're only going to be able to sell so much. With a salesforce we've been able to tremendously improve our growth. We've grown double the industry average over the last three or four years. And our sales approach has been a big part of it, because we've been able to cover more territory, find more opportunities, qualify them, and then the salespeople bring in the right managing director to close the deal. We have targeted accounts. We focus on those accounts, we call on them, we talk to clients about what their problems and issues are, we build value propositions. That's what's selling today. Not solutions. Value propositions.

Rick: Expand on this "value proposition" concept.

Ken: You can't go into a client today unless you can talk about how much money you're going to save them, how much money you're going to make them, and how you're willing to put skin in the game. They want to know you're going to put fees at risk, that you're willing to take some of your fees based on performance. They want to know if you've done it, and are you willing to stick with them through it. And they want to see numbers. They don't want to see "I want to analyze something."

Rick: And they don't want the fuzzy platitudes about increased customer satisfaction.

Ken: We don't even put soft benefits in presentations any more. If it doesn't have a number, achievable within twelve months as a return on investment, they're not interested. If they need infrastructure, some of them are realizing some projects have to go over a year, but they're going to break it into chunks so that they measure it and they don't commit to multiple years. That's the way we're selling right now. There have to be value propositions, and to do that we have partnerships. One of the key things we've found as one of our strengths is our channels. I think if you look at KPMG and at our Oracle, Cisco, SAP, or Microsoft alliances, we try to identify alliances that are going to give us channels to the marketplace. And we're going to provide them channels in return, and that helps grow their business too. If you just depend on yourselves and smart people, it isn't enough. You've got to have solutions; you've got to have channels to get to other clients and to help those clients solve problems with some of your channel partners. And you have to stick by them. You have to pick some players and you have to go to market with them. We hardly ever do selections for evaluations of packages.

Rick: Some consultants and consulting groups say it's a conflict of interest to say "We're aligned with Oracle," but to also say "We're focused on your best interest and the best solution for your particular needs." You don't see a conflict?

Ken: That's right. If clients are asking for us to be independent, we will be. And we do Oracle and SAP. But there's no need to do Oracle, SAP, PeopleSoft, JDEdwards, BAAN, Lawson, and so forth.

Rick: No need to start from ground zero and do an evaluation every time out.

Ken: We're good with Oracle; we're very strongly partnered with SAP; we do PeopleSoft; we do some things with JDEdwards, but after a while you have to say you believe in certain solutions for certain industries.

Rick: You mentioned that you have three tiers of targets: your named accounts, your key targets, and your general targets. What kind of criteria do you apply to put somebody on your target list?

Ken: First, to be a key target, we look at the Global 2000 and the Fortune 1000 and we see how they line up against our lines of business and our expertise. Then we look at how big they are and their IT spending. That's a predictor—this is a company that believes in technology and systems and it's worth taking a shot. On the other hand, there are smaller companies that actually spend more than you think for their size. There are a lot of electronics and high technology companies that spend way more than you would expect just going by size. That's one predictor; the other is where they are on their growth cycle. We tend to look at that. Based on that we see, who are the market leaders? Then you go through those and say which should be targeted. Can you get the named account? When we move them up to the named account status, it is a company that we're going to do a consistent amount of revenue with year after year and in different solution areas, because they believe we're a trusted advisor. They're going to spend a certain amount of money with other firms. It's probably going to be competitive. Almost everything we do today is competitive, but we're going to be able to compete within that client because they believe we bring value.

Rick: You're moving beyond the transactional scenario and you're moving toward more relationship-oriented business.

Ken: I think this is what really destroyed a lot of the upstart companies—they had no relationships. We find that if you have great solutions but don't have relationships, you might win, but it's going to be tough and your win ratio is going to be lower. But if you have relationships and you have good solutions and a good solid value proposition, you will have the opportunity to help that client and obtain add-on work with them, as long as you can execute. That distinction is key. Then you're in a good business model. The other thing is that too many people live in "vendorville." They don't understand that you have to keep your salesforce focused on calling at the right level in the account—and the same thing with partners. It's very easy, no matter how good people are and no matter how good our relationships are, for people to gravitate to working with people lower down in the organization, folks who don't have enough freedom to make decisions.

Rick: So let me take you past the sales cycle now. You're starting to focus in with the client on some areas where you think you could add value. How do you go about defining and scoping exactly what you're going to deliver? How do you make sure that what you're visualizing as the end result is the same thing that the client is visualizing?

Ken: One of my favorite things to ask clients is "What are the five things that keep you up at night?" It's amazing how few people ask that question, and it's amazing the great answers you hear from it. It's boom, boom, boom—most CEOs, presidents, CFOs, CIOs will tell you right off the bat, it's this, it's this, it's that. There's a common thread through a lot of them, like supply chain, or customer relationship management (CRM), but they don't say CRM, they don't necessarily say supply chain. They talk about business problems that relate to those areas. Once we find out what their pain areas are, we say, "We'd like to ask for permission to get access to your people. Tell us who we can interview. I'd like to spend maybe two weeks talking to your folks. We'd like to come back to you with an idea of how we could attack those five areas." And we'll break them down into specific functional areas. When they give us access, and sometimes they'll give it to you just to try you out. Then we go back and talk to their people on our own nickel. We scope out a solid value proposition, based on our experience, best practices, and technology, where they could save money. And then we come up with a short-term game plan of how they can pick some low hanging fruit, as well as a longer term game plan. We go back and run that by them or, if they prefer, with the executive sponsors. That's the first step.

Second step, if they want to proceed, we scope out the specific solution and the requirements with the people in their functional area. It has to have functional support. One thing we've found is that working with IT people alone on projects is a recipe for failure. If there isn't a functional champion, we probably will not proceed. I won't invest time and energy in it. Lack of departmental sponsorship means the organization will never commit, and even if they give you money, it won't be a successful project and it won't be reference-able.

Rick: Because they're not capable of building the consensus that's required to change the organization?

Ken: Yes. After we have an agreement on the scope, the next thing we'll talk about is how they want to do it. For example, some people are willing to just pay for performance. Time-and-material contracts are a thing of the past. At the very minimum, people are paying for a fixed price. And equity's a joke, a scam. So we'll scope out how they want to engage and what the deliverables are, the specific deliverables and the specific performance measurements that they and we are willing to commit to. And sometimes they still decide to shop out the work, at which point we still think we have a much better chance than anybody else. And a lot of times they won't shop it out because they realize we're putting skin in the game.

Rick: You've made such a compelling proposition.

Ken: And they torture us to death on price. But in the end, because you've put a good compelling proposition in place, you're able to defend your price, and sometimes even have upside on the fact that you're willing to take risk on the back end. Another thing we have is quality review after the engagement's going about a month, no more than two months. We have an organization of very experienced partners who have been doing this a long time and know practice management inside and out. We tell the client up front that we do this. The quality management partner goes out and is totally independent. These quality control people report to our CEO.

Rick: They're in a separate quality organization?

Ken: Right. They meet with the client, they meet with our team, they go through a very specific questionnaire. Then they review all the work papers, the schedule, the charging on the contract, making sure we have good integrity, the products and the deliverables are on time and are what the client wants. Then they put together an independent report that gives the project a red, a yellow, or a green light. And if it's a green, then everything is fine. The client's happy; people are following our best practices and procedures. And then the quality guys send out a message to everyone, including the CEO or CFO, all the way up the chain. If it's a yellow, you have to come back with very specific answers on how you're going to make it a green. If it's a red, you have to come up with even more specifics and the thing gets laser surgery and usually an executive call and a weekly, serious review. We've found this has improved our delivery quality significantly. It's decreased our write-offs and made for happier clients because they feel that we actually care about how this is going to be delivered. When we first started, we used to do these quality reviews at the back end of an engagement. We figured out it was better to do it earlier. We found that the earlier you did it, the better the quality of the projects, and the more satisfied clients. And also, you can recover. If you do your quality review early, you have the chance to recover, to make the client satisfied, to meet their goals, and to meet yours. The firm's exposure to risk, as well as the client's, is greatly reduced.

Rick: Plus you have a mentoring opportunity with those folks who are actually engaged, to help them understand what they're doing right and what they're doing wrong.

Ken: Absolutely. And since we use very senior and experienced partners, a lot of them have retired and just work half-time because they love doing it. They get to travel and it's worked out very well. It's dramatically reduced our write-offs.

Rick: So now that you've executed well and you're approaching the end of an engagement, how do you make sure the client is prepared for the operational aspects of whatever you've built for them? How do you get the client to sign on the dotted line and say, "Yes, what you've delivered is what I expected"?

Ken: We tend to take a "toll-gate" approach. We go through certain toll gates on a project. We're almost always deliverable-based. As we hit our different milestones or toll gates, we have signing events where the client signs off on the deliverable, so you don't have to wait until the end for the client to tell you whether they're happy or not; each milestone is a go or a no-go. And we very often are paid at these milestones or on deliverables.

Rick: So you're also talking about a collection philosophy as well, where you are incrementally paid as you reach certain deliverable milestones?

Ken: Some clients let you collect monthly or twice a month, but a lot of clients like to tie a certain amount of the fee to the deliverable itself, which is fine. It's a smart approach. Every deliverable becomes a quality event, because you have to make sure that you and the client are in agreement. They have to sign off on the deliverable for you to be paid. By the time you reach the end of the engagement, you know whether you've gone in the right direction or not. The other thing we do at the beginning of an engagement is that we'll build into the contract a transition plan and a change management plan. We won't necessarily sell change management; it's up to the client. The client can manage their own change with our support, or we can do it for them. We find the clients more and more do it themselves with some support from us. And it includes a communication plan. We're not really interested as a company in staying behind and running the system day to day. We're happier if the clients are confident that they can do it and don't have to call a lot; then we'd love to do more work for them if they have any, but we don't want them to feel dependent on us to make the system that we put together for them work.

Rick: So building client self-sufficiency is one of the key goals?

Ken: Right. And that leads to what we really want: a reference-able client. We feel that reference-ability is crucial to follow-on work, not only with that client but with the people that client does business with and other prospects that we'd like to reference back to the client.

Rick: You mentioned that some proportion of the folks you bring in don't come from consulting backgrounds but come from a domain-expertise background. How do you take someone who has been a product manager or line manager and turn that person into a consultant?

Ken: First of all, we don't do it by bringing them in as a partner. Not overnight. Let's take something like Oracle. We've taken people who are controllers who've worked with Oracle, brought them into the Oracle practice, brought them in as a junior consultant, and put them through Oracle training. We have a consulting training course as well, to teach people the basics of practice management and how we go about it. Then we assign them to a practice, give them a mentor, and start putting them on engagements that are related to what they know how to do and bring them along that way. We have mandatory training several times a year. We have a lot of web-based training, and people learn on the job.

Rick: Is your mentorship program a formal program?

Ken: It's becoming more formalized. For example, every senior manager, who may in the next eighteen months make partner, has a managing director, somebody other than who he or she works for, who's assigned as mentor and meets with the person once a month, sits down, talks to him or her, and works out what the person needs to be doing to be successful. We're starting to do that at a lower level as well, but it's not as formalized yet.

Rick: If I'm a rookie in your organization and I step into your office and ask, "What do I need to do to be successful in your organization?" how would you advise me?

Ken: The first thing I'd tell you is to find an area of interest that you felt you could add real value to that is emotionally exciting for you. Second: Make sure you're the type of person who communicates your interests to the people you work with and for. You're going to be working engagements other than just for the people you officially report to. We move people around. Make sure people know who you are and what you are interested in doing! To really do well at KPMG you need to be flexible and you need to be the type of person who's going to reinvent yourself, because our business requires that. And so the people who do the best are the ones who volunteer, who raise their hands and say, "I want to work on that engagement." Then people know, there's a go-to person. What matters is your enthusiasm and your willingness to take on challenges. We're pretty good at giving people the challenge they ask for. A lot of people don't always ask. They wonder, "Why aren't I getting more opportunities?" Well, have you asked anybody? "Aren't they supposed to come to me?" That doesn't work well in our culture. We tend to be pretty entrepreneurial and have a buffalo hunter mentality.

Rick: So you own your own career?

Ken: You own your own career. You could ask people to be your mentor and that's usually something people are willing to do. We're a pretty open organization. But a lot of times they don't ask. They go out on an engagement and their connection back to the organization is partly our responsibility and partly theirs. You need to call your engagement manager once in a while to say, "I'd like to talk about the next engagement you'd like me to work on." Because of the distance and being on engagements in different cities, you have to manage your career.

Rick: Thanks, Ken. Any final thoughts?

Ken: In consulting the key thing to remember is that people don't hire us just for technology. They hire us because they have a relationship with us, and that relationship has to be based on understanding their business challenges and problems, on being able to interpret what their business challenges are, and to translate those into business solutions that have direct impact on their business. The biggest mistake you can make is to just focus on technology and forget the relationship. What KPMG is good at is getting close to clients, building long-term relationships, and helping them through when times are tough, like they are now, or when times are hot. That's what keeps you going.

End Notes

1. Interview with the author, "Listen More and Talk Less," Independent Consultant Advises. *TechRepublic.com,* February 6, 2001. Used by permission. All rights reserved.
2. Interview with the author, "Quality Is Key to Ongoing Relationships," says KPMG exec. *TechRepublic.com,* June 18, 2001. Used by permission. All rights reserved.
3. Maister, D. *Practice What You Preach.* New York: The Free Press, 2001.
4. Brooks, F. *The Mythical Man-Month* (2nd ed.). Reading, MA: Addison-Wesley, 1995.
5. DeMarco, T. *Peopleware: Productive Projects and Teams* (2nd ed.). New York: Dorset House, February 1999.
6. Humphrey, W. *Managing for Innovation: Leading Technical People.* Reading, MA: Addison-Wesley, 1997.
7. Humphrey, W. *Managing Technical People.* Reading, MA: Addison-Wesley, 1997.
8. Curtis, B., Hefley, W.E., & Miller, S. *The People Capability Maturity Model.* Software Engineering Institute of Carnegie Mellon University. Available at www.sei.cmu.edu/cmm-p.
9. ibid.
10. The concept of fee capacity is based on material in *The Intellect Industry* by Mark C. Scott. Chichester, England: John Wiley & Sons, 1998.

The Basic Financial Model

chapter
THREE

The old cliché tells us that the difference between a professional services firm and an industrial firm is that in a services firm, the assets go home at night. Like the industrial enterprise, IT services firms must utilize assets to their best advantage in order to maximize their profit and productivity. Human assets, however, are not like industrial assets. The ability to churn out maximum productivity from human assets is subject to human forces such as satisfaction, consensus, and motivation. We'll talk in depth about the most effective management styles for motivating teams to deliver at their highest level. We'll review the values, vision, and culture that are required to build and retain high-performance teams. In this discussion of financial matters, however, suffice it to say that the human factor influences our ability to generate profits and achieve our financial goals for the firm.

What are those goals? How do we go about setting realistic financial objectives for the firm? What are the key metrics that IT consulting firm managers must oversee in order to have a clear picture of the health and future of the firm? Unfortunately, my experience advising IT consulting firms has exposed me to far too many firms that never go through the financial discipline of understanding their revenue potential, their break-even point, and their profit requirements. They just hire the best technicians they can find, go after every deal that pops up, and hope for the best. Whether our IT consulting practice is a publicly traded corporation, a branch office of a large national firm, a partnership, or a small local shop, our financial goal is to generate sufficient fees and manage costs well enough to maximize our profitability. Applying the fundamental disciplines of calculating your fee capacity, understanding your break-even point and profit requirements, comparing your key ratios to competitive firms in order to benchmark your performance—all contribute to your ability to maximize your returns from the practice.

Before we plunge into our discussion on the financial metrics of the firm, let's work through some common professional services language.

UTILIZATION

Professional services firms, from lawyers to accounting firms, are fixated on utilization rates. Utilization is the *simple measurement of billable hours.* It, along with billing rate, is the central measurement of every professional services firm. Whether we're lawyers, doctors, architects, or software developers, the most basic element of our business model is that clients pay for our time. Utilization is usually expressed as a percentage, as in "Jane was 50 percent utilized in September." Of the forty hours a week that Jane was available for billable activity, she worked on billable matters for twenty hours.

The professionals whom services firms hire to build their teams are expensive, and their costs are typically not variable based on how much they bill. They receive their salaries whether or not the firm is able to keep them busy and billable. Therefore, it would seem to make obvious sense that the goal is to keep these expensive resources as busy as possible. As is the case with many obvious answers, however, the measurement of utilization in the IT services business is not quite as clear as it may seem. Is 100 percent utilization the ultimate target, and is anything below that number a failure? What about the time required to record the work performed? What about developing new client relationships? What about marketing activity such as presenting seminars or networking? What about consultant development activities, such as keeping on top of the rapid changes in technology? What about preparation time for an engagement or for a sales call? How about the time senior staff spends in mentoring and coaching?

Targeting appropriate utilization rates is a subtle exercise that requires IT services managers to consider the skills, desires, interests, and best use of each consultant individually and to set a utilization target for each individual that encourages him or her to contribute in the best way possible to the firm's growth and profit. Senior individuals, whether they are partners or designated "rainmakers," need to spend a significant amount of time in non-billable activities in order to keep the firm focused on the future. Senior staff would actually be doing the firm a disservice if they only focused on generating billable hours. Even junior staff will need to participate in non-chargeable activities, such as simple administration and training, in order to keep the wheels turning. There will be some technicians whose best contribution to the firm is to bill as many hours as possible. This is not an attempt to rank them as better or worse than others; some individuals have an interest and proclivity toward participating in sales calls or trade shows, for instance, and others just do not. Some consultants should be targeted for 50 percent billable utilization, because their ability to articulate the firm's methodology and competitive advantage is so pronounced that it would be a disservice to the firm for them to be unavailable for sales calls. Other consultants are so suited to mentoring and developing their peers that they can save the firm thousands of dollars in training and retention costs if they are given some leeway to participate in team development activities.

It's also absolutely critical for managers to realize that there is a huge employee satisfaction and retention element to the proper use of utilization targeting. Employees who receive the message that they are revenue-generating machines and that in spite of their additional talents or desires they can only serve by billing are likely to have a much different view of the firm than those who see that their individual skills are noticed and honored. The utilization targeting process is a part of the ongoing relationship between the firm and its professionals, and the messages and communications inherent in the targets set for each individual must be respected by the firm's management. I've seen many firms develop damaging employee retention issues because managers took a simplistic and one-sided view of the utilization targeting process, seeing it as merely a stick with which to beat more dollars out of each staffer. On the other hand, I've seen enlightened firms develop lifetime loyalty from their consultants by using the utilization process intelligently, either to tell people that their unique contribution was recognized or to set challenges for folks to help them grow. The main point that IT services managers must understand is that blanket pronouncements or rules regarding utilization targets send the wrong message and are counterproductive. Using the utilization targeting process as a motivational, cultural, and reward mechanism, as well as a revenue-generating one, obtains the best results.

RATE

In the industrial firm, one of the key elements of strategy is the pricing decision. If a firm decides to be a low-price provider, that decision has broad implications across the business, driving everything from location to marketing to materials. Firms that decide to differentiate on premium quality or in a specialized niche likewise are driven by that decision to operate in a certain way. In the professional services world, however, any decision to compete solely on price would likely dilute the quality of the firm's deliverables quickly. Our asset is human, as we discussed before, and spending less on human assets, either in their recruitment and hiring or in their subsequent development and satisfaction, seems to lead to an inexorable downward trend in quality. Overemphasis on price often leads IT services managers to make the mistake of trying to staff engagements with lower-cost, which typically translates into less experienced or less skilled, consultants. The pricing decision in the services firm is clearly a bit more complex than in the product firm.

How does a professional services firm develop a pricing policy? While it's clear that senior consultants, with years of experience and the associated credibility, may bill at rates that are a multiple of the rates juniors can capture, is that the only basis for setting fees? And once fees are set, how are they used by management to maximize the profitability of the firm? Since the senior practitioners can charge the most, is it simply a matter of hiring a lot of senior folks and making them as billable as possible?

As you can probably guess by now, my response to these rhetorical questions is that there's a lot more complexity here than meets the eye. Professional service firms need to make some fundamental strategic decisions when considering pricing policies. Every firm must develop a profit plan in which management does a rigorous analysis of the firm's cost structure, including not only salaries and benefits but also sales commissions, facilities, marketing, travel, training, recruiting, and all other costs. This cost model must then be the basis for an honest breakeven analysis, and then expected margins, based on industry standards, must be applied to develop a target profitability number or range. Industry standard operating margins and other operational metrics can be found in the *VARBusiness* annual "State of the Market"[1] survey, in the Dun and Bradstreet annual *Industry Norms and Key Business Ratios*[2] or in Prentice Hall's *Almanac of Business and Industrial Financial Ratios.*[3] This type of baseline analysis is the only disciplined way to set rates and pricing strategy, yet I'm often disappointed when I ask my clients if they've gone through this process. Without a clear understanding of your cost of providing services, how can you set rates that will deliver the profitability you expect? How can you know how low you can go to snag a project you want from a targeted prospect, or how much you must charge to produce the excess revenue necessary to grow the firm? Only by running the numbers in various permutations and combinations, against a realistic and honest set of industry baselines, can managers make the best pricing decisions and optimize the profit potential of the firm.

In terms of fee setting, there is a significant level of controversy over even this simple metric. Obviously, the setting of fees is tightly connected to what the market will bear. In the age of the Internet, it's easier than ever to determine with some precision what rate each technical specialty can command in each geography. For example, RealRates.com,[4] managed by Janet Ruhl, author of *The Computer Consultant's Guide,* is a valuable resource for checking the going rate for a particular technical skill in a specific city or region. Ruhl collects rates contributed by consultants around the country who volunteer to participate in her informal, but extremely valuable, ongoing rate survey. Other resources, such as *VARBusiness* magazine's annual "State of the Market" survey, are also useful guidelines into the pricing policies in the IT services marketplace. While every consultant has special skills and attributes that will affect his or her ability to charge a specific rate, it's obviously meaningful to have access to a database of rates, submitted by real practitioners, to use as a baseline.

Yet even this simple element of the services mix is subject to debate. The concept of "value-based" pricing has become a standard topic of conversation whenever IT consultants gather. If, by developing a website for my client, I enable that client to generate $20 million that otherwise would never have been generated, is my $25,000 consulting fee based on an hourly billable rate fair compensation? Shouldn't I have an opportunity to participate in the riches that I, through my technical expertise, helped realize? The ability to separate the value of the deliverable from the cost of creating it has an obvious lure for service firms. On the other hand, why would the client pay me some percentage of profits when all the financial risk was his or hers, and when there are legions of other consultants out there willing to take on the work on a pure pay-for-hours basis? Further complicating the debate is the fashionable practice of pay-for-results or risk-reward-based pricing, in which the service provider puts some percentage of fees at risk if the system is not on time or on budget or does not deliver the expected business benefit, and the client agrees to offer some financial incentive for delivery of outstanding results.

This is not merely a rhetorical debate. Some of the gurus of the consulting world, such as Alan Weiss, author of *Million Dollar Consulting*,[5] insist that consultants who don't migrate to value-based pricing are allowing themselves to get stuck at the lower end of the value chain. It does seem a bit unfair that clients should profit exorbitantly based on our ability to deliver technical functionality. It takes a lot of credibility, based on a track record of demonstrable success in delivering business value, as well as a rock-solid client relationship, before consultants can move to a value-based pricing scheme, in my opinion. Nevertheless, this is a topic that all IT services managers should consider when they strategize on setting rates and pricing policies within the firm.

If it's true, as we noted, that senior consultants can command higher rates, is hiring more senior players and deploying them on more jobs the answer? Of course, senior folks not only charge more, but they cost more as well. In addition, as we discussed before, senior staff often contributes much more to the long-term health of the firm through mentoring, development, rainmaking, and quality activities than by simple revenue generation. Most professional service firms have learned that informed use of leverage makes the most sense for the firm. The judicious and strategic use of senior staff for quality, experience, and relationship skills, and junior staff for their ability to hunker down and grind out work (and billable hours) maximizes profit and client satisfaction. Understanding the subtleties of the proper use of leverage is a key learning that experienced services managers bring to the firm.

As is the case in any business, whether selling product or services, the prices we charge will affect the client's decision to buy. If we charge $50 an hour for an entry-level developer and $250 an hour for a "superprogrammer," that pricing structure will drive the client to certain decisions about how much of each commodity they wish to purchase. Wise service managers therefore use pricing to drive the sort of utilization behavior we've discussed. Senior talent is priced at a rate that encourages clients to use them in a supervisory, quality assurance role, rather than as heads-down delivery resources. Junior talent, which we as managers want to give the opportunity to get out into the trenches and develop their skills, are priced at a rate that drives client behavior in that direction. Many managers in the IT services business are afraid that they'll price themselves out of the market if they set rates for their senior staff that drive the right type of client behaviors. It's my experience that clients are most interested in the "blended rate," the overall cost to them of achieving their goals, and are not liable to be "spooked" by high senior rates. In fact, the old adage of "getting what you pay for" often comes into effect, and the fact of the rate alone can often add a cachet of credibility for a particular consultant.

FEE CAPACITY

Our returns may be called earnings per share, contributed margin, or profit per partner, depending on how we're structured. In any case, we as managers are focused on the same thing: understanding our potential for generating fees, realizing that potential, and controlling our costs. Our fee-generating potential, or "fee capacity,"[6] is calculated by multiplying the number of billable consultants in the firm by the average billable rate and then multiplying that by the utilization rate we have targeted for our billable team. So if we take the standard assumption of two thousand hours available annually, a team of twenty consultants with an average rate of $100 and a target utilization rate of 75 percent displays a fee potential of $3 million (see Table 3.1).

Table 3.1. Calculating Fee Capacity

# Consultants	$ Rate	Annual Hours	Utilization	Fee Potential
20	100	2000	75 percent	$3,000,000

This illustration is oversimplified; there are any number of complicating factors. This calculation assumes that all consultants are at the same level, with the same utilization targets, the same fee-generating capacity, and the same number of hours available for billable activity. Any consultant or manager who has spent any time in the real world of professional services knows that this is far from the case. There are senior partners who act as rainmakers, spend most of their time on relationship and credibility-building activities, and, when they do perform billable work, can generate fees that are many times those of the juniors. There are subject-matter experts who are targeted at lower utilization rates because of the intense training commitment they must make to stay current with the latest technology. There are rank novices who can perform only tactical and administrative roles at this point in their development—and yet are expected to achieve billable ratios of 100 percent and sometimes higher as they demonstrate their commitment to the firm and to their own growth.

This issue of varying levels of experience, capability, and fee-generating capacity among the staff is an important one. In fact, some commentators, including David Maister, whose *Managing the Professional Service Firm*[7] is considered by many the foundation reference in this field, call its management the paramount factor in determining a firm's health. Maister states that "many factors play a role in bringing [the firm's] goals into harmony, but one has a preeminent position: the ratio of junior, middle-level, and senior staff in the firm's organization." Senior partners who can keep an active role in the client engagement, while allowing more junior staffers to perform the bulk of the work, are said to be *highly leveraged,* and esteemed and cherished for that ability. Entire firm structures are built around the ability to develop highly leveraged engagements, and this capability is recognized as a margin-building strategy. Astute control of leverage is, like the elements of rate and utilization, a key success factor for firms. The ability of senior partners to leverage their client relationships across many engagements, and to turn those relationships into deeper and broader engagements that can be delivered by junior staff, is often a make-or-break issue for firm success.

MEASURING PERFORMANCE

Utilization, billing rates, fee capacity, leverage—all boil down to one key number, profit per partner (or profit per share in a corporate structure). Firm managers have a financial responsibility to the firm to keep their eye on the ball and ensure that the engagements they take on, and the manner in which they deliver them, maximizes that profit. Managers need to be constantly monitoring, tuning, and optimizing the following financial elements:

- *Utilization Rates:* Are the members of the team targeted at the rate that best suits their talents and potential?

- *Yield:* Are team members actually realizing the potential revenue that they should be realizing? Are they achieving their utilization targets, are they efficiently delivering the quality product and services that clients expect, leading to satisfying and beneficial ongoing relationships?
- *Margin:* Are costs under control so that the firm is achieving the expected margin on hours billed or engagements delivered?

By keeping on top of these few metrics, IT service managers can have a clear idea of how the firm is performing financially. Of course, there's much more to firm management than the financials. As we discussed at the beginning of the chapter, the service firm differs from the industrial firm in that the assets are human. The management of human assets requires us to be masters not only of financial achievement but also of human relationships, enabling us to manage other critical metrics such as staff retention, satisfaction, and turnover rates. We'll discuss these elements in detail a bit later when we talk about organizational culture. In the context of financial responsibility to the firm, however, IT service firm managers must recognize that financial success does not take care of itself and that simply throwing IT talent against whatever projects arise is not a viable business strategy. Only by judicious strategic planning for utilization and pricing, and by constant oversight and adjustment, can we realize the potential for profitability that we and our teams work so hard to achieve.

End Notes

1. www.varbusiness.com.
2. *Industry Norms and Key Business Ratios.* Murray Hill, NJ: Dun and Bradstreet Information Services, 2001.
3. Troy, L. *Almanac of Business and Industrial Financial Ratios.* Englewood Cliffs, NJ: Prentice Hall, 2001.
4. www.realrates.com.
5. Weiss, A. *Million Dollar Consulting.* New York: McGraw-Hill, 1997.
6. The "fee capacity" concept is adapted from *The Intellect Industry,* by Mark C. Scott. New York: John Wiley & Sons, 1998.
7. Maister, D. *Managing the Professional Service Firm.* New York: The Free Press, 1993.

Vision and Mission

chapter **FOUR**

In my consulting work with IT services firms worldwide, I'm often dismayed to find that many firms lack a clear vision of their business model and their place in the competitive landscape. When asked where they fit along the spectrum of IT services companies, whether they are "body shops," application development firms, web boutiques, network consultants, or application service providers, the answer is often "yes!" Many firms are trying to be everything to every client, following the "one-stop shopping" competitive mantra of many of the Big Five firms. Many startup firms in the IT services industry often try to be whatever their clients want them to be at the moment, to grab any contracts that come in the door and figure out how to deliver them later. Does this approach make sense, and is it even possible, given the complexities of providing all of these different types of services? Divergent sales and marketing messages, differences in operational and project methodologies, and the challenges of recruiting and retaining skilled professionals all conspire to make offering a broad range of IT services a delivery nightmare. Perhaps just as importantly, can an IT services firm be all things to all clients and still present a consistent message to its staff, one that inspires them to think and act as a unified team? I'm convinced that this consistency of message is the key to enabling IT professionals to deliver high-quality services and stay connected and motivated.

BROAD OR DEEP?

This strategic decision, whether to generalize or specialize, whether to go broad or go deep, is as old as the professional service business itself. From legal firms to investment banks, and from medical practices to architectural firms, the question of whether it makes business sense to offer a broad range of services or to pick a niche and become the dominant player is one of the central strategic decisions managers need to make. The idea that whatever the client needs, "We can do that!" is certainly attractive from a marketing point of view. When it comes to delivery, however, it becomes more complex, especially in our field of information technology. While it might be true that, whether an architectural firm specializes in residences or office buildings, it's all architecture and all follows some similar patterns, in our business that's clearly not the case. The very structure of the work that an application development house must do to provide value to clients is inherently different from the work that a network management outsourcer or an ASP does. The types of individuals we hire, our project lifecycles and methodologies, our measurements and deliverables are so divergent that it's valid to ask whether these are even the same business. Just because they're both called IT consulting doesn't mean that the same teams of engineers can deliver these services successfully, that the same teams of managers can manage them, or that the same sales teams can market and sell them.

In fact, this human aspect of the company vision is a critical one. My experience working with IT service teams indicates to me that it may be the most important element. Over and over again I encounter in my work confused and unhappy engineers and consultants, grousing about the lack of vision and the inconsistent message they're hearing from their managers. Again and again I hear the same questions and complaints:

- "Are we a consulting business or are we here to move products?"
- "Are we doing projects or are we an outsourcing business?"
- "All they care about is billable hours. What about client satisfaction and building relationships?"
- "They're judging us on the number of scope-of-work documents we generate. It's no trick to pump up the number of prospects—just pursue every deal, even if it's a bad fit!"

These typical comments indicate again one of the central components of my philosophy: Vision is not just a slogan, it's a message that informs every decision the firm makes, from the type of business we pursue, to the way we're measured, to the quality of the work we deliver. It's a virtual contract between managers and consultants that defines our expectations for the way we conduct ourselves.

If we turn the tables a bit and look at this question from the client's side, it may seem like a no-brainer to say that clients want to work with full-service firms. One of the buzzwords that swept the IT services industry in the late 1990s was the idea of "one throat to choke," one vendor with responsibility for the client's entire portfolio of IT requirements, who could be held accountable for the business and technical results without the finger pointing that has bedeviled clients since hardware and software were unbundled in the 1970s. Once a client has been through a troubleshooting scenario in which hardware vendors point at software vendors and vice versa, their tolerance for divided IT responsibilities is severely diminished. Clients want "SBK," a single butt to kick, when projects or IT operations go awry. Larger clients with global IT operations, multiple concurrent projects, and diverse operational requirements are especially likely to look for partners with the same type of global breadth, both geographically and in service portfolio. This is one of the driving reasons behind the well-known adage that big firms like to work with big firms. For a company like Citicorp, for example, a relationship with a Big Five provider that can offer a complete range of services, take a strategic global view of the company's IT needs, and develop relationships with top managers worldwide makes a lot of sense.

Yet even global firms like Citicorp typically have niche relationships with specialist IT firms for their unique expertise in a particular technology or subject matter. Banking firms may trust their data center operations to a generalist, for instance, but may seek a relationship with a vertical market expert in banking for that unique currency-conversion application or for management of its ATM network. Geographic expertise may also be a factor in selecting relationships, as cultural differences between, say, Malaysia and Brooklyn may drive a multinational bank to develop relationships with local service providers to help them navigate local cultural issues. Fortune 500 companies often cultivate multiple service-provider relationships simply as a vendor-management tactic, to keep their Big Five partners honest by ensuring that they never become complacent or believe they have a lock on the business.

STRATEGIC PLANNING

The "broad versus deep" dilemma is not the only decision before us. We need to plan for the culture of the firm, the management style we'll practice to develop high-performance teams. We need to design metrics and programs that will ensure accountability and quality. Will we use benchmarking, quality circles, and 360-degree feedback mechanisms? What type of project methodologies will we select? Will we have a flat management structure or use a "team leader" approach? All of these operational and cultural issues have to be determined. If our firm is a startup, growing from a concept into a real business, we have the luxury of working these issues through in theory before we open our doors. In many cases, however, we have the additional operational burdens of attempting to keep a business running while we work through strategic questions. Either way, we have a responsibility to the future of our business to plan and strategize, rather than just to grab whatever projects we can scare up and hope that a business model emerges.

In essence, the task ahead of us as we try to decide the shape of our IT services firm is a strategic planning process. Strategic planning is the best method for performing a disciplined analysis of the business landscape and then setting out goals, objectives, measurements, and tactics for building and growing the firm. The strategic planning process has fallen into disrepute over the past ten years, criticized as elitist, academic, and stifling. As discredited as the strategic planning process has become in some circles, however, it is still the best framework for the necessary tasks of analyzing your skills and competencies, gauging the needs and competitive landscape of your marketplace, and assessing your own desires and proclivities in order to create a firm in your image that also has relevance in the marketplace. This is a critical point; the strategic planning process, when done right, is an exercise in understanding your own strengths and weaknesses, and then placing those attributes in the context of the external marketplace in order to understand your competitive advantages and disadvantages. A clear and honest assessment of our own competencies and the realities of the market are two key elements of any strategic plan. While it's true that some extraordinary companies can create markets where none exist and lead the buying public to a whole new place, for most of us, especially if we haven't invented some world-shattering new technology, the market leads us, and we're wise to follow. Especially in this post-Internet environment, the IT services landscape is littered with the corpses of consulting firms that thought they were smarter than the marketplace, only to find that customers actually do know what they want and are smart enough to vote with their dollars for the services that add value to their endeavors.

Many strategic planning methodologies often have "vision and mission" as the first step on the road toward the development of a five-year plan. The problem with putting this first is that, until you've completed the other steps in the planning process, such as inventorying your skills and competencies and evaluating the needs of the marketplace, it's hard to know what the focus of the firm should be. Therefore I believe that strategic planning, especially for a new or developing firm, should be looked at as a loop rather than a path. By working with your partners, staff, and clients to draft a vision everyone can support, then subjecting that vision to the realities of both the marketplace and the consensus-building process within the firm, IT services managers can craft a plan that can guide the actions and efforts of the team as it competes in our crowded and challenging market space.

Strategic planning is sometimes referred to as "anticipatory decision making." This definition implies that, by agreeing on some broad principles and guidelines for the business before a decision is required, we can make the evaluation process easier and more consistent. For instance, by deciding that we have no competitive advantage or special competencies in application development, we preclude the debate when that application project comes in the door and we're tempted to drop everything and become a Java development house. The vision and mission component of strategic planning goes deeper than just telling us what our core business is, however; it sets up ethical and cultural norms as well, so we have a framework for making the moral determinations that are central to hiring, firing, promoting, and evaluating individual contributors, as well as the everyday dilemmas of pricing, competition, and customer satisfaction that every business must face.

So what is this planning process and how do we apply it? For consultants, this process should be ingrained into our way of looking at any problem, for it's the basic consulting method at work. From a macro view, strategic planning, like any consulting engagement, is the process of answering three top-level questions. The first, "Where are we now?"—often called the as-is analysis—requires us to do an honest assessment of our current state, both in terms of our skills and resources and of our needs, desires, and inclinations. If we're an existing firm, we ask ourselves what our team members can deliver with quality, what technologies or skills we possess and excel at, and what our experience and training prepare us for. If we're a startup, we focus on our vision for the firm, what type of team we want to build, and where we'd find the talented technicians, consultants, and managers needed to realize our vision. This current-state assessment is also our opportunity to consider the competitive backdrop, to do the research and analysis required to understand who is in our market space and how we'd stack up against them.

Question two is "Where do we want to go?" This "to-be" vision is the driving force behind our entrepreneurial work, the common vision the firm will share of what we can achieve, what the tone, tenor, culture, and business model of our joint enterprise will look like and feel like. This is an art and a science; the *art* is to create a vision that will motivate and inform the team, that will create a consistent and heartfelt message that teams can rally around and feel connected to. The *science* is the development of an explicit, detailed operational plan that guides the actions of the firm as it invents itself or continuously improves its results. In our exercise in planning for the vision and mission of our firm, we need to stay focused on the real, daily decisions that we and our teams will need to make every day. This is the real meaning of anticipatory decision making.

The third question we answer in our planning process is "How do we get there?" This is one of the areas where strategic planning has gotten a bad name. Too many plans focus on the creation of a poetically worded vision statement, then neglect to design a tactical plan that tells them exactly what steps they need to take to achieve it. What actual, concrete, daily actions do we take to build the firm we want to build and create the culture we want to create? How will we recruit, select, and hire the teams we need, both in sales and delivery? What will our marketing program look like? Will we sell by referral and reputation, or will we mount a large advertising campaign, or some combination of both? How will we motivate and compensate our sales and delivery teams? What kind of clients are we looking for, and what kind of projects? How will we manage the projects we win? Do we have a consistent process and methodology we follow to ensure the delivery of quality services, and how is it enforced? What are our rates, our utilization targets, our expected margins? This is just a sampling of the questions we need to consider as we plan and build our IT consulting practice.

Now that we've looked at the strategic planning process from a high level, let's examine these planning elements in a more detailed and structured way. The first step in any planning process is deciding who should be included. In both startups and existing firms, the answer to this may seem obvious—it's the managers, owners, and executives who participate in planning, and they then broadcast the results to the team and encourage them to get on board. While it's evident that the commitment and sponsorship of these folks is required, I believe it's a dangerous error to limit participation to just executives and managers. In fact, in my consulting experience with IT firms, this error is one of the key causes of discontent and lack of consensus around the company mission. Vision can't be imposed or broadcast—it must be believed and internalized. The most effective way to achieve this is to include individual contributors and other team representatives in the planning process. Not only do team members take pride and ownership in the strategies to which they contribute, but they also are on the front lines of client engagement every day and can contribute real intelligence and insight to the process. They know what both the marketplace and individual clients value, and they understand what enhances or detracts from customer satisfaction. Their insight and contribution is a central element in the creation of a vision that is based on real market needs and that has a chance of being embraced by the staff. This inclusive style of planning also creates a cadre of evangelists for the vision, rather than a bunch of resisters and snipers.

Once we agree on the "who" of planning, the next question is how. I'm a strong believer in the use of facilitated work sessions for this kind of activity. Facilitation is a process that is specifically designed to drive meetings to conclusion in spite of conflict, disagreement, or competing agendas. I won't go into the details of running a facilitated session here—there are many excellent references on that topic (see Bibliography). The sessions that lead to a vision and mission statement need to be run in as neutral and open an atmosphere as possible. Too often, managers will come to a conclusion before the meeting and then use facilitation as an opportunity to feign participation, subtly (or not so subtly) manipulating the process to arrive at their preconceived conclusions. It should be obvious, but unfortunately it is not universally recognized, that people are not stupid and can tell when they're being manipulated. This not only breeds resistance to the vision, but also creates an atmosphere of distrust and discontent that bleeds through to everything from retention statistics to client satisfaction.

When we've determined who to include and how to run these sessions, the obvious next question is, what will we consider? I ran through a litany of questions earlier. Now let's structure them as an agenda so that entrepreneurs and managers can address them in a structured manner. One of the lessons of the Internet bubble is that the business fundamentals do in fact hold true and that entrepreneurial passion and great technology do not in themselves assure business success. A disciplined approach to planning is widely regarded as the single most effective method of creating a business with a chance of success and longevity. Let's start to construct a planning agenda that will serve as our framework for deciding what this IT services firm we're creating will look like, what it will do, and who it will serve. To do this, as we discussed earlier, we need to start with an assessment of the current status. Whether we're a working firm re-examining our objectives or a brand-new startup figuring out where we're going, we need to start here.

THE PLANNING PROCESS

Environmental Analysis

The current state of the business world we live in must be the backdrop for all planning efforts. This consideration can be further divided into four components:

The Economic Environment. Responsible businesspeople will analyze macroeconomic factors and allow them to influence the decisions they make about the timing and shape of our business activities. Is the economy in recession or expansion? Is technology purchasing on the upswing or downswing? Do tax laws encourage or discourage business investment? If IT analysts such as The Gartner Group determine that most companies will skip this generation of Windows migrations or that Linux will only penetrate into 5 percent of corporate accounts instead of the 25 percent forecast earlier, should that influence our strategy? If we know interest rates are high, causing businesses to delay the expansion of their technology infrastructures, perhaps a network implementation firm that specializes in new buildings is not the best idea. Ignoring the macroeconomic trends is a classic error of naïve entrepreneurs.

The Competitive Landscape. Thinking competitively requires us to consider both industry and marketplace. On an industry level, we need to research the state of the IT services marketplace and of our particular niche, to be sure that we have a clear understanding of the industry we're about to enter and our place in it. Does it make sense to open another general ASP now, with the knowledge that scores of well-capitalized ASPs are dropping to the wayside? Is an outsourcing business right for the moment, or is outsourcing shrinking due to oversupply or other factors? The smart entrepreneur uses resources like the financial press, financial websites, industry associations, and other research tools to broaden his or her understanding of the current state of business in the pertinent segment of the market.

Local Market Conditions. Entrepreneurs or firm managers need to review their local markets to understand how they would compete successfully given local conditions. Is another web design boutique firm a great idea in a town that has more Internet designers than clients? Is there a dominant player in our area of operations that we'd need to dethrone in order to gain a foothold? The old adage of "hitting them where they ain't" is one of the best bits of advice any entrepreneur can receive. Understanding where dominant players and strongly capitalized national firms have built practices and reputations in your area is one of the first pieces of research any IT services manager or entrepreneur must do.

Core Competencies. Finally, entrepreneurs or managers must do an internal evaluation and understand their own values, strengths, and weaknesses and those of the firm. The old standby consulting tool, the SWOT analysis, is a great method for doing this analysis. SWOT, named after its components of strengths, weaknesses, opportunities, and threats, is an easy way of structuring a facilitated discussion among all the parties participating in planning the firm's future. By asking the simple questions of the team: "What are our strengths and weaknesses? What opportunities exist for us? What are the main threats to our business concept?" in turn, and then digging down into the issues that arise, managers can gain valuable insight into the areas where the team has or lacks confidence and can make planning decisions based on those issues. This doesn't simply mean that we play to our strengths and downplay our weaknesses—the realities of the marketplace won't allow that. It often means that, when we understand the totality of the macro economy, the industry and competitive landscape, and our own competencies, values, and aspirations, we need to devote our resources to developing our weak areas in order to compete successfully.

Values Scan

Another part of the internal assessment is often called the "values scan."[1] While this may seem "softer" than the competitive analysis we've just talked about, it actually is equally important, some would say more important, to the firm's vision and mission. The standard definition of values was supplied by M. Rokeach in his book *The Nature of Human Values,*[2] as follows: "A value is an enduring belief that a specific mode of conduct is personally or socially preferable to an opposite mode of conduct." Values can address issues such as the following:

- Risk tolerance,
- Quality focus,
- Importance of growth,
- Personal aspirations,
- Commitment to employee development,
- Community participation,
- Formality or informality of the business atmosphere,
- Commitment to a diverse workplace,
- And a host of others.

It's also important to include quality-of-life issues, such as expectations about workload, time in the office, commitments to work on weekends or holidays, and other work-life balance questions. Especially now, when telecommuting and flex schedules have become an integral part of our business environment, it's important to flush out these expectations and address them directly, so that there are no misunderstandings.

While some businesspeople will scoff at these issues and insist that the marketplace and the bottom line are the only values we need to worry about, the trends in recent business prove otherwise. The most celebrated business leader in recent memory is Jack Welch of General Electric, recognized by *Fortune* magazine as "The CEO of the Century."[3] Welch was the embodiment of values-based leadership. Welch has a well-known disdain for strategic planning, opting instead for leadership based on a few simple principles such as:

- Face reality as it is, not as it was or as you wish it were;
- Don't manage; lead;
- Change before you have to; and
- If you don't have a competitive advantage, don't compete.

Welch's philosophy is based on the concept that, rather than managing folks on a task-by-task basis, the key to successful leadership is the development of some overriding values and principles that guide people's decisions. This style of leadership has become the norm rather than the exception and has been adopted by successful leaders from John Chambers of Cisco Systems to Andy Grove of Intel. Especially in the high-tech world we work in, where talented contributors require autonomy and participation, this style of values-based leadership is a perfect fit.

There is recent research that goes beyond the trends and anecdotal evidence to draw a clear correlation between organizational values and profitability. In *Practice What You Preach*[4] by the dean of professional services analysts, David Maister, the hypothesis is presented that "the most financially successful businesses do better than the rest on virtually every aspect of employee attitudes, and those that do best on employee attitudes are measurably more profitable." Maister goes on to argue, and to back up with extensive research and field surveys, that organizations that focus on positive values such as participation, recognition, ethics, loyalty, fairness, and trust do better on all measures of business success, from profitability to recruiting to retention and client relationships. The ability to understand the values of both the individuals and the organization, to create an enterprise that embodies those values and adheres to them consistently, and to communicate those values convincingly to both the team and the market is, according to Maister's research, the most powerful business tool available. So it becomes even more clear that it is incumbent on IT services entrepreneurs to take the values scan seriously and to devote as much attention to it as we'd devote to a marketplace analysis.

Remember that values can be both personal and organizational. I've worked for companies that were highly participative and informal and for others that were authoritarian and reserved. Organizational values can be driven from the top, but they also develop over years and are the cumulative result of the circumstances, histories, and personalities that pass through the company. In a startup situation, it's critical to ensure that the founding partners have values in common—or at least negotiate among themselves to determine how their personal values will be applied to the firm's direction. In an existing organization that is stepping back and reassessing its direction, managers and entrepreneurs must confer with their teams and determine whether the values that have evolved are consistent with their personal values.

How do we assess these values? Often the process begins with a survey, and there are many pre-designed surveys available that can be used for this purpose. (Maister's *Practice What You Preach* includes a complete list of the surveys he used to prepare his findings.) Facilitated work sessions are also frequently used as a follow-up to the surveys, to dig deeper into the values, attitudes, and opinions expressed throughout the enterprise. It's important to make the values scan process as participative as possible. As we learned in the first chapter, recruiting and retention in the IT field is highly dependent on a cultural as well as a technical fit, and firm managers need to stay focused on this reality. Understanding the values of the management team is important, as they will be the examples and mentors for the organization. The values and expectations of current and prospective employees are just as important. Remember that values are often in conflict, and disagreements must be worked out. This is an excellent opportunity to gain a clearer understanding of your partners, team, and staff, and again, it's the process as much as the outcome that's valuable.

Finally, how do these values manifest themselves in the vision and mission exercise? Almost any organization's mission statement includes declarations regarding the company's desire to be tops in its market or to be the preferred supplier. Most mission statements also include language about the culture and values of the organization. Hoechst Celanese, for instance, states that their core values include: "Respect for individuals, diversity accepted and valued, informed employees through open communication."

Johnson & Johnson states that "We are responsible to our employees. We must respect their dignity and recognize their merit. We must provide competent management, and their actions must be just and ethical. We are responsible to the communities in which we live and work."

Marriott Hotels has a mission statement that is an exemplar of conciseness and clarity. "We do it right" was the mission that J.W. Marriott, Sr., handed down to his team, and that simple statement guided the actions of thousands of employees who faced the customers every day.

These brief examples illustrate the importance of ensuring that any company vision encompasses individual and organizational values as well as pure business goals. "Eighteen percent earnings before taxes and depreciation" may be what the shareholders or investment community wants to hear, but that statement will never energize a team the way Jack Welch's exhortation to "be number 1 or 2 in every market we compete in" or the Marriott motto "We do it right." These types of statements, deeply connected to the personal, social, and organizational culture that you're trying to create, are the rallying cries that motivate achievement.

Business Modeling

The next step in the planning process is the development of a business model. Our environmental analysis should have helped us set some broad parameters in terms of the businesses we may want to go into and the ones we'll stay away from. Our values scan will have given us guidance in terms of issues like growth plans, recruiting, and culture. Now it's time to select our lines of business, create detailed operating plans, and define success in our chosen lines of business. This is the moment when we address questions such as:

- What is our overall business? Are we an application development shop, a network outsourcer, an ASP, or a "rent-a-tech" house?
- Within this overall business, exactly what offerings will we be presenting to the marketplace?
- What actions must we take to prepare these offerings?
- What staffing decisions must we make to be ready to fulfill the projects that arise from our offerings?
- How will we be organized to deliver on these lines of business?

One of the most successful methods for finding the answers is the use of *scenario planning.* This technique is widely used in the world of business planning and is also becoming a valuable tool in the IT planning world. It's important to emphasize that this is not simply an exercise in figuring out how to acheive better results in the businesses we're already in—it's about envisioning a new and unique future for the organization and then figuring out the steps we'd take to reach it. John Scully, the ex-CEO of Apple Computer, in his book *Odyssey: Pepsi to Apple,*[5] described Apple's planning process as projecting Apple five years into the future, visualizing not just the company and the computer industry but also the world economy. The planning team worked toward developing a consensus regarding their predictions, how the expected events and environment would affect Apple, and what the best outcomes for Apple might be. Then they set about the nitty-gritty work of figuring out how to attain the optimal results based on their predicted scenarios.

Some would say that scenario planning is an exercise in speculation and fantasy that has no place in the down-and-dirty world of business. While scenario planning must be tempered with the reality of competitive analysis and industry research, it does give managers and entrepreneurs an opportunity to allow their creativity and aspirations to guide the organization's future. Russell Ackoff, one of the pioneers of corporate planning, in his classic book *Creating the Corporate Future,*[6] called this type of scenario planning "proactive futuring," a term that highlights the benefits of this approach. It's not just about dreaming of some happy ending; it's about taking responsibility for actively building toward that goal. Rather than being the subject of changes and events that come down the pike, the organization takes responsibility for its own future. It's this type of planning that is responsible for creating some of the most successful products of the late 20th Century, from the disposable diaper to the Walkman. These were markets that didn't exist, but were foreseen by agile planners who synthesized their understanding of their customers and the capabilities of technology to envision new products to serve emerging needs of new markets.

How does it work in practical terms? It's a brainstorming process in which the entrepreneurs, managers, and team members can take what they know about their industry, what they've learned from their analysis, and what they have uncovered in their values scan and apply that knowledge to visualizing the ideal IT services organization. This exercise can utilize many of the tools we've described earlier, such as surveys, facilitated sessions, and executive planning sessions. I've seen some creative organizations use innovative techniques for this process. One group of managers asked their team members to write essays describing what the firm would look like in five years, what their jobs would be like, and what they would need in order to make their vision a reality! Handing out homework assignments is not the usual order of business in many firms, but in this firm the team members got behind the exercise with vigor and took personal responsibility for championing their visions and for taking on the tasks they identified. Again, this is not just an exercise in creating a plan, but another opportunity to show your team members that their opinions matter and that their desires for a fulfilling work life congruent with their plans and dreams is an important component of the firm's makeup.

The business modeling exercise takes as input the competitive analysis we've done and the values scan we've performed and then applies those results to the following questions:

- What are the lines of business we'll develop?
- What are our goals and measurements of success in those businesses?

- What are the operational details we need to master in order to achieve those goals?
- What other strategic thrusts, such as alliances, partnerships, development programs, or other activities, must we pursue to build long-term success in these businesses?

The answers to these questions will guide us toward the overarching vision and mission statements we'll develop as the end result of this process and will start us on the road to the creation of detailed operational plans and procedures for the daily management of the business.

Our honest assessment of the marketplace, of our proclivities and aspirations, and of our talents and knowledge will be our guiding lights in this exercise. We may decide to focus on developing banking applications in Java or on installing and managing large data centers. We may determine that we're more interested in working with high-tech manufacturers or with the aerospace industry. We might decide as a team that the best use of our experience and knowledge is to consult with Fortune 500 companies on the deployment of Internet technology. The honesty and judgment required to navigate this exercise successfully is intense; we must balance our desires and hopes with the hard reality of the marketplace and of our team's strengths and weaknesses. The ability to match true competencies and experience with the needs of the market and the competitive landscape is one of the defining characteristics of the entrepreneur.

If we do decide, after an honest appraisal and evaluation, that developing banking applications in Java is our niche, we'd better have come to that decision based on the realities of the marketplace and our abilities. This may seem obvious, but it's my experience that many would-be entrepreneurs in our business are more driven by their interest in a particular technology than by a clear-eyed assessment of the real market potential of that technology. This is not the moment for falling in love with a particular technology and hoping that the world will share your affections, yet I see this approach frequently. Often the would-be entrepreneur responds to my criticism of this approach by stating that "We'll lead the market to this technology." While it's true, of course, that companies from Intel to Netscape have created markets where none existed, it's also true that the conditions were ripe for these developments. If you are planning to lead the market, your attention to the realities of the competitive landscape, your competencies, your plan for surviving the "years in the wilderness" before your technology takes off, all of these elements must be clearly defined if you intend to be successful.

Realizing the Vision

After your team has done the "as-is" analysis of assessing the marketplace and your competencies and has visualized the "to-be" state and the services and offerings that the firm will provide, the next step is to create an execution plan. Operational plans in the IT services world are based on five key components, as follows:

- Targeting and servicing clients;
- Developing a compelling mix of services;
- Managing the financial metrics of rate, utilization, and leverage;
- Developing and enforcing processes and methodologies; and
- Recruiting, retaining, and developing talented consultants.

Let's take a look at the creation of an operating strategy for each of these elements.

Targeting and Servicing Clients

Targeting clients in the IT services business is one of the most critical components of an operating strategy for a number of reasons. Unlike the product business, services are delivered person to person, so the development of client intimacy and trust is an integral part of the transaction. Services firms often develop long-term relationships with their top clients, and so compatibility and mutual understanding are essential to success. The profit potential of different clients varies widely, depending on their IT spending habits, their use of outside partners, their economic condition, and a host of other factors. The cost of courting, nurturing, and retaining clients is high. For all of these reasons, IT firms must devote special attention to their target marketing programs.

In the strategic planning process, we must formulate a target market strategy that will keep us focused on the right clients and the right appeals that will attract them. Rather than relying on such broadcast techniques as advertising, cold calling, and direct mail, successful services firms develop targeting techniques based on a sophisticated understanding of the competition, of the prospects in their area of operations, and of the macroeconomic factors, both by geography and business segment. We'll talk about this in more depth when we delve into marketing, but at this stage in the planning process we need to begin articulating our vision of the clients we'll target. Are we focusing on a particular industry or segment? Do we have actual firms in mind, such as the top three Fortune 500 companies in our state? How will we learn about their current relationships with competitors and their current projects or initiatives? How will we ensure that we don't fall prey to the "honey trap" of professional services, namely over-dependence on a few plum clients? During this vision and mission quest, entrepreneurs need to think through their client profiles and develop a plan of attack for their targeted markets.

Developing a Compelling Mix of Services

Is it enough to say, "We're an application development shop"? Or is it more prudent to further qualify that and say, "We're a Java shop specializing in the development of web-based supply chain management solutions"? The creation of services is an especially subtle exercise. Many firms try to "product-ize" their service offerings. This is especially prevalent among those with a history in the product business, such as system integrators or the professional service arms of product companies, such as software developers or hardware manufacturers. Their sales teams are comfortable selling products, their accountants are used to counting in units, and their managers and executives are comfortable forecasting in units. We therefore see the packaged migration service, the packaged network design service, or the packaged eCommerce solution. The problem with this approach is that, to the client, it's not reassuring but disconcerting. Clients understand that every engagement is unique and that their needs are different from the last migration or eCommerce solution you provided. Packaged services may be more comfortable inside the firm, but they lead prospects to fear that, rather than giving them individualized services, you'll try to fit them into a pre-packaged "box" of services.

Therefore firms must walk a fine line when developing their services portfolio. It's obviously critical to have a story with which to go to market so that you can explain exactly what it is you do. On the other hand, that story has to portray enough flexibility so that the prospect hears the message that you'll be flexible and easy to work with—and that you won't try to make them fit a pre-conceived mold. We'll talk about ways to walk this tightrope successfully further on, but for now, remember that thinking through your portfolio of services with your team and determining the actual steps it will take to create that delivery capability are key outcomes of this vision quest.

Managing the Financial Metrics of Rate, Utilization, and Leverage

We discussed in the last chapter the basic financial elements that all IT services firms have in common. Now you and your team must knuckle down and make the hard choices. Will you be a low-cost provider of commodity techs-for-rent, hiring PC jockeys out of technical school, or a high-dollar strategic partner, with the attendant need for more senior and experienced staff? Will you charge a premium rate or try to compete on price? Will you target high utilization and attract talent by offering top dollar, or will you target moderate utilization and recruit based on opportunities for training and development? All of these decision are part of the mix of strategies you and your team must weigh as you develop your financial approach to the business.

Developing and Enforcing Processes and Methodologies

The reengineering craze, the quality movement, and the process improvement bandwagon of the last twenty years have revolutionized the manufacturing industries, yet the professional services firms have been largely untouched, doing business the same way they have for eons. Sure, we may be using Microsoft Project instead of a napkin to track our project status, but our fundamental process of people delivering hourly services to other people has remained pretty much the same. Even in the IT niche, we've been slow to adopt the improvements available through new technology and methodologies.

This can't last. With the advent of professional services automation software and the market pressures of pay-for-performance engagements, service firms will be forced to compete on process efficiency and on methodology. Clients become more sophisticated every day, and it's not uncommon, in my experience, for IT services firms to walk into client sites and find that the client's project methodologies are far more robust and disciplined than the provider's. We'll devote the entire next chapter to an in-depth discussion of the place of process and methodology in the services firm. I'll just say here that smart entrepreneurs will acknowledge that they must compete, not just on the basis of superior technical talent, but also on the ability to harness that talent to deliver results efficiently and consistently.

Recruiting, Retaining, and Developing Talented Consultants

It's all about talented people. As with a basketball team or an orchestra, the physical assets, the brand and relationships, have no value without the players to make it all come alive. And, as in music and sports, the contribution of management is to scout, motivate, and develop those players into a competitive team that can deliver the goods. As we plan for the future of our team, we must develop strategies for finding and attracting the best candidates and for helping them mature into seasoned senior contributors.

How do you find the best technical contributors? IBM, with its 2000 workforce of 149,000 in the Global Services business, obviously needs to identify and attract talent continually. In 2000 alone, IBM hired 19,000 professionals worldwide for its services business! In order to assure that they were identifying the strongest candidates, IBM surveyed their IBM Fellows, an elite group of engineers and scientists, and asked them what attributes top technical contributors have in common.[7] The most frequently mentioned indicators of superior technical performance, in order, were

- Selection for technical task forces;
- Selection for special projects;
- Professional society publication;
- Professional society awards;
- Professional society presentations; and
- Company or team awards.

The message from this survey is that talented technical professionals are best identified by their peers, as evidenced by their selection to participate in high-visibility projects or to present or write for a technical audience.

Equally interesting is a study by Alon Gratch, a doctoral candidate at Columbia University. Published by *The New York Times* as "Tamed Rebels Make Good Managers,"[8] Gratch's study tested the attitudes of seventy corporate leaders and found that one of the key indicators of success was their degree of non-conformity. Other criteria for success were their degree of autonomy, their ability to motivate themselves without outside reward, and their deep concern for the autonomy of others.

Finally, we must remember that we're not looking for back-room technicians who can hide away in a data center. Because we're building a business around trust, advice, and personal service, we need individuals who, along with their technical skills, have communication, negotiation, and presentation skills, who can apply technology to business needs, and who are mature, presentable, and likeable. As

I've mentioned, one of the fatal mistakes I've often observed is hiring for technical skills alone.

How do these studies help IT services entrepreneurs? My experience is that the best way to recruit for the technical disciplines is to ask technicians for candidates. Technicians have an informal hierarchy of respect that develops from working together, from word of mouth, and from visible achievement. I've found that incentives that encourage technicians to bring their peers into the organization are highly effective. I've also known services managers who will scour the trade papers and even the local business or computer newsletters and reach out to anyone who's contributed an article or is listed as a seminar presenter or speaker. Using the technician's grapevine and offering cash incentives for bringing talent to the table has been my staple recruiting mechanism throughout my consulting career. The data on non-conformity confirms the conventional wisdom that top performers are not afraid to bend the rules, are not looking for outside impetus but are instead self-driven, and are autonomous workers who don't need to be managed on a task-by-task level. This is especially true in the IT world, and I look for these attributes when recruiting. Identifying the interpersonal, business, and project skills required for successful consulting is also a necessary element of the recruiting mix.

Retention is one of the most intractable issues in the IT services business. In flush economic times like we experienced in the late 1990s, it wasn't unusual for IT consulting firms to experience 40 percent annual turnover! Obviously, with the expense of recruiting and developing consultants, including the costly technical certifications that are common in our business, this can devastate a firm. Although the leaner economic backdrop of the early 21st Century has limited the options for our technical players looking to jump ship, the inevitable return to growth will again offer lots of alternatives for strong contributors. Of course, it's always the best performers who have the most options, no matter what the economic backdrop looks like.

The threat to retention of talented consultants comes from both ends of the spectrum. At one end, there is the problem of consultants "going native." Consultants, especially those on long-term assignment, start to lose their social connection to the firm and substitute social connections within the client. These, after all, are the people they work with every day, the folks they go out to lunch with and interact with and, in many cases, especially when the consultant is traveling to the engagement, the firm is far away. These consultants are frequently lured away by the client, or even volunteer for open spots within the client's business. Defection to the client is, in my experience, the number one cause of attrition in IT services firms. Consulting managers must develop strategies to counteract this phenomenon, from frequent home-leave to executive site visits to team activities and recognition.

At the other end of the spectrum is the consultant who is always seeking the grail of deeper technical challenge. Consulting draws people who need constantly escalating exposure to new technology, new challenges, and new experiences. These folks become bored as soon as they solve the technical problem and are often ready to jump ship whenever the next big thing comes along. Smart IT managers will create development programs that allow people with these personalities to keep on top of technical developments and will schedule resources on projects with an eye toward their interests and development, rather than focusing only on driving the best profitability or the highest utilization.

Consultant development is such an important area that I've devoted an entire chapter to it (see Chapter Eight). While profitability and client success are the driving forces behind our business, the true life achievement for many entrepreneurs comes from helping talented rookies develop into mature advisors, outstanding contributors, and great earners for themselves and for the firm.

THE VISION THING

Vision, like faith, is hard to define, and harder still to capture. How do you know when you've achieved it? I have a simple indicator: *belief.* If the team believes that the vision that you've developed and articulated together reflects the group's desires and aspirations, if it believes that together you can achieve the goals and objectives set forth, if it believes that you've brought together the right mix of talent and ambition and is ready to march together toward the future you've visualized, then you've achieved a common vision. If that level of common belief is not there yet, it doesn't mean you've failed; it just means you have a bit more work to do. The strategic planning process can't be short-circuited. If consensus and common belief have not been achieved, then go through the loop again and try a little harder to work through the areas of disagreement or confusion. While we don't want to allow "analysis paralysis" to stop us from going out into the arena and competing, we need to take whatever reasonable efforts we can take to ensure that we're creating a mission that our team can act on. If anyone has issue with the services we're proposing to offer, working that out can only be a positive. Either it will uncover a hole or unrealistic expectation, or it will bring on board a reluctant participant. The process is the point. By allowing all contributors to participate, we build a future that everyone has a stake in, and that everyone owns.

FROM PRODUCTS TO SERVICES

The migration from products to services is being navigated by many of the industry giants. From Oracle to Microsoft to Intel to Compaq, every product manufacturer is being driven by customer demands or shrinking product margins to mutate from a pure product company into a provider of services. This is not just an IT phenomenon; Jack Welch and GE Plastics is a classic business school case study in the migration from product to solution selling. In the IT industry, however, this migration has a checkered past that should be sobering to any IT services manager. For every success story like IBM Global Services there's a nightmare like Compaq's bid to buy services capability through its acquisition of Digital Equipment Corporation. The large PC resellers like ComputerLand and BusinessLand attempted this migration in the 1990s, and judging by their recent acquisitions at bargain-basement prices or their outright folding, they didn't navigate the change very successfully. The giant IT hardware and software companies have much at stake as they, too, attempt to make this change. Will their sales teams, skilled at selling products, be able to successfully morph themselves into services sales professionals, with the added complexities of selling intangible services and benefits? Will their product-oriented lifecycles and methodologies make the transition to the world of IT services? Will their engineers, accustomed to internal development in teams of like-minded and like-cultured teammates, learn the delicacies of providing fee-based services to external clients? Can executives transition from counting units sold, and instead focus on relationships, utilization, knowledge management, and practice development, as IT services managers must? Let's take a closer look at some of the issues involved in making this transition from products to services. The history of IBM Global Services makes a great case study to guide our understanding of the complexities of this strategic business model transition.

IBM: Moving from Products to Services

One of the big stories in the IT services industry has been the migration from product-centric offerings to offerings focused on services. As I'm writing this, the IT business press is featuring the announcement by Compaq Computer that they will be the latest to refocus their business model on the services segment. This move by Compaq continues an industry trend that is exemplified by the transition made by IBM under the stewardship of Lou Gerstner. In fact, Compaq's CEO, Michael Capellas, explicitly cites IBM's success in making this migration as his touchstone. "We're definitely looking at the IBM model," he told *Information Week* magazine. "Our combination is to blend superior systems engineering and services, so it results in the kinds of platforms that we think are going to be the future of the Internet."[9]

Of course, pulling off these kind of migrations is easier said than done. Compaq purchased Digital Equipment Corporation in an attempt to take advantage of Digital's huge services practice and stumbled badly in the integration of the two companies, in the opinion of most analysts. Even Capellas acknowledges the difficulties faced by his predecessor, Eckhard Pfeiffer, in that acquisition. "Digital was huge. That was a foundation-changing, wrack-the-rafters, entirely different business model," Capellas told *Information Week.* "Within the company we don't even talk about Digital integration anymore. That is long gone. I have a very simple rule: You work with the culture, not against it."[10]

Looking back at the successful migration of IBM, it seems inevitable that the world's most powerful computer company would be able to pull off this sort of company turnaround. Like all corporate rebirths, however, the reality was a lot messier than it appeared. In 1993, before Gerstner took the helm, IBM was losing billions of dollars, watching its stock fall through the floor, laying off tens of thousands of staffers (in an "employment for life" culture), and seemingly headed for a breakup. Now, on the eve of Gerstner's retirement, it's a very different story. In the midst of a tech meltdown, IBM shows steady growth, has successfully tied its name to the eBusiness revolution, and has regained its edge in hardware and software. It's in the services division, however, that IBM has really rocked the IT playing field. IBM's Global Services, formerly a small backwater of bundled offerings that were typically given away with hardware, supplied $8.5 billion of revenue in 2000, accounting for 40 percent of total sales and nearly half of profits.

As noted in a recent article in *The Industry Standard,*[11] the turnaround in IBM was based on a lot more than just Gerstner's special skills. "It's tempting," said Jonathan Weber of *The Industry Standard,* "in light of this history, to give all the credit to Gerstner. Indeed, one obvious moral of this story is that leadership matters. But the turnaround is also a credit to the deep strength of the company's culture. Behind it were real principles: belief in the power and importance of technological advancement, commitment to excellence in everything from R&D and product development to sales and marketing, and attention to the complexities inherent in managing a very large organization."

The landscape of players who have tried to make this shift is littered with corpses, however. The entire PC reseller industry is a case study in the difficulties of making the transition from products to services. In the interest of full disclosure, I'll note that I was a general manager at Entex Information Services, one of the top players in the reseller space, during the 1990s, when we tried to migrate from selling PCs and networks to becoming an outsourced services provider, so I had a front-row view of the challenges involved.

In the 1980s, when the PC began to attract the interest of the corporate world, a new business segment arose, which came to be known as the value-added reseller, or VAR. Companies such as ComputerLand and BusinessLand tapped the corporate hunger for PCs by first opening retail storefronts and then expanding those businesses with outbound sales forces. These businesses had huge success at first because the IBM and Compaq computers and the Visicalc and dBase software they sold were in high demand. Margins were often in the range of 40 percent or more. Thousands of small computer shops sprouted in every mall and downtown area, servicing local businesses and offering installation assistance and training in the use of these new devices. As the PC landscape settled, a few clear trends emerged. Many of the early entrants into the PC manufacturing marketplace, such as Osborne, Kaypro, and Columbia, disappeared as the dominant players like Compaq, Apple, and IBM began to take more and more market share. The same phenomenon occurred in the software world, as the hundreds of small developers offering niche software products were overtaken by Microsoft, with their offering of bundled Office Suites that, although perhaps not the best product in each area, offered the convenience of interoperability and one-stop sales, support, and service.

Resellers in the 1990s were hit with a whirlwind of change, and many of them were swept away in the maelstrom. First, their suppliers and partners turned into their competitors. As the Compaqs and Microsofts of the world gained a foothold in the corporate marketplace, both they and their corporate customers decided that a direct relationship had significant advantages. For the vendor, direct corporate sales obviously offered larger margins and an unfiltered relationship with the customer. Compaq and Microsoft fielded their own direct corporate sales teams and distanced the VARs from their most lucrative and profitable customers. For the corporate customers, the value that the value-added reseller provided was diminishing rapidly, as more of the workforce became computer literate and so needed less of the training and support the VARs offered, and as in-house IT teams became more PC and network savvy and more able to perform their own support and installation work. Then, Michael Dell threw another monkey wrench into the reseller's business model by creating "Dell Direct," a program that disenfranchised the resellers completely. This innovation was based on the final recognition that the value was completely gone from the value-added model. Corporate clients and home users alike decided that they would forego the supposed added value to save a few bucks on the PC. Starting in a University of Texas dorm room, Dell chipped away at the VAR-distributed PC business until, in 1999, Dell overtook Compaq as the largest PC company in the world.

As the VARs saw this storm approaching, they all made the same decision: migrate from products to services. In an effort to distance themselves from their product-oriented heritage, many of the resellers shed their skin and took on new identities. ComputerLand became VanStar, BusinessLand became Entex, and resellers like CompuCom and MicroAge tacked "services" to their corporate names. Most of these players attempted to hold on to their product businesses, even as the Dell and Gateway direct sales model cannibalized their customer base and nibbled away at their margins. From the 40 percent margins common in the glory days, margins on PC gear for most resellers plummeted to the 1 to 5 percent range by the late 1990s. Worse, their split focus on selling both hardware and services confused customers and undermined their marketing message. Were they independent advisors working with their clients to select the best solutions based on the client's needs? Or were they just trying to move boxes? This product/services hybrid model created other difficulties. The sales talent required to sell hardware and the skills required to sell services are very different, and the focus of the customer relationships diverge as well. In large organizations, PC purchases are typically done through a purchasing department, while services are typically sold to CIOs, IT managers, or departmental executives. The sales teams that excel at the detailed minutia of product lines, serial numbers, licensing agreements, and product compatiblilities possess very different skills from the successful sellers of services, who bring an understanding of the client's business requirements, the ability to recommend various solution architectures, and a gift for gaining the client's trust as an advisor and resource. The attempt to turn product salespeople into "solution providers," the VAR buzzword of the 1990s, in most cases was a bust.

The events of the last few years are a clear indication that the demise of the reseller is at hand, if it hasn't in fact already occurred. The once mighty ComputerLand became VanStar and then was absorbed by Inacom. Inacom closed up shop in 2001, unable to keep up with the Internet-inspired changes sweeping the industry. Entex, which in the mid-1990s was listed as number one on *VARBusiness* magazine's list of the top VARs in the world and boasted revenues of over $2 billion, was recently purchased by Siemens for less than $120 million, and now exists only as a division within the giant Siemens organization.

THE LESSONS OF MIGRATION

What are the lessons for IT services entrepreneurs and managers from this history? The VARs made a few obvious errors as events overtook their business model. First, of course, just calling yourself "value-added" doesn't mean that the marketplace will perceive you as such. Many VARs continued to insist that clients valued their ability to offer training, installation, and service even as the success of Dell and Gateway proved the opposite. This head-in-the-sand attitude cost these companies dearly, and the lesson for IT services firms is that the marketplace rules, and the value perception of customers must drive every decision we make. In my practice as an advisor to IT services firms, I often see companies so focused on their own products or services and their own perception of the value they bring that they forget to include the customer in their calculations. All business models, and all products and services, must be tested in the crucible of the marketplace, where customers decide to spend or withhold their dollars and so tell us what they value. This is especially interesting in light of the ITAA study we reviewed earlier, in which 70 percent of IT services companies surveyed stated that they are not good at developing new products and services. As noted by ITAA and its consulting partners, IT firms need to continually survey the marketplace and develop new service offerings and should use techniques such as user groups and customer councils to gain a clear customer's-eye picture of the needs of the marketplace.

This history should also remind us that the sales and relationship skills required to sell IT services are rare and unique and that IT services can't just be "grafted on" to an existing business. Many of the advertising agencies or network integrators that tried to jump on the eConsulting bandwagon during the Internet explosion learned this lesson the hard way. Just because your customer is prepared to buy a PC from you, or trusts you to design a logo, doesn't mean that you can then migrate to become a trusted advisor with mission-critical IT systems. In the IT services world, experienced, business-savvy, technology-literate individuals who can develop executive-level relationships are a key to success. Many of the resellers, in their hunger to migrate up the value chain by offering services, tried to "productize" their services by creating off-the-shelf network design or Lotus Notes products. Unfortunately, clients are sophisticated enough to recognize that one size doesn't fit all in IT services, and these canned offerings were spectacular failures. IT services managers must resist the temptation to focus on their internal selling needs when designing service offerings and must let the voice of the customer into the company to drive their selection of services. Through focus groups, customer feedback forms, regular customer satisfaction surveys, and executive-level interactions, IT firms can hear what the marketplace values and design services that fit those needs. As the demise of the VARs illustrates, those firms that believe their own hype or neglect to change with the changing marketplace are doomed.

Does this mean that there is no place for IT services providers that also offer hardware or software? While the huge national VARs have mostly disappeared, in fact there are many local resellers who are still doing well with this model. These local firms have developed deep trust relationships with their small-business customers and often act as the outsourced purchasing, R&D, support, and training organization for their clients. The trends that decimated the large national resellers, such as direct sales by the manufacturers and increased PC literacy of the workforce and IT staff, have, in many cases, passed these smaller players by. Their small business customers never gained the attention of the Compaqs and Microsofts of the world, and they typically have little or no internal IT support. For these small companies and the local resellers that develop relationships with them, the product/service hybrid business model still adds value. If small to medium businesses are your target market and you are interested in focusing on a local scope, this model may still have much vitality left in it for you as an IT services entrepreneur.

On a larger scale, we return to the Compaq and IBM product/services hybrid. While few entrepreneurs have the wherewithal to enter into competition with, or to emulate, these giants, there are still some lessons we can learn from them. The IBM turnaround miracle, for instance, teaches us, as we discussed earlier, that the power of culture and values can go a long way toward sustaining an organization through tough times and can provide the fuel for a turnaround when the conditions are ripe. Entrepreneurs and managers who can build supportive, collaborative, and participative cultures around values of achievement and pride can rally the troops to make the difficult changes necessary to survive through downturns. Another point to recognize is that IBM's turnaround was based on a ruthless focus on business fundamentals. As noted in the recent article in *The Industry Standard,*[12] "The company's transformation hasn't come easily. It has, in fact, been hard work—the roll-up-your-sleeves, nose-to-the-grindstone, pencil-to-the-paper kind of work that a turnaround specialist like Gerstner understands and preaches. That's what Gerstner did, meeting with each operating unit and going detail by detail through each department's business plan. The result was a plan to reduce $7 billion in expenses. Tens of thousands of IBMers left or lost their jobs." While these wrenching changes are never easy, they stand in sharp contrast to the dilly-dallying and self-delusion that conspired to finish off the resellers. In our exploration of the IT services industry, we'll return again and again to the themes sounded here, the themes of hard-nosed attention to the business fundamentals, and of complete concentration on the dictates of the marketplace.

End Notes

1. The concept of the "values scan" is based on material in *Applied Strategic Planning,* by L.D. Goodstein, T.M. Nolan, & J.W. Pfeiffer. New York: McGraw-Hill, 1993.
2. Rokeach, M. *The Nature of Human Values.* New York: The Free Press, 1973.
3. The Greatest CEOs in History. *Fortune,* December 1999.

4. Maister, D. *Practice What You Preach.* New York: The Free Press, 2000.
5. Scully, J. *Odyssey: Pepsi to Apple, a Journey of Adventure, Ideas, and the Future.* New York: Harper & Row, 1987.
6. Ackoff, R. *Creating the Corporate Future.* New York: John Wiley & Sons, 1981.
7. The IBM survey is based on material in W. Humphries, *Managing Technical People.* Reading, MA: Addison-Wesley/Longman, 1997.
8. Gratch, A. Tamed Rebels Make Good Managers. *The New York Times,* February 10, 1985.
9. McDougall, P. One on One with Capellas. *Information Week,* July 2, 2001.
10. ibid.
11. Weber, J. The Fall and Rise of IBM. *The Industry Standard,* May 28, 2001.
12. Boslet, M. Big Blue After Lou. *The Industry Standard,* June 4, 2001.

Process and Methodology

chapter **FIVE**

Consultants often develop a jaundiced view of their clients. In the same way that cops begin to believe that everyone is a criminal or divorce lawyers start to think that everyone is an adulterer, IT consultants often develop the opinion that every IT staffer is a bungler with no idea how to manage a project. Like members of these other professions, our clientele is self-selected—in other words, if they weren't in trouble (or at least in need of assistance), they wouldn't call us. And like these other practitioners, we're at risk of becoming cynics if we start to believe that our sampling of troubled clients is representative of the whole world. Still, it often seems that every project I see is in trouble and that every IT organization I engage with lacks basic project processes.

I look back at my career in IT consulting and find that a large proportion of my projects have been "saves," projects that were in danger of failing or had already failed due to poor project management. While some of these were internal projects, attempted by IT departments that were then overwhelmed by complexity or politics, an equal number were projects run by IT consultants, who, of course, should have known better. From SAP projects costing millions of dollars that never reach completion, to network integration projects that never integrate, to application development projects that only deliver a fraction of the expected functionality yet overrun budget and schedule by orders of magnitude, the horror stories abound. And while lawyers have bar associations and doctors have review committees that evaluate their performance and, in extreme cases, can even revoke licenses, we as IT consultants have no judge but the marketplace to appraise our results. And judging by the consultant jokes, the disparaging TV ads, and the swift demise of many high-flying Internet consultancies, the market's judgment has been harsh and unforgiving.

No architect or builder would consider beginning a complex construction project without a detailed plan. No responsible construction firm would have a bunch of tradesmen, no matter how skilled, just show up at a job site and start laying bricks or pouring concrete. Yet, amazingly, there are still many IT services firms who believe that just applying good technical resources to a project is a recipe for success. When in my work as an advisor to IT services firms I interview clients to hear their assessment of the services they received, I often hear a story similar to this:

> "They told me they had the best network technicians in town. Since we had a network project, they seemed like a good fit. It was true—their technicians were very talented. The problem was, they just showed up—no preparatory meetings with our IT team or our departments, no project planning meetings, no communication. Just a bunch of engineers showing up at our data center and starting to do stuff. They never stopped by to tell me what they were doing that day, what they had accomplished, or what they planned to do next week or next month. Their idea of an IT project was just to throw a bunch of technical bodies at it and hope they'd figure it out. And then we got this bill. . . ."

I wish I could report that this was an exaggeration or an isolated situation, but unfortunately that's not the case. Especially among the smaller, more entrepreneurial IT firms I work with, this is the rule rather than the exception. Managers of IT service teams often make the mistake of assuming that, just because an engineer is an expert in the technical matter of the engagement, that it automatically translates into expertise in the process of engaging. The techniques required to deliver an IT result that fulfills the client's expectations, with quality, on time, and within budget incorporate a complex set of disciplines and methods that technicians don't just learn by osmosis or pick up by accident. They must be defined, formalized, and enforced by the firm, and the firm has responsibility for ensuring that they are applied consistently and successfully for the benefit of its clients.

This topic of methodology and process is broad and encompasses many components. Project management is obviously a critical part of it, but it's not all. The development of service-specific toolkits is also an important part of a firm's process portfolio. So is the development of a set of standards around the way documentation, training, security, contingency planning, and knowledge transfer to the internal IT staff are delivered. IT consultants at client sites delivering services often must deal with complex and dynamic technologies, integration challenges, political turf battles, and organizational quagmires. They shouldn't have to make up a process for delivering services on the fly each time they engage!

There is, however, a danger in swinging the pendulum too far in the direction of pre-packaged service delivery. I've chatted with many IT consultants who have left the Big Five consulting universe because there was so much methodology around every move they made that they felt all room for creativity and personal expression had been squeezed out of their work. I've often heard from these folks that they became disgusted when they realized that, whether they were building an enterprise-level data center or moving a PC from one desk to another, they still had to fill out the same seventeen binders full of risk forms and checklists and still had to navigate the same series of approvals and counter-approvals. The best firms are those that have discovered the fine balance between methodology and creativity.

The movement toward lighter methodologies is one manifestation of the push toward this balance. The old waterfall methodologies (so-called because project activities moved in only one direction, forward, with no opportunity to revisit a previous activity), developed in the early days of programming as remedies for chaotic and undisciplined programming practices, have since gained a reputation for being burdensome and unresponsive. The revolutions that have occurred in computing, such as the PC, personal productivity software, and client/server or network-based applications, have brought with them new expectations on the part of the user community. No longer are users prepared to wait years for an application to be delivered from on high by a priesthood in a glass house—their exposure to applications like Lotus 1–2–3 and dBase changed all that. Once they realized that they could, in a few days and with little prior experience, develop their own applications without waiting or begging, the tolerance for heavy, stringent, bureaucratic methodologies was significantly diminished. This led to a new set of expectations, in which users expect to participate in the application development process, expect applications to be available quickly, and expect to see prototypes and mockups of their applications before they are delivered so they can be sure that what they're receiving matches their needs and desires. These expectations have resulted in a new philosophy of project development, the light methodology movement, in which development teams, rather than following an inflexible and invariable set of disciplines for every project, select the appropriate tools from a toolbox of forms, checklists, and procedures, based on the needs, risks, and complexities of the project at hand.

These new, less restrictive methodologies are iterative, meaning that clients see prototypes during the development process so they can make modifications before it's too late (and too expensive). They are participative, meaning that the client is part of the solution development process, rather than just someone we go to for a requirements statement and then never see again until we deliver the final result. They are change–friendly, because they assume through their iterative and participative nature that clients will see things that aren't as they expected and will request modifications. This doesn't mean that scope or requirements can change without controls, but it does mean that, unlike waterfall methodologies, these methodologies are not designed to discourage change. Change management procedures are still an integral part of the process, and the impact of changes on schedule and budget still needs to be analyzed. These new lighter methodologies are not, as some waterfall methodology proponents insist, the road to anarchy. They are a step toward freedom and responsiveness that, when properly applied, deliver the benefits of structure without the undue restrictions of bureaucracy. We'll talk about these in more detail and I'll point you to some excellent references later.

For entrepreneurs and managers in the IT services business, making the right decisions about project methodology is a critical success factor in more ways than one. Obviously, having a methodology that is robust and flexible enables our teams to deliver quality projects in a consistent way, without having to make it up as they go along. An often overlooked benefit of a strong methodology is its sales value. I believe I've sold more projects by talking to the client about *how* I would deliver than about *what* I'd deliver. Too many IT services managers and sales teams still think that their best sales pitch is something along the lines of "We have the best technology" or "We have the best technicians." What they don't realize is that every competitor is saying the same thing, thus diluting their competitive advantage to a "me-too" proposition. Sophisticated IT buyers have learned the lesson that just throwing technical bodies against a project does not result in success. They want to hear about your methodology, your project process, and your approach to solving problems. Obviously, technology and expertise are essential elements in the delivery of an IT project; sophisticated buyers have learned that they are not sufficient. Without the discipline to plan, manage, and control the projects we undertake, all the expertise in the world won't solve the client's business problems.

What are the indispensable elements that make up a methodology for delivering IT services? I see these components as a path that leads from the initial sales contact through the development of a scope of work and project plan, then through the control documents required to manage the design, development, and delivery of a solution, and finally through the post-project support and assessment activities. Let's list these elements here, with the understanding that we'll be fleshing out each of them in detail later in this chapter. The essential components of an IT project methodology are

- A sales planning process;
- A proposal process;
- A scope of work standard;
- A stakeholder participation process;
- A risk analysis process;
- A project planning process;
- A status reporting process;
- A set of solution-specific toolkits;
- A change management process;
- An issues management process; and
- A post-project review to assess customer satisfaction and gather lessons.

This list may seem long, and it does in fact require a lot of us as managers and practitioners. I've learned from bitter experience, as a consultant delivering services and as a manager and coach of other consultants, that leaving out any of these elements is a recipe for disaster. One of the main benefits of these disciplines is that they limit costly rework and after-the-project debate, both of which can easily drain the profit out of any project. I've seen many unfortunate IT firms that spend more of their time fixing project errors for free, or debating with the client about what was and wasn't delivered, than they do performing billable work. And yet many of those firms, the ones that need these disciplines the most, like them the least and resist them with the most vehemence. So if this list looks long and cumbersome to you, just think back to the last project that you needed to re-deliver due to poor planning or weak communication. Recall the last time you or your firm spent more time debating with a client than you spent delivering the project in question. Every experienced consultant has gone through these nightmare experiences. I often tell consultants and consulting managers to look on these disciplines as debate-elimination (or at least debate-limiting) measures, and that description often helps them see their value.

As we've done throughout the book, let's now expand this list and discuss each of the elements in detail.

A SALES PLANNING PROCESS

One of the adages of the professional services business is "Everyone sells." From the receptionist to the accounts payable clerk to the consultants and partners, every individual, through the way he or she relates with clients and teammates, creates the experience that builds the reputation by which services firms grow. Consulting companies often say "consultants sell consulting." Does this mean that every consultant must become a salesperson? Not necessarily. Does it mean that all consultants have a part to play in the sales process? Absolutely!

First and most obviously, the consultants themselves are the product. Their entire portfolio of skills, including technical skills, as well as relationship, communication, and project skills, is part of what the client buys. The client also is buying a relationship with an individual. Most clients want to meet and interact with the consultants they may be trusting with their critical project. They know that they're also trusting them with their reputation and perhaps their livelihood. They want to gauge technical competency, of course, but they also want to judge such less-tangible elements as cultural fit and maturity. They also want to test their gut reaction, to see if this individual is "simpatico." Sales coaches theorize that most sales decisions are made at a gut level, and then the facts and figures are brought into line later in a process of after-the-fact rationalization. After the sale, consultants onsite can be valuable sources of information about new initiatives and emerging needs. The best consultants can also build trust and reputation while they deliver value to the client.

Although we'll talk about the process of selling IT consulting services in detail in a later chapter, I want to emphasize the unconditional connection between selling and the IT services delivery process here. In my practice of advising IT firms, I can often gauge the health and prospects of a firm simply by evaluating the degree of integration or separation between their sales and project teams. In organizations with conflict between the sales and delivery teams, the archetypal complaint from the delivery teams is this:

> "The sales guys tell the client we can do this thing within some arbitrary schedule and budget, and then they come and tell us to do it. Sometimes they don't even come and tell us. They just send us an email telling us to show up at this client on that day. They never consulted with us, estimated, figured out what it would take to do the project, or even if we *should* be doing it. So now we've got this impossible death march, and they're off to lie to the next client."

On the sales side the typical complaint is

> "If we get these guys involved in every deal, we'd never sell anything. Every client problem is an opportunity for an endless technical debate. Most of them have no business skills. They don't add much in front of the customer. We've tried it and lost deals to competitors while they were debating the most elegant solution or arguing about how long it takes to install a server. We're better off selling the stuff ourselves; then they can have their debates."

Like all clichés, these both have elements of truth or they wouldn't be so universal. Sales teams are typically more interested in establishing the broad requirements, closing the deal, and going to the next one. Consultants and technicians can turn the sales cycle into an academic debate and lose sight of the competitive requirement to sell the deal. I've been in some firms in which the collaborative atmosphere has become poisoned. Even less combative firms, however, are often deeply divided between the sales and the delivery functions of the business. Sales teams take responsibility for targeting and penetrating accounts and for tracking their pipeline of potential sales. They often must present for each potential engagement a "probability of close," a lie that salespeople tell their managers and that has become a part of many sales forecasting methods. Sales teams meet with sales managers to review sales forecasts, and no one from the delivery side of the business is invited. In many IT organizations, a delivery team member hears about a project for the first time from a phone call or an email from a sales counterpart informing him or her of the need to join a conference call with a prospect in fifteen minutes or to attend a sales presentation the following morning. On the delivery side, team members often encounter major project problems or uncover major opportunities at the client and never inform the salesperson, because they never developed a collaborative relationship.

This level of disconnectedness and lack of integration is common. This disconnection is so great in some IT organizations that a salesperson will hear about a new project through an RFP that comes in the mail and then find out his or her firm has ten consultants on the client's site every day. The consultants have had the inside information, but not understood its value, who to take it to, or how to benefit from it. I'll discuss remedies for this situation in detail later, but I want to make a couple of fundamental points in this discussion about process and methodology. If we accept the proposition that our methodology is a framework that guides us through the entire engagement from beginning to end, it should be clear that the process begins the moment we become aware of a possible engagement.

The sales process is a project process of its own. Every prospective opportunity should be managed as a project, with a project manager, typically the sales person, and a pursuit team, selected because their particular skills are the best available for winning that deal. This applies not only to technical skills—some consultants are great presenters or excellent solution designers, some may have existing relationships with the client or particular credibility in a key technology. Whatever the attributes or talents required to pursue and win the deal at hand, IT service managers should assemble a team and then set about creating a "win strategy" for capturing that business. Just as the underpinning of successful delivery is a robust project methodology, so the foundation of successful sales is a vigorous sales methodology.

This doesn't mean only technology—while there are great technical tools out there from CRM and contact management software providers, the tool doesn't make the process. I recommend these tools for those services managers who haven't yet implemented them. Having a database that records and categorizes sales activities and creates an ongoing record of your relationship with every client and prospect is an invaluable part of the sales process. We need to make sure, however, that we don't make the same mistake many of our clients make of believing that installing a system solves a business problem. Managers must manage and enforce the process by ensuring that every prospective deal is captured in the system. They must review and analyze the pipeline of deals to ensure that sales teams are devoting their energies to deals that have a high probability of closure and that are a good fit for the capabilities and strategy of the organization. And most importantly, they must ensure that every qualified prospect is being pursued with a strategy, by a team composed of both sales and delivery folks. They must ensure that their process is a catalyst to cooperation and collaboration between their sales and technical experts, because only the mix of technical understanding and relationship expertise can deliver the best results throughout the engagement.

Again, we'll delve into this more fully when we flesh out the sales and marketing function, but I want to make one additional point. Many IT services organizations have a weekly sales meeting, presided over by the sales manager or the "rainmaker." Project teams have project meetings at which they walk through the technical and delivery status of each project. In most IT services firms, the twain never meet—sales and delivery never meet together as a team. This is a core mistake. Sales and delivery teams should participate in periodic joint working meetings. Only in these joint meetings, which may occur every month or so, do you have the chance to uncover those breakthrough synergies that never happen in siloed organizations. It's been a gratifying feature of my career to see the quantum leap in innovative thinking that occurs when sales teams and delivery teams work together to figure out how to craft a solution that will appeal to a specific client. Sales teams, especially in siloed organizations, are often amazed to find that consultants can actually help them be successful in the sales process by adding some bit of insight into personalities or politics they gleaned while delivering services. Conversely, consultants are often surprised to find that their advisory and technical skills can add a lot of value to the sales process. Both are often thrilled to find that together they can achieve results that neither could accomplish alone.

A PROPOSAL PROCESS

Just as some IT services firms will try to change their spots just to snag any project, many firms will jump on any RFP or proposal opportunity, whether or not they have a chance of winning the deal. Some shops respond to every blind RFP that comes over the transom, even those that are not a good fit for the capabilities of the firm, on the hope that they'll win the job first, then figure out how to deliver it later. Is developing as many proposals as possible a good strategy, with the assumption that it's a numbers game and more entries means more wins? Or is it a better tactic to target your proposal process to jobs in which you have a competitive advantage, that you can deliver successfully, and that you can win?

The answer seems clear to me. Developing proposals is a costly and resource-hungry activity that can tie down your best sales professionals and technical resources. The win rate on blind proposals, with no prior relationship and no account penetration, is dismal. The frustration factor of repeated rejection is dispiriting. The lack of discipline of trying to mold the business, your capabilities, and your references to fit the needs of the prospect is dangerous—it leads some firms to stretch the truth or to try to morph the business to fit the RFP-of-the-week.

Let me reiterate the concept of the engagement methodology as a path through the project. The proposal process is the next step in the path, in which, once we've targeted and qualified leads and decided to pursue them, we solidify the pursuit team and focus them on delivering a competitive proposal. I deliberately included two important concepts in that last sentence, the concepts of *qualification* and *competitiveness.* Qualified prospects are the only ones we should be spending time on, prospects on which the basic homework has been done. Prospects are qualified in our business when we have confirmed that:

- There's a real potential project;
- There's a budget for the project;
- We're engaged with the right decision makers;
- We're a good fit both technically and culturally; and
- We have a reasonable chance of winning the deal.

If any of these elements are absent, this doesn't necessarily nix the prospect outright. Every door is not going to open for us automatically, and in some cases we need to create business where none existed before. If all or most of these elements are absent or undefined, however, managers need to start asking themselves if they're chasing rainbows. As with many of the things we're discussing, there's a finesse factor involved here—some deals should be pursued, even if not high-percentage prospects, to grow the business and challenge the sales team. But considering the expense and commitment required to turn out a quality proposal, managers need to think analytically about which proposals to pursue and which to respond to with a polite "no bid" letter.

So when we are considering whether to respond to an RFP or other proposal opportunity, we need to ask ourselves the questions above, which should lead us to an honest self-assessment of our capabilities and competitiveness. Are we really a good fit for this work? Can we deliver the level of quality the client is expecting? Are we engaged at the right level in the organization? Is this a real project, with support, budget, and realistic expectations? Is there a real chance of winning the deal, or is the proposal process a "fair bidding" exercise with a pre-determined outcome? What's the positioning of our competitors? Where are we strongest, and weakest, in comparison? The proposal process is the place to honestly ask these questions and avoid wasting time on unproductive activities.

The proposal itself is best managed as a project, with a short plan and schedule developed and the deliverables from each member of the pursuit team clearly defined. A standard proposal template, and even some standardized language, is a real time saver in this process. The critical success factors with the most impact on the proposal process, in my experience, are

- Selecting the right ones to respond to, and
- Managing the response effort like a project, with strict responsibilities, deliverables, review processes, and objectives.

Exercising the discipline to review each prospective engagement critically, to select those prospects that are in the firm's strategic interest and capabilities sweet spot, and then applying a project mentality to the pursuit of those deals conserves the firm's resources and amplifies the percentage of wins exponentially.

A SCOPE OF WORK STANDARD

Ask any IT analyst—IT projects fail because of scope creep. From the CHAOS studies of the Standish Group[1] to the academic work of Barry Boehm[2] or Capers Jones,[3] the theme is clear and consistent. Scope creep, feature creep, creeping requirements, moving target, whatever we call it, it's the bane of IT projects.

In fact scope creep haunt all projects, not just IT. Why is it so much more of a problem in our world? One obvious answer is that our product is *soft.* Hardware, once it's built, is material and tangible. It seems obvious, once a building or a spaceship is built, that moving the door or changing the placement of a dial will require significant rework. Our product, unlike the spaceship or building, is not material, tangible, or even visible. This is especially, and obviously, true when our work is application development, the ultimate in soft wares. Lines of code compiled into a routine on some disk has no physical reality for the client, unlike the building or spaceship, and so changing them seems simple. Even system integrators have this perception problem, although their combinations of hardware and software into systems should seem more concrete. But to the client, it's all part of *the system,* and the system is nebulous and insubstantial. And since it's so soft, nebulous, and insubstantial, why can't we just change one more thing?

This tendency toward fluid project definition and constantly changing client expectations has been the central problem of IT design since the beginning. The structured programming disciplines of the 1960s were a direct response to ever-changing requirements, and they were designed to ensure that the requirements were defined, agreed on, and then frozen before program development would begin. These methodologies, often disparaged today as "waterfall methodologies" and considered bureaucratic and inflexible, were an attempt to take something vague and soft, namely software, and make it concrete. The consensus in the IT community is that these methods went too far toward rigid control and process, but they did give us the foundations of scope management. Even though the new lighter methodologies are probably a better fit for most of the work we do today, the fundamental disciplines of IT scope management began with the structured methods of Yourdon,[4] Wirth,[5] and Constantine.[6]

The scope of work is the central contract of the consulting engagement. Every IT services engagement should have a written documentation of the expectations, agreements, commitments, and deliverables that define the project at hand. It's surprising to me how many engagements I see have no scope of work or only the vaguest all-purpose document. I've been called in by clients to review problem engagements, asked to review the project documentation, and found scope of work documents like this real example:

> "Standard Computer Systems will install and implement your accounting information system."

This seems a bit wide open to me. Kidding aside, this is a recipe for unhappy consultants, unsatisfied clients, unfulfilled expectations, and a lifetime of indentured servitude. Are we installing hardware, software, infrastructure, and cabling? Does this mean that every upgrade, patch, and fix will be installed under this scope forever? Does implementation imply training, documentation, support, security, disaster and recovery planning? One thing is certain—the client's view of what this includes and the provider's view are quite different. It's also a sure bet that there will be a lot of debate on this project before any bills are paid or client acceptance documents signed.

And, of course, this is not the worst scenario. Many projects have no documented scope statement at all. Some IT services managers believe that this protects them, since "We never agreed to provide anything specific." Of course, legally you did agree when you met with their teams or accepted their checks. Now the question is: To what did you agree? It's much safer to explicitly document both what's within the scope you've agreed to take on and what's outside its boundaries. The scope of work is the indispensable document of the IT services relationship. It defines the work to be done, the expected results, the approach to delivering it, the relationships between the parties, the resources and time to be expended, and the measurements of success. It must include all these things, plus more.

The essential elements of a scope of work document include the following:

- Executive summary;
- Project background;
- Objectives statement;
- Scope statement;
- Project approach;
- Roles and responsibilities;
- Deliverables definition;
- Stakeholder analysis;
- Estimated schedule and budget;
- Risks;
- Assumptions; and
- Constraints.

As should be clear, the process of developing the scope document also enforces the disciplines of risk planning and stakeholder analysis. It forces us to decide with the client which elements of a system, such as training, documentation, and security, are in or out of our scope. It also forces us to go through the discipline of project planning, because without a plan we can't estimate budget or schedule. I use the word "estimate" deliberately. IT services firms that provide budgets and schedules before they plan the work are not estimating—they're guessing. There's no shortcut to the estimate. The only way to reach an estimate is though the project plan.

To state this another way, I believe that the project plan is actually an essential component of the scope of work. Not only do we want to describe the broad scope of the work, but we want to illustrate for the client the tasks and activities that will be required to reach the goal. As we discussed, IT can be an intangible entity. I want my sponsor or client to have as clear a view as possible of the actual daily work we'll be performing. This may sound like a case of too much information, and many clients will not have much tolerance for plowing through a twelve-page project plan. That's OK; the plan is important but it's not the point. The process of thinking through, as a team, exactly what you will deliver on this project and how, in detail and in writing, is the central discipline of project work. Unless you do a scrupulous job on this, all the other techniques and processes lose their value. Change control, issue management, cost control, schedule management—all become meaningless without a detailed scope that's agreed on by all.

A STAKEHOLDER PARTICIPATION PROCESS

Studying project success factors is all the rage. Every IT trade magazine seems to have another article about the success factors for IT project management. The importance of user participation is one common thread through all the commentary. The Standish Group, for instance, has concluded that "user involvement" is the number two success element in IT projects. As their top analysts recently stated in an article on software development projects, "Lack of user involvement traditionally has been the number 1 reason for project failure. Conversely, it has been the leading contributor to project success. Even when delivered on time and on budget, a project can fail if it doesn't meet user needs or expectations."[7]

User involvement is just one element of the overall activity that is often referred to as "stakeholder analysis." I prefer to call this a stakeholder *participation* process. Stakeholder analysis is a critical activity, but it's just the beginning, not the end, of the road. Once we've analyzed the needs, desires, attitudes, and influence of the stakeholders, we must actively incorporate that input into our project planning. We have to take what we learn in the analysis process and build it into our solutions and plans.

At the heart of the stakeholder participation process is the question: "Who is the client?" Inexperienced project managers often make the error of focusing only on the project sponsor, as if satisfying that individual alone will lead to a successful implementation. For internal IT professionals, this is a serious error, as it creates situations where the needs and expectations of both the users of the system and others affected by it are not integrated into the design. This leaves stakeholders, with no ownership or investment in the project, free to kill it by gripe and indifference. Internal IT teams at least have the benefit of insider insight into the politics, culture, and personalities of their organization and are usually smart enough to include at least the key influencers in project design, even if they include stakeholders only because of the "hot stove syndrome," namely that they (or their projects) have been burned before.

For IT consultants, ignoring the stakeholder participation process is more than an error. It is a potential disaster. Failure to engage the broad spectrum of stakeholders in the project process is one of the fastest routes to project failure, client dissatisfaction, and unfulfilled expectations. IT consultants are at increased risk for a number of reasons. Unless we have a strong relationship with the client, we're often in the dark about the inner circles of influence, politics, and "fiefdoms" that drive the enterprise. We're often brought in after projects have already derailed, so tensions are high and nerves are frayed. Many times, these projects are in jeopardy precisely *because* the organization lacks the skill or inclination to give stakeholders a voice in the outcome. And, of course, we're being paid the big bucks, so the pressure is on for results quickly and with minimum disruption.

And there's the rub: In the perception of many clients, stakeholder participation is in direct conflict with both quickness and minimal disruption. Many project sponsors believe that, although stakeholder participation is a nice concept, we don't have time for it. When they think of all the fears, emotions, and rumors that will be roiled up by interviewing every clerk and customer service rep, they decide that this stakeholder thing seems like less and less of a good idea. So in order to use the stakeholder participation process, we first must convince the client that it makes sense. We have to persuade the client that bringing all constituencies into the project can lead to better results, with less internal conflict, delivered faster.

How does stakeholder participation lead to better results? First and foremost, stakeholders bring intelligence to the discussion, a fact that is often overlooked by executive project sponsors. Contrary to the widespread conceit in the board room, all intelligence about what people require in order to do their work effectively does not reside in the executive suite. The folks who actually do the work, deal with the customers, and use the systems every day have valuable insights into the way things should be done. I worked on a large relocation project for a company that, although it called its employees "associates," was not very good at permitting them to contribute to the design of projects. Against the advice of their consultants, they designed the floor layouts of the new building without sounding out the various departments and issued a move list based on their ideas. This resulted in a complete firestorm, as departments realized that the groups that they interact with every day were now in a different building on the other side of the campus. Individuals went wild as they discovered that their best friends who sat down the hall were now in a different building. From the distribution of mail to the logic of work flow, every convenience and efficiency that the stakeholders cherished was disrupted by the new floor layouts. In this case the stakeholders forcibly inserted themselves into the process in the form of an internal revolution. As should be clear, when stakeholders need to enforce their participation, the project starts with a black mark against it.

The psychological benefit of drawing stakeholders into the process is even more important. If they don't believe that they've had a chance to influence the design of the project, users have no ownership or vested interest in the outcome. This is the key cause of resistance, sniping, rumor, and sabotage. Real participation is the only reliable method I've found for converting resisters. I recently heard a story of a determined resister to a project who, when finally challenged by the project manager about why she was against the project so vehemently, sputtered that the system would never work because the font size on the input screens was too small to read. Once this was changed, this resister became an evangelist for the project. She even began referring to it as "her" system—the ultimate validation of the theory that participation creates psychological ownership. Allowing stakeholders to participate in the process is not a time-consuming excursion—it's one of the deciding factors in project success.

Many projects today reach outside of the four walls of the enterprise. Many enterprises perform some of their core functions through outside entities with relationships such as strategic partnerships, supply-chain extranets, and outsourced manufacturing. In ventures like Internet-based supply chains, partners along the chain of production, from suppliers to designers to shippers and customers, all share information and common systems. In these multi-enterprise IT projects, the stakeholder imperative is even more powerful and certainly more complex. Identifying and analyzing the stakeholders inside the enterprise is at one level of difficulty and complexity. Imagine the complexity of identifying, gaining access to, and then interviewing all the stakeholders in a complex multi-enterprise system! Yet is there an alternative? I contend that it's impossible to deliver a system that will span the needs and expectations of this broad constituency without a thorough stakeholder process. In intricate and dense projects like these, the art of stakeholder participation becomes the defining task of project management.

In Figure 5.1 we examine an example of the supply chain extranet I've been referring to. If your project sponsor is the CIO for your client company, is it possible to design a system that will be embraced and supported by everyone across this spectrum by engaging only with your sponsor? Clearly, both within the client company and in its partners across this spectrum, the range of requirements, agendas, and expectations will be broad. Good IT consultants will think broadly of their constituencies and will gather needs and manage expectations across the spectrum. IT services managers can reinforce these habits by building stakeholder analysis into the firm's methodology.

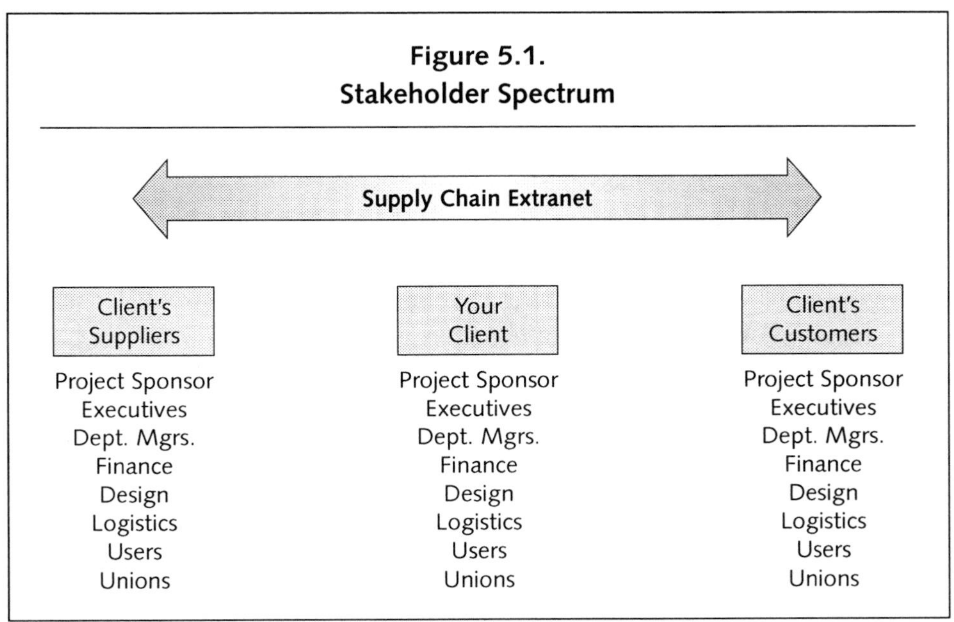

Now that we've argued the merits of the stakeholder participation process, let's review its mechanics. As IT services managers, what tasks, activities, and disciplines should we expect our teams to follow on every project? I think of the stakeholder analysis process as "four I's," as follows:

- *Identify Stakeholders:* Work with your project sponsor, your sales rep, client staff, and business managers to determine who the stakeholders are. Look both inside the client enterprise and at any possible outside players.
- *Inform:* This is a two-way conversation, in which IT consultants and project sponsors educate stakeholders about the project, and stakeholders help consultants understand their needs, desires, and expectations for the end product.
- *Influence:* This is another participatory activity, in which the project team uses communication and interaction to influence stakeholders, and stakeholders become project participants by reviewing designs, contributing ideas, and testing deliverables throughout the project. This is as much about being influenced as it is about influencing.
- *Impact:* Stakeholder participation can't be an empty exercise—it must have an impact. Stakeholders can smell a phony feedback session in an instant. This is an important point, as many executives interpret the stakeholder process as another opportunity to convince their teams that the executives are right. In other words, it becomes another broadcast rather than a conversation. Plans must be fluid enough that stakeholder input actually is taken into account and reflected in the solution. Input, suggestions, and comments are integrated into the final deliverables and publicized to emphasize openness and responsiveness.

I've seen methodologies that have very robust and detailed stakeholder procedures, including the creation of influence maps that categorize teams and individuals as sponsors, resisters, or coaches. I've seen techniques that emphasize facilitated work sessions and interviews to obtain individual feedback on project issues. I'm not going to try to impart a specific technique here. IT services managers and their teams need to collaborate and develop a process that allows them to identify, inform, and influence the stakeholders on their projects, and they must ensure that the stakeholder input has an impact on the project.

A RISK ANALYSIS PROCESS

As an IT services manager or a project manager, there is no phrase uttered by a team member that irks me so thoroughly as "How was I supposed to know. . . ?" This typically is heard when some critical technical element is not working as expected and is holding up the progress of the entire project. It's usually something like the following:

- "How was I supposed to know the hard disk would crash?"
- "How was I supposed to know the server would be D.O.A.?"
- "How was I supposed to know the data would be incompatible?"

These are real examples from my experience. They have something important in common: The most elementary use of risk management would have prepared any prudent project team for these contingencies. If you're doing a server room rebuild project with twenty servers and you don't prepare for the eventuality that one of those servers may not come up, you either haven't done many server room projects or you didn't think about the risks. The same is true with each of these examples; experienced professionals must foresee obvious risks.

Of course, technical risk is not the only sort of risk we need to worry about. While technical risks can sink projects, organizational and political risks are far more dangerous, in my experience. Strong technical resources can, with some guidance from an experienced project manager, learn to anticipate risks to their technical deliverables. Observing, analyzing, and anticipating the organizational, political, and human issues that could arise on a project is far more challenging. Senior sales pros and mature consultants are especially sensitive to these nuances and undertones. They've usually been burned by them before and so have grown antennae that are finely tuned to turf wars, empires, and agendas. This innate sensitivity is valuable, but firms shouldn't depend on it; they must create a formal risk management procedure that provides every consultant with a framework for uncovering, recognizing, and handling risk.

I've taken formal risk management training and found it to be overly complex and technical. While there is certainly tremendous value in doing cumulative probability curves and risk simulation models, these advanced techniques of risk management often serve to frighten off the novice and make risk management seem like some deep and mysterious art. Our problem in the IT services industry is much more basic. Our technical resources tend to have high confidence in their abilities and are known to estimate all tasks optimistically and under the assumption that everything will go perfectly. Many of us don't have project management training and so have never been exposed to disciplined risk management. We therefore are not thinking about the obvious risks, a task which must necessarily come before the more systematic risk management techniques.

Let me illustrate what I mean. When I train consultants in risk management I emphasize four simple questions, questions we should be asking about every element of the project throughout the engagement. These questions are

1. *What can go wrong?* This question should be asked about the technical elements, of course. It also has to be asked about the personalities and key skills sets. Ask not only "What if the software doesn't work?" but also "What if a key team member quits?"
2. *What if it does?* What is the impact if this particular module, or report, or router doesn't work as planned? What happens if Juan, the C++ programmer, decides to change jobs? What are the possible showstoppers that we need to prepare for?
3. *What's the likelihood?* Is there a high probability that this problem will arise, or is it an outside chance? Which risk items are the most likely to pop up? Which long shots can we safely ignore?
4. *What should we do?* What risk mitigation or preparedness actions should we take to be sure that this risk, if it occurs, can't hurt our project?

We ask these questions both on a macro and a micro level. We ask what can go wrong both on the project as a whole or with some major deliverable, as well as on individual tasks. Using a series of common-sense questions, rather than a ponderous risk analysis technique, seems to be more palatable to technicians I've worked with. Don't misunderstand—you must ask these questions with rigor. Whether it's the project manager or the services manager asking the questions, they must be asked until they expose the risks both to the project and to its individual tasks. Understanding the risks is the only way prudent IT services managers commit to projects.

If risk management is such an obvious boon to project success, why is it so often neglected? It's important to remember the psychological undertones of risk analysis. Risk is perceived as a negative. Many sales reps don't like it when we talk about risk to their clients. They're afraid it leaves the impression that projects are dangerous and uncertain and that we're not sure we can deliver. Technicians are resistant to risk conversations because they see them as questioning their technical abilities. It's just human nature to engage in wishful thinking, hoping that things will go well and we won't hit any snags. Because thinking about risk is against our temperament, we need to build it into our methodology.

Risk analysis is not a one-time event. It's an integral part of the project management process and should be revisited at every team meeting. As a project manager I will ask my team at every meeting the four questions we listed above. I'll challenge my project team aggressively to ensure that they've thought about the possible barriers, obstacles, and snags that could derail our project and force us to miss our commitments. Good IT service managers mentor their teams over and over again that thinking about the potential risks and problems up-front is good practice and good business. It protects us from the surprises and the showstoppers and minimizes the rework and "free work" we need to do after the fact.

A PROJECT PLANNING PROCESS

"Plans are nothing; planning is everything," said Dwight D. Eisenhower, in the crispest, most concise, and most significant comment I've yet heard about project planning. It's the process of project management, the give and take, the discussion and debate, the team interaction as solutions are considered and discarded or adopted that brings projects to life. Only through a team process in which we examine the scope together, consider the risks and contingencies, weigh stakeholder opinions, and divide the tasks and the responsibilities can we create a project that reflects everyone's intelligence and passion—and that everyone supports and owns.

I've seen weak project management across the spectrum of IT firms, from the global powerhouses to the local web boutique. Proficient project management isn't guaranteed simply by working with a Big Five shop. The literature bristles with horror stories of never-ending software implementations, application development efforts from hell, and all the other familiar scenarios. Books such as *Con Tricks*[8] and *Dangerous Company*[9] are rich with stories of failed projects taken on by the global consulting firms. I've also seen excellent project management at all points on the spectrum. Many of the large multinational consulting firms have project management tools and techniques that have been honed over decades of use in all kinds of engagements, and they have developed into formidable assets. More to the point, they have a culture and a set of norms that instill respect for the process at every level.

In many firms, especially as they start up and go through their initial growth stages, project management is an afterthought. Most firms are technology-centric and tack on project techniques after the fact. This is not necessarily bad, as each firm must develop a project management style that's suited for the culture they've built and the type of projects they take on. This is why I don't recommend "canned" project methodologies—they never fit properly. What is crucial is that every IT services firm quickly and aggressively create a standard project process, explain why the firm's reputation and future are tied to it, and enforce its use by everyone on every project.

There's typically one small IT service firm in every market that has made project management its primary competitive advantage. This has been true in every marketplace I've ever competed in. One consulting shop was always visible and influential beyond its size and annual revenue. These firms in every market had great relationships with some of the premier companies in town. Their sales calls emphasized project process instead of technical issues. The overriding impression working with these firms is of professionalism. Everyone on the team represents a company philosophy of quality, responsiveness, and discipline. They often are not the first with the latest technology. In fact they're often behind the curve, waiting for lessons to be learned and knowledge to be gained before implementing new technology on the client's time. Clients love these firms because they deliver as promised. That simple attribute is enough to build a business upon, although actually achieving it isn't simple.

What are the difficulties of creating a project planning process and sticking with it? First, there are still some firms that aren't convinced that project management is a good fit for them. I work with firms that are small and entrepreneurial, in which the founders or managers run the business based on personal relationships with some key clients. The founders of these firms are typically very involved in the daily operations, especially in the sales cycle. They like to be able to say yes to the client, and they bristle at any controls that proscribe the commitments or concessions they can make on scope, time, and cost. The structure of a project process, in which the consultants who would do the work were involved in planning it, was too restrictive for their style of real-time deal making with customers. The first step, obviously, is for the firm's leadership to believe that a robust project process is a prerequisite for success.

Many consultants are also conflicted about project management. There is an inherent tension between the creative process of IT solution design and the rigors of project process. Whether it's writing code or designing IP networks, the creative process is a freewheeling and unrestricted place where bright IT minds can collaborate and brainstorm. Project management is a place where forms are filled out and status reports are due. Creative IT people clearly gravitate to the former. Many consultants and technical experts have never been trained in project management, and, worse, many of them have never seen good project management in action. Any project methodology must strike a balance between creativity and structure, between freedom and process. IT consultants must be convinced that the project methodology the firm adopts addresses their creative and cultural needs. It's the responsibility of firm management to aggressively promote the benefits of project management and to back up their words with actions.

Finally, clients also struggle with the idea of adhering to a structured project process. Every veteran consultant has been asked by a client, "When do we stop planning and start doing?" Every veteran has had a client ask, "Why do you have to be so bureaucratic?" And most veterans would agree that it's the clients who need project management the most who respect it the least. In order to gain a competitive advantage from having a strong project process, we need to help clients understand the power of project planning. This is an education process and, in sales terms, a process of creating demand. We need to create demand for strong project management in the mind of our target client. When we win the engagement, we need to show them that good planning results in quality delivery.

Why was I so impressed with the quote from Eisenhower? For its emphasis on the process, the interaction. Project planning is a challenging and fulfilling process in which consultants can brainstorm, try out solutions on the fly, debate and contest ideas, and ultimately craft the best solution for the client's needs. It's also a discipline in which the exact tasks required to deliver that solution are identified, estimated, and documented and through which the details of project execution will be monitored and managed. No IT services methodology is complete without some standards around both of these activities.

The creative activities of project design and planning make significant use of techniques such as brainstorming, facilitation, and prototyping. These activities, such as facilitated planning sessions, should include both sales and technical delegates to ensure that solutions make both business and technical sense. They should result in options that can be presented to the firm's management—and ultimately to the client. Clients like to choose, and smart consultants know that we want them to participate in their own solutions design. The structured activities of project management require the use of standard forms such as a project plan, a change request form, a status report, and a timesheet. Studies agree that selecting an experienced project manager to take ownership of the project is a key success factor. It's not just the process that's important; it's the capabilities of the individual managing it that count.

I won't attempt to convey an IT project process here. I've included lots of great references in the bibliography for IT service managers who want to implement a project process. These references include not just written works, but also Internet-based resources targeted at the project management community. From the worldwide organization of project managers, the Project Management Institute, to the dozens of project management websites run by individuals or companies that offer excellent templates, lifecycles, and forms for use in your own practice, there are many excellent "jumping-off" spots that IT managers can use as a basis for their project planning efforts.

A STATUS REPORTING PROCESS

Status reports are the project manager's lifeline. Only by keeping a finger on the pulse of every team member and every deliverable can the project manager truly be on top of the project. In the projects I manage and the teams I mentor, I insist on a written status report from every member of the team every week. My standard status report is very simple, containing only three fields for my team members to fill out:

1. Five top accomplishments last week;
2. Five planned accomplishments for next week; and
3. Issues or risk encountered or anticipated.

That's it. I don't want the status process to become a burden that interferes with the team's ability to do the actual work. I don't want it to be so cumbersome that people will avoid it or procrastinate. And frankly, I don't have the patience or desire as a project manager to read through voluminous recitations of technical details. I want a short, crisp, and concise rundown of the essential activities past and upcoming.

This fundamental discipline is necessary for a number of reasons. Not only does it give me an opportunity to peek into the status of every deliverable, but it also enforces a constant planning process under which every team member thinks through what he or she will be delivering in the next reporting period and what risks or issues might arise. I've seen many status reports that include the first two questions, but not the third, which I consider to be a serious omission. By requiring each consultant to think through the possible issues that could derail his or her efforts, we eliminate the "How was I supposed to know. . . ?" factor. Every professional must understand that foreseeable risks must be foreseen and that assuming the best is not an acceptable approach. Of course, it also puts a burden on me as a project manager and as a coach. I must dive into the fray and do whatever I can to eliminate or minimize the risks outlined.

The status process is both a document and an interaction. I've seen too many project managers who simply collect reams of status reports, but never go out and interact with the consultant to understand the actual state of affairs on the ground. Project managers should be collecting status information not just on paper, but face-to-face. Written reports don't have the inflection and nuance that a conversation can convey. They don't allow for the interaction and the problem solving, the mentoring and coaching that can only occur in person. Use the status reporting process as a chance to keep in personal contact with your team, to keep them motivated and informed, and to constantly develop them in project, business, and problem-solving skills.

A SET OF SOLUTION-SPECIFIC TOOLKITS

What are the assets of a professional services firm? Professional services firms may have physical assets, such as their offices or their sets of law books, or, in the case of IT service firms, our prototype laboratories or development networks. Unlike manufacturers or other industrial firms, our physical assets are not the source of our advantage, and we can typically pick up and move from one site to another without losing much. We also have relationship assets, the client affiliations we've built over the years, and the trust and rapport that we've been able to develop. These obviously have significant value, but are transient and subject to the whim and fortune of the client and therefore hard to quantify or value. Finally, we have the human assets, those managers, consultants, technicians, subject-matter experts, and support teams that actually deliver our services and develop the client relationships. It is within these human assets that the competitive advantage, the ability to create relationships, and ultimately the accumulated knowledge of the firm resides.

How does a professional services firm gain the most value from the knowledge it holds? Is the knowledge that consultants have gained in their engagements with clients just a personal experience, or is it an asset of the firm that must be collected, codified, and managed? The general consensus in the business community is that the knowledge that employees have gained through their work for the company is actually a valuable competitive asset that the firm must assemble and administer. Knowledge management is a movement that has gained momentum across the spectrum of firms, from manufacturing and retailing all the way to the professional services world. Software has been developed to assist organizations in capturing and benefiting from their inherent knowledge, and consulting firms have arisen focused on this niche. From manufacturing to professional services, the language of knowledge management, from "best practices" or "best known methods" to "knowledge portfolios," has become part of the business lexicon. How does this concept apply in the world of IT consulting?

This concept of capturing knowledge so it can be reused shouldn't be new to anyone who comes from the programming side of the shop. It's similar to the concept of modularized functions that has made the C programming language so popular—why rewrite a function for outputting a character to the screen, for example, when you can write it once and then capture it as a compiled function that can be called by many different programs. The concept of reusability that has been so influential in the programming world is analogous to the concept of best practices in the services world. Why reinvent a Windows migration project when we can write a set of tools, forms, and checklists and then reuse them whenever we need to?

Knowledge management is a huge topic, and many books have been written about how its precepts can be applied in different business segments. I won't attempt to re-create that material here, but direct interested readers to the references cited in the bibliography. What we'll discuss is the most fundamental aspect of knowledge management, the idea that we shouldn't have to figure out every engagement and every solution from a completely clean slate. This is popularly known as "not reinventing the wheel." Professional services firms provide similar services to many clients, and, although we acknowledge that each engagement is different, we also must acknowledge that many elements are the same project to project. It's true that every Windows migration or network design is different because the personalities, cultures, and circumstances are different. It's equally true that every Windows migration has some elements in common. There are certain tasks, such as auditing the client's current operating systems and applications or assessing the client's network architecture, that will probably be done on every migration project. If we take a broader view and look across the landscape of projects and practice areas, it should become obvious that there are a lot of project-specific tools and techniques that shouldn't have to be reinvented for every engagement.

There are circumstances that conspire against the creation of company-wide best practices. Collecting them is difficult—you must have practitioners who have not only done the work, but who have gained some valuable lessons from doing it and who can then document those lessons in a manner that's coherent to others. This in itself is a real hurdle, as there are not many technicians who are also good writers and instructors. You must convince consultants that they can actually gain from using the captured knowledge of others, an idea that will often meet with tremendous resistance, as many consultants have developed their own ways of working and will chafe at compulsory practices or methods. Management can also be an impediment. I've met many managers who make the mistake of thinking that they can send out a directive telling their teams to "document the best practices you pick up on this engagement" and then think that they've created a knowledge management program. Managers must prepare a complete program around collecting, codifying, standardizing, disseminating, and enforcing the use of these firm-wide practices, as they will not just happen, but must be actively—and aggressively—managed.

I've met managers who have developed some creative techniques for going around these obstacles and creating powerful knowledge management programs. Some managers have targeted those consultants who have the best skills at documenting and training and sent them to training to enhance those skills so they can take a lead role in capturing best practices. Other firms have brought in knowledge management consultants to help them develop programs that encapsulate their innate knowledge for reuse by the entire team. Some creative firms have gone further. They've made the development of best practices an integral part of every engagement, and they've assigned teams of their best and most experienced consultants the task of reviewing every engagement and developing reusable toolkits from each. They've created websites where their teams can go to review and grab the tools they need for any engagement. They've created training programs so that the experienced consultants can share their knowledge with the rookies. They've created technical mentoring programs so no "newbie" needs to figure out technical answers that the firm already knows. They schedule periodic consulting summits, where experienced practitioners can impart their knowledge to the rest of the organization.

The important point here is that IT services firms, although we may not have physical assets like General Motors or Boeing, still have valuable assets in the form of the knowledge, expertise, and experience we gain every day in the field. If we don't capture that and use it as a competitive advantage, we're squandering our most valuable capital.

A CHANGE MANAGEMENT PROCESS

Is there a successful construction company or home remodeler anywhere in the world that doesn't have a change order process? Of course not, because the principle of survival of the fittest would drive that company out of business in short order. Every builder knows and understands that changes are an integral part of the job and that, in fact, the smart player can make the bulk of his or her profit on changes. There's a big difference between the outcome visualized in the client's mind, or drawn on a blueprint, and the actual physical result. Smart builders make it easy for clients to ask for the door to be a bit wider or the color to be a bit brighter. They don't, however, make it free. And they certainly don't allow changes to be made on the fly with no record—and no signed change order! In our new world of iterative, prototype-driven system development, change is a constant, inevitable, and beneficial element of the process. This doesn't, however, give us license to disregard the need to document changes, to put them through an approval process, and to measure their impact on the schedule and budget so that we can keep the client informed and manage expectations appropriately.

Why do we in IT persist in allowing changes to occur on the fly and unrecorded? As we discussed earlier, the intangible nature of our product makes clients believe that changing a screen or a report is a trivial matter, with no impact on the schedule or cost and no implications for the rest of the project. We also conspire in our own harm by allowing "covert," off-the-cuff changes to be made in the false pursuit of customer responsiveness. It's not unusual, in my experience, for a client to develop a friendly relationship with a rookie consultant and then use that relationship to manipulate the consultant into changing the deliverables on the fly. "Could you just change this one report, as a favor to me?" The rookie, of course, sees compliance as customer focus, not realizing that it will, in fact, jeopardize both the project and the relationship. Salespeople resist robust change management processes because they force the client to adhere to a discipline, and clients will often go crying to the salesman with the complaint: "Why are you guys so bureaucratic!?" The first step, therefore, in enforcing a change management discipline is education, both of the client and, especially, of your team.

Once the necessary education has been done, the process itself is not complicated. Clients who want to make changes to the scope or deliverables of a project must document their requests, and there are forms galore on every project management website for this purpose. Clients must indicate what they want to change, why, and why it makes sense to do so. The impact of the change to scope, schedule, and budget must be estimated, so that the client makes an informed opinion on whether the change makes business sense. As in the original project planning process, it must be the individuals responsible for actually doing the work who estimate the impact. Changes must be approved by a change control authority, usually established at the start of the project. Whether this is an individual or a steering committee, the client must take ownership of the approval process, as it's their money and time that will be impacted by any changes. Changes must be reflected in the project plan, so that the plan is an accurate depiction of the delivery schedule. All of these activities are part of the basic discipline of project management. As we discussed, no construction company worth its salt would neglect these elements, and neither should we.

A couple of additional points. As I said, some builders make their profit from change orders, and many IT firms do so as well. At some large firms, "scope expansion school" is a part of every consultant's basic training, as consultants are taught to look for the opportunity to expand the scope and generate additional revenue for the firm. I think this trend is unfortunate, as it confirms the client's worst fears about us and distracts consultants from their primary role, fulfilling the customer's expectations. If the intent is to prepare consultants to manage change in a structured manner, I'm all for it. If, on the other hand, the idea is to get into the client's house under the pretense of a minimal scope and then wangle our way in deeper and deeper, this seems to me to undermine the trust relationship to which we all strive.

Also, change control must be introduced at the beginning of the relationship, not when the first change request comes up. I've seen projects and relationships become derailed because the client feels sandbagged or "baited and switched" when the change discipline is introduced deep into the project. Help the client understand your project disciplines from the beginning, and educate the client so he or she understands how these disciplines protect his or her interests as well as yours. The best surprises in any business relationship are no surprises at all.

AN ISSUES MANAGEMENT PROCESS

Every status report, every team meeting, and every interim deliverable will inevitably flush out issues that need to be addressed. From the late delivery of a server, to a glitch in the software, to a necessary expert who decides to leave the firm, issues are an inevitable part of the project delivery process, and they must be hunted down and managed to resolution without mercy. Every robust project methodology has an issues management process, which usually includes a small database or spreadsheet on which all issues that arise are captured and documented, assigned to a team member for resolution, and tracked through to closure.

A POST-PROJECT REVIEW TO ASSESS CUSTOMER SATISFACTION AND GATHER LESSONS

Every robust system is a loop, not a path. The post-project learning process provides the feedback required to continuously improve the process and as such is one of the most important elements of the discipline. I consider this so important that I've devoted an entire chapter to it, titled "Growing and Improving the Firm" (see Chapter Nine). Suffice to say at this point that we need to resist the temptation, at the end of the project, to pack our stuff and run out the door and on to the next paying engagement. The lessons we can learn from our completed engagements, and the relationship benefits of simply asking the questions, are immeasurable. Clients want to have an opportunity to tell us where we succeeded and where we need to improve—and we need to hear it. Teams need a chance to step back and analyze their own performance, clear the air of issues that may have arisen in the heat of battle, and think about how they can work together more effectively. Managers need to illustrate their commitment to quality delivery and constant progress, to both their clients and their teams.

Customer satisfaction surveys are not, as some firms believe, the entire feedback loop. They are just one element, and they don't substitute for a face-to-face encounter. Every questionnaire, by its structure and the questions it asks, influences the response. You won't, obviously, get answers to questions you don't ask. Holding a free-form, facilitated session that allows the conversation to go in unexpected directions creates the opportunity for some real revelations that would never be uncovered from an impersonal survey. Take the time and make the effort to meet with your client and key stakeholders, and be prepared to take the good with the bad. Avoid the blame game, and focus on organizational and process issues rather than individual failings or errors. Stay focused and keep your client focused on the key question: "How can we improve our processes and disciplines so we can serve you better next time?"

This set of disciplines is just the beginning, but my experience tells me that the majority of firms do not have even these fundamentals in place. Firms that want to make project management their competitive advantage in the marketplace can go much further, using standards such as the Software Engineering Institute's Capability Maturity Model[10] to build a world-class engineering capability. The key point is that complex system projects cannot be delivered off-the-cuff, no matter how talented your technical team may be. It's unfair to your teams to expect them to deliver successfully without the tools and techniques to guide them, and it's a disservice to clients to approach engagements without the structured disciplines required to deliver consistent quality.

Interview with Malcolm Frank

NerveWire is an innovative consulting company that focuses on the integration of complex, inter-enterprise systems for Global 2000 clients. NerveWire has been named by *Red Herring* magazine as one of its Future 50, the fifty firms that best represent the future of technology, and by *ComputerWorld* as one of the Top 100 Emerging Companies in the IT business. NerveWire is especially interesting because it differentiates itself based on some pioneering engagement methods, which I discussed with its chairman, Malcolm Frank.

Rick: Malcolm, what I'm focused on is a simple question: How does an IT services firm use its methodology as a competitive advantage? There are a lot of look-alike methodologies. They might put different names on them, but they all follow the same approach. It seems like NerveWire has come up with some innovative ways of thinking about the client engagement. Let's talk about how those ideas evolved and how you use them as a competitive advantage.

Malcolm: The IT services universe is a pretty broad one. So I think you have some variables that firms really have to think through in doing this. The first is, specifically, what do you do as a firm. And that's really important because there are so many different flavors of IT services, and one type of solution area may require one type of methodology, while another requires a different one.

Rick: Absolutely. If you're an outsourcer it's a completely different approach than if you're an application development house.

Malcolm: Exactly. So the methodology differs if you're in the outsourcing or application development business; and within application development, there are different types of applications. So the approach you need to take on an SAP death march, for example, is very different from a fairly codified and well-contained executive management system. Where I think firms get into trouble is when they aren't true to themselves and don't really understand what they're trying to address in the marketplace.

Rick: The guys who run after every project and then try and figure out what they're going to be when they grow up.

Malcolm: That's exactly right. I think number one is that your methodology has to be defined by looking in the mirror and being very honest with yourself and making choices. In other industries, it's very clear the choices that you make. If, for example, you're a manufacturer of any segment, you're going to make one type of product, and you're just not going to make other ones. It just wouldn't make sense. Because we're selling human skills, we try to convince ourselves that, even though we've never done that before we could do it now. It would never occur, for example, to Ford Motor Company to start building motorcycles tomorrow. So I think you have to really stay focused on and answer those basic strategic questions: "What do I do better than anybody else in the world?" and "How do I make sure I have the discipline to stay focused on that?" If you do that, then I think a methodology starts to unfold pretty elegantly.

And I think a second thing is: Are you going to try to compete on speed? If you are, then you have to have a methodology that has underpinnings with that.

Rick: In other words, are you going to make speed of delivery one of your core competencies?

Malcolm: That is a deep cultural and philosophical decision for an IT services firm. I had a conversation with Michael Hammer a couple of weeks ago on this, and he said that change programs, reengineering, and such are all so tough to do if organizations can't change staff enough. So he said that, to a sophisticated buyer, the time argument isn't that critical. He knows it takes time for a firm to internalize this stuff. But other firms, some of the Internet-born consulting firms, pushed speed-to-delivery very aggressively. So your methodology needs to reflect that.

I think a third area is cost, obviously. A fourth is what type of contract you want to have with your clients. Is it going to be basic time and materials, fixed time, fixed price? Is it going to be some type of value-sharing arrangement? And there are huge implications relative to that for your methodology.

Rick: I would see that as probably one of the central drivers. If you're going to be doing value-based pricing, or if you're going to be doing some type of risk-reward scenario, you'd better not be making it up as you go along. You'd better have a pretty robust methodology that's focused on all of those milestones and deliverables.

Malcolm: You got it. You know, fixed time, fixed price, I lived through that for ten years of my life. It's interesting. Many of the speed-to-delivery firms, who were leaders in doing fixed price and fixed schedule bids during the 1990s, gained a reputation with their clients as being methodology Nazis, and the reason was, as with any project, you are three months into it, the client's thinking starts to evolve, they understand more, and the scope changes. What you're forced to do is to say no. You pull out your contract and say, fixed time, fixed price. I'm going to deliver what we decided three months ago.

Rick: Even if it doesn't have any relevance to what you really need.

Malcolm: Because we have a contract that says I'm on the hook for delivering this. If I change it you're going to kill me.

Rick: And that's always kind of a trade-off with the client in terms of how flexible you can be versus how much you need to nail down those things.

Malcolm: But then there's the Big Five model, where in some of those firms they actually have scope expansion school, teaching their consultants how to grow the scope with the client, because their methodology and type of client contract allows them to do it. So I think that the type of contract you sign is another really important point. Those are, I think, the critical issues that go into the development of methodology.

Many folks have become cynical about the attempt to use methodology as a differentiator in the IT services business. Wall Street, for example; five years ago they would really focus on a firm's methodology to justify its valuation. Now they don't even talk about it. They just assume you have one. And the reason is, they really trivialize it. It's like building a house: you've got to spec it out, you've got to architect it, you've got to develop it, and you've got to help the new owners move in. So you're going to have a four-stage methodology that's scope, design, develop, and roll out.

Rick: And who cares what you call it, it's pretty much the same thing.

Malcolm: Exactly. But those in the industry understand just how important it is, because you've got to make some very honest decisions around each of the four decisions to say who you are as a company. Then it leads to a fifth. Over time, you see it in almost every firm, your methodology becomes the firm. As

Churchill said, "First we define our structures, and then our structures define us." In an IT consulting firm, first we define our methodology and then our methodology defines us.

Rick: There's another quote from Churchill that fits here: "All history is personality." To kind of twist your statement around, the personality of the firm also becomes reflected in the methodology.

Malcolm: There's no question about that.

Rick: Personalities and human beings and the way people do things and the way the firm is comfortable doing things starts to become embedded in the methodology, so it becomes mutually defining.

Malcolm: That's right. Along those lines, it's how you treat the customer through your methodology. Some of the Internet-born consulting firms were the poster children for doing this badly. Many of them just treated their customers like idiots. Their approach was: "You don't get it, get out of my way and let me do this for you."

Rick: Right, "You're too stupid to live so it's a good thing you found me."

Malcolm: And that came from the personalities of the people who ran these firms, as opposed to other firms where they say, "The customer is king, and we need to truly collaborate with this firm." And that shows up in the methodology. They say to the client, "For our design session you need to have all of your key users here, because we're not so presumptuous as to think we know the answers. We'll have to collaborate with you to do this."

Rick: In my experience selling IT services, I found that I was much more successful selling on methodology that I was selling on technology. And my experience now, when I consult with consulting firms, a lot of them try and sell on technology. "We have the best network designers" or "We have the best whatever," rather than trying to explain to the client how they'll guarantee that they can deliver. How do you present methodology in the sales cycle?

Malcolm: It's vitally important that you do it. A lot of consultants think in terms of winning the contract, but the client's on the other side of the table thinking about making his business better, you know, rolling this thing out, getting it done. Seeing the benefits. So when you speak in terms of methodology, and how the clients interact with that and what it means to them, they start to visualize in their own minds how this whole thing is going to work and how they're going to see benefits from it. If you sit there and just talk about your own capabilities, you come across as narcissistic. Their defenses are up. The client's going to think, "Well bully for you, but how does that help me?"

Rick: It's my observation that most clients, and the higher they are in the food chain the more this is true, have been burned in IT services before. So they come to the table with a certain degree of skepticism to begin with. It's my experience that you need to reassure them. One of the most elementary things you need to do is reassure them, "We're not like those other guys. We can actually deliver."

Malcolm: But the sophisticated buyers, they take it as a given that you're going to know Oracle or you're going to know Tibco or the other specific technologies that you're dealing with. You shouldn't be in the room if you don't know that stuff. But they want to know how you are going to take that knowledge and make something work in their environment.

Rick: We've been talking generally. Let's drill down a little bit into NerveWire specifically. In your world, do you personally become involved in the sales cycle a bit?

Malcolm: Yes, for select opportunities.

Rick: It's nice for the sales guys to bring in the CEO and have a more strategic conversation when executive level folks from the client side are in the room. Do you personally have an opportunity to have these kinds of conversations: Why we're different and why we can deliver?

Malcolm: All the time. In the market segment that we've selected, what we've focused on is really simple. There are two aspects to it. First, we focus on strategy through architecture. It's a bit of a distinct model, because we compete against the more strategic management consulting firms rather than the technology focused ones. But then we can take the strategic advice we give the client and build a business architecture and a technology architecture that support it. Then we build the underlying systems. That makes us a bit unique as a smaller firm. And second, we typically are focusing on a specific problem set, to deliver services that take the client strategies from strategic architecture all the way through building the solution. Whether it's on the buy side or on the sale side of the business, or design, we help our client become a true collaborator and share their processes with their business partners.

Rick: A lot of firms out there are really struggling with the complexity of stakeholder analysis. You are doing a lot of value net and supply chain work, and obviously your stakeholder universe is enormous within the sponsor/client organization and then from the supplier's supplier to the customer's customer. There are so many stakeholders you need to touch, how do you know what to prioritize, that is, how to negotiate through that? Does your methodology give your practitioners any guidance in that area?

Malcolm: We've had a lot of experience. We have deep experience on the strategy side, navigating through those things specifically. It's done through numbers of interviews and then workshops and really facilitating the process where our clients need to make trade-offs and turn something from an opinion into a consensus. You can put the objective criteria up and facilitate everybody through making those decisions. And if you don't get that right, you can just forget about everything else, particularly with the types of solutions that we're trying to put in place for our clients. So in our methodology, we've leveraged a lot that came out of the Future Mapping® approach and really drive that through with our clients.

Rick: If I were a new recruit at NerveWire, how would I become immersed in the methodology? How would I learn the NerveWire way?

Malcolm: You first go to "Wired Week," a generic one-week immersion. It's fascinating that you put your finger on the whole cultural issue. We actually spend the whole day on culture: This is who we are, and these are the values that we live up to. We spend a lot of time on that. And then they go on to the nuts and bolts. They spend two weeks in training on their specific areas. So whether they are project managers or technical architects or business architects or strategists, they will spend time there. Then we typically have them shadow for a period of time on a project to really see what we're doing and become immersed in that manner.

But I think the key prior to all that is having a very rigorous interview process so we know if this person is a fit or not. It's a very collaborate process. We've run folks through a lot of interviews and a lot of the questions are not focused on technical competence; we assume people are going to have that. To be sitting in that chair, they have to have that. So a lot of the conversation is around what motivates this person. For our collaborative approach with a client, do they define things personally or do they define them as a team? When they talk about their greatest achievements, are they team achievements or personal? How many times do they use the word "I" versus the word "we"? The interview process is exceedingly important to us to make sure people come into the firm properly.

Rick: There are behaviors that you can enforce through methodology, and then there are other behaviors, what I sometimes hear referred to as "soft skills" or consultative behaviors, that really can't be codified but are probably just as important or more important in terms of the client's experience. How do you make sure people either have those or are capable of developing them, and then how do you develop them?

Malcolm: We're lucky to have a very senior team. We have a lot of mentorship going on in terms of the engagement. The second approach that we've employed is we have a solution-center model. We actually have a number of our engagements happening on our site and not on the client's site. There are a lot of benefits from this for the client. But one of the benefits for us internally is great mentorship by your most senior people. So when we send one of our junior consultants on a project in Philadelphia or Cleveland or Dallas, we have no shot of mentoring that person. But when they're working in a solution center here in the building, that person can receive hands-on mentoring in real time on the project. This is where people truly learn. It's analogous to the airplane pilots in training. They don't learn in the classroom. They learn when they're at 36,000 feet and hit a nasty problem. That's when they need the guy sitting next to them in the cockpit saying, "OK, I've seen this twenty times; here's how we're going to get through it." Similarly, we have to have that approach to help our colleagues mature and learn on the job.

Rick: Do you see clients who don't value project management and methodology? You know the mentality, "When are you going to stop planning and start doing?"

Malcolm: We might be a bit skewed because the clients we have are very sophisticated IT services buyers. These are people who know how to consume this stuff. And for them it is very, very important. There's a basic theme here, which on one hand is very obvious but on the other hand too many consulting firms ignore it. It's similar to what I said a few minutes ago, that if you select the right recruits, they're going to assimilate well into the company. The same is true about selecting the right clients or having the right clients select you. If you are one of those firms that will do anything and have no true methodology, you're going to have mismatches with your clients all the time. But if your culture is very distinct, and if your methodology is very distinct, that client is going to make a better determination.

Rick: So it's self-selecting. The right clients pick the right partners.

Malcolm: Our firm is very similar to some of the clients that we deal with. We work hand in glove with them because we are a Type A, high urgency outfit, so dealing with firms on Wall Street or in high tech, there's a nice fit. I don't mean to sound like I'm prioritizing here, but if we were working in some more conservative industries, we might be really offensive to some people. It just may not work. It's important to say, "Hey, this is who we are," and then you can fit it to a firm pretty well. It really helps to have that manifested at the project management level, because the project manager is integrating your team and your culture into their team and their culture and is making that methodology come alive in front of the client.

Rick: I noticed on your website that you have a "Program Management Office" rather than a project management office. Most of the organizations that I've worked with who've tried to create a PMO have really struggled with defining what it is. Is it an enforcement agency? Is it an air traffic controller agency, watching the gauges? Is it a training agency? What is it at NerveWire?

Malcolm: I think it's mostly a mentoring and a service agency. It's one of these things that you know it's done right, because there's a line outside the person's office. And you know it's done wrong when people can't stand the person or there's a lot of politics surrounding it.

It's the ability to really harvest from a project, get set practices, and then inject them back into engagements that we're working on.

Rick: It sounds to me like it's a knowledge-management function.

Malcolm: That's right.

Rick: It's one thing to know that you have a robust methodology; it's another to develop that image out in the world. How do you develop that image in the world?

Malcolm: For us, methodology is a cornerstone of our competitive advantage. We can walk into the client and say, OK, here is how it's going to occur and we're going to carry the ball all the way down the field. Now this requires a couple of things. Number one is, you have to have vertical expertise, because when we're talking about externalizing these key prophesies of where the market will be in the next five years, whether a high-tech manufacturer in their procurement of direct goods, a Wall Street brokerage house in how they view their customer relationships, a global pharmaceutical company in how they approach IT and strategic alignment, you must understand the business exceedingly well. That's one important ingredient. The second is you have to do it with senior talent who have lived through these things before and have done this before. So that's the approach we've been taking. We have found that it's a very powerful model. That's been the Holy Grail of the IT services industry for a long time. How do I integrate strategy and implementation into one? We started NerveWire with that vision. We said that as businesses become more and more technologically centric, their IT service partners must be prepared to talk about strategy and talk about technology in one conversation. You can't get the value out of one without talking about the other.

Rick: And without actually delivering, rather than just theorizing.

Malcolm: We started with some very senior folks out of places like Cambridge Technology Partners, Computer Sciences Corporation, and Accenture and said this is the right market vision, but the only way to get there is to build it organically from the ground up, with one methodology and one culture. We might offer a brilliant strategy, but if the client starts referring to IT as plumbing and tactical and implementation stuff, a bell goes off telling us we're talking to the wrong person. You're speaking to the converted here in terms of culture and methodology and how those things can differentiate the best IT service firms in the market. Culture, methodology, strategy, technology. . . it's all one and the same. You can't separate one from the other.

End Notes

1. The Standish Group. *Chaos Study.* www.standishgroup.com, 1995.
2. Boehm, B. Understanding and Controlling Software Costs. *IEEE Transactions, 14*(10), 1462.
3. Jones, C. Revitalizing Software Project Management. *American Programmer,* June 1994.
4. Yourden, E. *Techniques of Program Structure and Design.* Englewood Cliffs, NJ: Prentice Hall, 1975.
5. Wirth, N. Program Development by Stepwise Refinement. *Communications of the ACM,* April 1971.
6. Constantine, L. *Concepts in Program Design.* Cambridge, MA: Information Systems Press, 1967.
7. Johnson, J., Boucher, K.D., Connors, K., & Robinson, J. Collaborating on Project Success. *Software Magazine,* February/March, 2001.
8. Ashford, M. *Con Tricks: The Shadowy World of Management Consultancy.* London: Simon & Schuster, 1998.
9. O'Shea, J., & Madigan, C. *Dangerous Company: The Consulting Powerhouses and the Businesses They Save and Ruin.* New York: Times Business, 1997.
10. www.sei.cmu.edu.

Sales and Marketing

chapter **SIX**

The most important fact underlying every discussion about marketing IT services is that services are totally different from products. They are marketed and sold differently, they're judged differently, they're delivered differently, and they're perceived differently. Products are marketed based on the "four Ps": *product, price, place,* and *promotion.* Products are typically a mass-consumer business, with the goal to sell as many copies of the product to as many consumers as possible. The car dealership or bookstore sells a commodity, which is basically the same wherever you buy it. The differentiating factors are the convenience of the location, the price, and the brand image that, via marketing, the seller can plant in the prospect's mind.

Services, on the other hand, are sold based on the "four R's": *reputation, relationship, referrals,* and *references.* Rather than being a mass business, professional services are delivered in a personal, one-to-one relationship. Professional services such as IT consulting are different each time they're delivered, and prospects look for reassurance, credibility, expertise, and a solid history of delivery. We've already looked at some of the challenges of migrating from a product to a service business, and we've explored some of the special skills that services sales professionals need. How does the IT services manager or entrepreneur bring all these concepts together and create a sales and marketing program that uncovers potential clients, delivers the right opportunities, and helps close deals and develop lasting relationships? We'll use the framework of the "four R's" to explore how firms can create a comprehensive marketing program for IT services. First, let's discuss some of the issues that mitigate against an effective marketing and sales program in the IT services world.

CHALLENGES

It's important to remember that IT has special obstacles to overcome. While all services are intangible, at least when a firm hires an auditor or an architect, the outcome is material and tangible. Whether it's a set of financial statements or a new building, the client of those professionals can reach out and touch the result of the engagement. In IT our result, often an application or an amorphous "system," is less tangible, less understandable, and less measurable to the client. To complicate matters, even if our deliverable is material such as a web property or a data center, measuring its value to the organization is difficult. There are many disciplines out there specifically designed to measure the value of IT to the enterprise, and there's a deep controversy over whether IT has actually delivered productivity benefits in proportion to the expenditure. Finally, many organizations have been burned before. It's sad but true that there are many IT services firms that, through their undisciplined and unfocused delivery methods, have failed to produce the promised outcomes and have left a bad taste in the mouth of their clients. That bad taste lingers through your sales cycle. All these circumstances conspire to make selling IT an especially challenging endeavor.

Many of the IT services firms that I advise struggle with this element of their businesses more than any other. Looking back at the ITAA Chicago IT Survey we reviewed in the first chapter, let's remember that less than 15 percent of the firms surveyed rated themselves as excellent marketers, and only 23 percent said they were meeting their marketing goals. Only about 30 percent thought their sales efforts were as good as their competitor's. Clearly IT services firms don't have a lot of confidence in their marketing programs. For those IT consulting firms that have a product heritage, either as PC resellers or systems integrators, the predisposition to fall into product-based marketing and selling patterns is tempting. This leads to the "product-ized" services we described before and to the attempt to fit clients into a box of pre-packaged offerings. On the client side, this often leads to the perception of inflexibility, of the dreaded "you'll work our way" syndrome that many of the Big Five are often accused of.

For IT services managers or entrepreneurs coming from the technical side of the business, selling and marketing don't often come easily or naturally. In fact, for many technicians the very concept of selling and marketing has a whiff of the unsavory about it. Consultants often see selling as hucksterism, a glorified form of lying in which the bigger the lie, the greater the reward. Others have a deep resentment for the sales professional, whom they believe has a knack for making unrealistic or impossible promises that consultants must then deliver, and then, to add insult to injury, be paid more to sell the stuff than the technicians make for delivering it! Technicians and consultants often see their technical design and implementation work as a creative achievement and look down their noses at the lowly salesperson, whose only talent, according to them, is tricking people into buying things they don't need. "No salesman ever created anything!" I've heard technicians and consultants say many times.

Obviously, for a healthy relationship to develop, these preconceptions must be swept away. Technical resources must be made to understand that sales and marketing are crucial components of the firm, that there are no opportunities for creative engagement without the sales team to uncover and close them, and that the future of the firm is dependent on their participation in, and support of, the sales and marketing function.

Sales teams need to understand that no commitment to client deliverables, such as project schedule, budget, or scope, can be made without the participation of the consultants responsible for delivery. The acceptance of these fundamental truths is the indispensable first step toward creating a healthy partnership between sales and delivery.

Partnership is indeed the goal. One of the key points that I'll make here is that the secret of success in IT services sales lies in a collaborative relationship between the sales team and the delivery team. The separation of sales and delivery into two separate camps, in which there is no interaction, no visibility from one to the other, and no team spirit, is the most counterproductive situation possible. Sales teams who don't understand the capabilities and competencies of their delivery team, can't articulate the firm's methodology or successes, and are uninvolved with the ongoing client relationship after the deal is closed are sabotaging the potential success of the firm. Delivery or technical teams who aren't helping their salesforce target the right clients and projects, who don't go on sales calls and convince clients that they're the right team to get the job done, and who don't participate in the marketing function by delivering quality and by building relationships and not just systems, are also failing the firm. We'll develop this theme of collaboration between sales and delivery further as we go on.

THE FOUR R'S OF SERVICE MARKETING

Returning to the concept of the four R's of service marketing, let's reiterate them and explore a little bit deeper:

- *Reputation:* Firms gain renown, credibility, and a positive image from activities such as writing, speaking, and networking, from memberships in professional associations, from publishing books and white papers, and from developing a record of achievement and quality.
- *Relationships:* Relationship equity is one of the most underutilized and underappreciated assets of most firms. Firms that target their existing client base for their marketing efforts gain a wealth of rewards. From delivering outstanding service to personal nurturing, to assisting clients in unexpected ways and cementing personal relationships, the investment in existing clients often pays back far more handsomely than does chasing prospects.
- *Referrals:* The most successful service providers I know understand how to create a network of partners who help each other and grow each other's businesses. This goes far beyond the typical chamber-of-commerce networking and consists of becoming an invaluable business resource to your clients by developing an ecosystem of relationships that you and your clients can turn to in order to solve a myriad of business issues.
- *References:* I'm a firm believer in using success stories, case studies, and the testimonials of satisfied clients as marketing tools. We'll discuss in detail the techniques that successful firms use to turn quality delivery and delighted clients into new business.

Identifying the basic elements is an important first step, but IT services managers need to look at their marketing efforts holistically. Each of these elements is but a portion of the whole. We should be striving to create an integrated program, in which our efforts in any area complement and amplify the efforts in others. Our discussion will be centered on this idea of an integrated, holistic marketing program—and the sales efforts that are a natural consequence of doing the right things in marketing.

Reputation

Reputation in the services business is analogous to brand in the product business. The creation of an accepted brand name is an attraction for the consumer, through familiarity, comfort, or image association. We buy Coke® because it's an American icon, because we know what we're getting, because "things go better" with "the real thing." From BMW to Sony, the lure and gravity of the brand is based on a complex interaction of memories, experiences, expectations, and images. As David Ogilvy, the dean of American advertising, stated, "Brand is an image in the customer's mind."[1] Apart from the obvious advantage of name recognition and automatic associations, brand has some hidden rewards as well. In his book *The Invisible Touch*[2], Harry Beckwith talks about what he calls "The Brand Placebo Effect." As he defines it, "Our belief that something will do such-and-such leads us to believe that it actually did—even when it didn't." Many people see brands as merely a way of attracting clients. The Brand Placebo Effect tells us that brands do far more than that. They influence the client's perception of what they actually received, of its quality and effectiveness. This is a powerful outcome. Reputation, like brand, can have this effect on existing customers.

The traditional methods of attracting new clients used in the product business, such as advertising, direct mail, and cold calling, are not a good fit in the professional services arena. While broadcasting a generic message about the features and benefits of a particular product may work when you're selling cars or televisions, the personal and customized nature of services is not well-suited for a one-size-fits-all campaign. While some professional services firms are successful with so-called "image advertising," this is another method of building reputation, and not the usual appeal to buy that we see in the product world.

In our business, the most effective method of drumming up new business is to attract prospects to you because of your reputation. Reputation covers a broad spectrum. Some of the areas in which firms gather a reputation are as follows:

- A reputation for expertise;
- A reputation for results;
- A reputation as a good partner;
- A reputation for quality; and
- A reputation for ethical behavior.

There are lots of firms that have very talented team members, with great experience and deep expertise, who never are quoted in newspaper articles or interviewed or published. Other firms, with equally talented practitioners, are always called on to comment or to speak. What's the differentiating factor? Those firms that are asked for their opinions typically make the building of reputation and credibility a focus of their marketing efforts, encouraging their staff to write, publish, network, and participate in the activities of their industry. From writing letters to the editor of a trade magazine to speaking at a trade show or seminar, each of these activities has a reputation-building result. But they must be undertaken as a program, not simply as a series of unrelated and uncoordinated actions. This is where many firms trip up. In my experience with IT consulting firms trying to build reputation, they will often have a few folks on the team who regularly are published or invited to speak, but there's no coordinating theme to their efforts.

To move from disorganized actions to a synchronized campaign of reputation building, firms need to be clear on the reputation they're trying to build. What are the key competencies that we want prospects to think of when they hear our name? If, as we discussed, brand is an image in the client's mind, what image do we want to call up? As we saw during the Internet boom, image can have a huge effect on success or failure. The image of speed, informality, exclusivity, and "with-it-ness" that characterized many of the eConsulting firms during their explosive growth phase may have been appropriate at that moment, but it clearly worked against them when the tide turned and clients wanted a stable, experienced, mature firm to guide them through troubled waters. Reputation is difficult to build, but once built and ingrained in the prospect's mind, it's extremely difficult to change.

Approaching the building of reputation purposefully requires us to analyze ourselves and our aspirations. Is the reputation we seek focused on our technical skills, our stability and maturity, our specific industry expertise, or our staff of recognized authorities? Each of these outcomes will require us to take different actions. Technical expertise is typically judged by technicians, so participation in user groups, technical testing and reviewing, writing for technical journals, and presenting technical seminars are the appropriate activities. Achieving a reputation for stability and maturity in the industry is often the result of years of experience and success, and it requires that you achieve longevity and then that you make the world aware of your successes and your depth and length of experience. This is one of the few areas where advertising can add value to your marketing efforts—like many of the Big Five firms, advertising can grant the appearance of permanence and solidity. The ads that the large firms place don't tout a particular service or offering, however. They're focused on a simple goal—planting an image in the client's mind. They seek name recognition and, at most, the connection of a short punchy message with the name.

I think of reputation-building efforts as active, as opposed to the passive activities of advertising, putting listings in phone books, or setting up web pages. Steps like publishing, speaking, presenting seminars, or developing white papers on specific topics all require action on the part of both the performer and the receiver. The performer, in this case the firm, must select the right venue, must do research, must prepare and polish their offering, and must present it successfully. The receiver is not in the passive posture of watching a commercial on television, but is an active participant, attending a seminar or reading an article. This active posture is much more likely to position prospects to engage in dialogue with the service provider, exactly the action that is required for a relationship to begin forming.

The most powerful of the reputation-building activities are

- Publishing either books or articles;
- Presenting seminars;
- Speaking engagements;
- Developing "white papers"; and
- Volunteering.

Publishing

Publishing is the best credibility-generating activity you can pursue. As I've learned from the experience of writing my first two books, nothing brings the instant aura of expertise like the words "author of. . . ." My life has completely changed since the publication of my books. Publishing creates your brand in a way that no other activity can, by permanently attaching your name to your area of expertise. It is the first step to the further credibility-enhancing opportunities of writing articles, being quoted and interviewed, and being asked to speak or present. It starts the ball rolling for your brand and reputation. If you or someone in your firm has the talent and discipline necessary to write a book or article, you need to think about the following key questions:

- *What's the best venue for my material?* If your practice is technically focused, your target audience should be technical, so a technical book or an article in a technical journal is your best bet. If you're trying to reach senior decision makers, a more strategic title or periodical might be a better fit.

- *What's the audience looking for?* If writing a book is your goal, do some research on what's out there and what's being noticed. Look at the listings on Amazon.com in your area of interest and see what's selling and what's new. If writing articles for a particular publication is your plan, be sure to review the magazine and see what they're printing. Nothing disturbs an editor more than receiving material that is not appropriate for the magazine or the imprint.

I won't go into the details of how the publishing industry works, as there are lots of great references on that topic (see Bibliography). What I will emphasize again is that writing, besides requiring the discipline of doing the actual work, which can be grueling and demanding, also requires us to think through exactly what we're trying to accomplish and what audience we're attempting to reach. With a little strategic thought and a bit of persistence, consultants can change their futures entirely by becoming published authors.

A couple of quick cautions, however: publishing can bring great credibility to the individual, but that credibility is not automatically transferred to the firm. Firms need to be sure, if their team members are writing for publication with the intent of building the firm's reputation, that the firm is named and promoted in the book or article. And, of course, the material must have intrinsic value besides simply touting the firm. I've seen many books that are little more than veiled brochures, totally focused on the firm and how great it is and bringing little of value to the reader. Readers are not stupid—they can tell the difference between a book and a hardcover brochure, and your book will end up on the trash heap if all you're creating is a vanity work.

Seminars

I learned from experience the sales value of seminars, and it's a lesson I've never forgotten. Early in my career, I worked for a small network integrator in New York City and watched as they grew their business from a small, product-oriented shop into a major player in the highly competitive New York IT services marketplace. Their main weapon was seminar selling. They had a small classroom built in their New York office, seating about thirty, and developed a seminar series that brought in a constant flow of CIOs, network managers, and other key prospects. What were their secrets?

- *They targeted their prospects.* They spent a significant amount of time researching the firms in the area, their industries, and the influencers and decision makers they needed to reach.
- *They brought in speakers of real interest to the audience.* Rather than getting up themselves and giving a "rah-rah" speech about the company, they brought in speakers from their partners, such as Microsoft, Novell, Cisco, and Compaq, to talk about issues that were meaningful to the audience.
- *They marketed the seminars to death.* For months before each seminar, they went through a regimented discipline that included a personalized invitation to each targeted attendee, then an executive phone call to personally convince that individual to attend, then a follow-up call near the date of the seminar to make sure that targeted attendees did not drop out at the last minute.
- *They made sure that the content had real value.* They had very little tolerance for partners who gave hard-won attendees a generic product pitch. They reviewed each presenter's material beforehand, had a dry run, and coached each presenter to stick to the valuable content and stay away from the advertising.
- *They worked the room.* The sales reps were required to familiarize themselves with the material so they could intelligently contribute to the conversation. Attendance was mandatory for a select group of sales reps so they could develop or deepen relationships with attendees. Key consultants in the technology being discussed were also in attendance in case the conversation was technical. Every seminar closed with a series of small-group discussions about the material, facilitated by a sales rep from the firm, to uncover the real-world issues that prospects and clients were facing.
- *They followed up.* The whole point of all this activity is to create opportunities for further discussion. Sales reps learned from these seminars who had an interest in the technology being discussed and had already demonstrated that the firm had the partnerships and the expertise to deliver technical and business results, so it was a short leap to asking for a next meeting to discuss how this technology could be applied in the client's situation.

For my money, this is a blueprint for successful seminar selling. Unfortunately, I often see firms do all these things wrong and then wonder why they aren't getting results from their seminars. They hold open seminars rather than targeting prospects, a sure recipe for giving away a lot of doughnuts, but hardly effective in creating targeted opportunities. They put their own technicians on stage rather than finding experienced presenters from their partner organizations. They put a small advertisement for the seminar in the local business journal and then hope for the best, rather than marketing and following up to ensure attendance. They allow their presenters to give an hour-long advertisement, leaving attendees wondering why they interrupted their busy day to be pitched. They let the seminar attendees drift off at the end, never engaging them in any discussion about how the subject at hand affected them. They never follow up or, because of their poor planning and performance at the seminar, are never allowed by the client to get any closer. Seminar selling is a discipline and, when managed properly, can be the best marketing tool a firm can have. The New York firm I mentioned always had a steady stream of attendees because their seminars had a reputation for delivering value. This led to a steady stream of new engagements.

Speaking

Every businessperson has attended a trade show or conference, and we all have seen the good and the bad of public speaking. Especially in the technical arena, I've experienced both engaging, interesting, entertaining, and informative presentations and boring, pedantic, and condescending harangues—and everything in between. How do these people get the opportunity to be in front of a captive audience? What are the elements that make a speaking engagement effective or counterproductive?

For those consultants or firms that have followed my previous advice and made an effort to publish, speaking engagements are a lot easier to find. Many consultants I know will log on to the Gartner Group website[3] or the TechRepublic website,[4] each of which has a listing of upcoming IT conferences, and then send a copy of their book or article, along with a press kit or introduction letter, to the conference organizer. This often results in an opportunity to propose a talk on a subject of interest to that particular audience. This is a bit more difficult if you have no particular claim to fame in the topic, but not impossible. I've known consultants who will simply call or write to the conference chair or organizer and make a pitch. Very often conferences are short on speakers and welcome the chance to have someone with even a tenuous connection to the topic stand up and talk. The point for the firm, of course, is to capitalize on the opportunity by using it to enhance credibility. Unlike seminars, speaking is not typically a direct route to building relationships on the spot. It's more like publishing, a general reputation builder that incrementally helps create an image of expertise.

As we discussed in the section on seminars, using a speaking opportunity to pitch to a captive audience is the cardinal sin. Audiences do not interrupt their busy schedules and spend rare travel dollars to attend conferences and be harangued or sold. The first rule of effective speaking is to speak for the benefit of the audience, not for your own benefit. Understanding the audience, its commonalities, interests, and motivating factors and then tailoring your talk to fit those interests is the key. Research, preparation, and a light, conversational approach are the most effective ways to overcome nerves and gain a positive response. Be sure to make yourself available for informal chats after the talk, and always have a follow-up conversation with your sponsor to be sure that you delivered what they expected and to develop an ongoing relationship that will result in more speaking opportunities.

Developing "White Papers"

White papers, often called position papers or simply research reports, are short, punchy, three-to-six-page documents that outline your firm's opinion or research on a particular topic. Again, these must be targeted to the reputation you're trying to develop. If you want to be seen as a strategic advisor, a paper on "Optimizing C++ Modules in a JavaBeans Enterprise Server Environment" might not be the best choice, even if the content is first-rate. Always be sure that your credibility-enhancing activities are focused on a specific result, and not just on what your engineers feel like playing with at the moment.

Companies like Oracle, Sun Microsystems, and Microsoft are masters at this art. Take a look at their websites and you'll find case studies, position papers, and "notes from the field" on every area of their operations. While these papers often have a distinct tinge of marketing, they're typically rich in meaningful content that brings value for the reader. Look at the sites of the big consulting firms as well. They'll always have a section on research or articles, where they publish their proprietary research for clients and prospects to review. Some, like McKinsey and Booz Allen, even publish their own magazines! Use these examples as your models—these organizations have been doing this for a long time and know just the right mix of content and promotion.

I'd include newsletters in this category, by the way. Many consultants and firms will periodically develop a short paper on a topic of current interest, use a desktop publishing package to format it, and then mail or email it to a targeted list of prospects and clients. While it's true that the majority of recipients will either discard this or put it into their "later" pile, the repetition alone can generate name recognition, and if the content is of value some prospects may read it and build an image of your expertise in their minds.

Volunteering

One of the most overlooked activities in marketing is volunteer work. By volunteering to assist your local mission, youth group, or social organization, you have the chance both to do good for the community and to contribute to the growth of the firm. It's no accident that the Fortune 500 firms always set aside part of their marketing budget for charity and community activities and that major law firms do pro bono work. I'm not attempting to disparage the altruistic impulses that drive this work. Most firms do this in part because it's the right thing to do and because it creates an outlet for their teams to feel like they're giving back to the community. It would be naïve, however, to suggest that there is no other motive. In fact, firms do receive substantial goodwill and networking benefits from these activities, and your firm can as well. In the IT world especially, there are many opportunities to assist in the development of systems, in the training of workers or kids, and in the presentation of training classes for career changers or retirees, to give a few examples. It's not inappropriate to publicize your participation in these activities through a subtle press release or website notice.

I've found that, apart from the charitable and marketing aspects of this work, there's a significant employee satisfaction effect as well. Folks want to be associated with a firm that's not just about money. One of the most effective employee retention tactics I've ever used was the Christmas toy drive, which I ran every year when I managed a consulting team. Employees and their families felt a completely different level of connection to the firm after they'd had the opportunity to work together on an activity that benefited others and spread the wealth and joy.

Other Promotional Activities

From advertising to direct mail, and including cold calling and putting your name on the back of Little League team jackets, the traditional methods of marketing just don't add much value in the world of professional services. Other passive forms of marketing, such as brochures and websites, fall into the area of must-haves, but are not lead generators on their own. No client has ever stumbled onto my website and called me for an engagement, and I doubt any ever will. These techniques are so ineffective, and so low on the totem pole of profitable activities, that David Maister, the dean of professional services analysts, calls them "clutching at straws" techniques.[5] Maister notes, and my experience confirms, that most consulting firms make an inordinate investment in the low-return activities, such as developing "capabilities" brochures and direct mail campaigns, and much less time on the high-value efforts. Even those firms that are prioritizing their efforts are often unclear as to exactly what effect they're aiming for. The key to success in the building of reputation is in having a strategy, and then in prioritizing your efforts so that they're aligned with your strategy and targeted at the right audience.

Relationships

There's one thing that every consulting and professional services analyst agrees on—the best bang for the buck in marketing comes from nurturing and delighting existing clients, rather than chasing new ones. This is true for a number of reasons. Clients who have had a good experience with the firm are highly likely to select it again, rather than go through the time-consuming, expensive, and distracting search or bid process. Professional services is a trust business, and those firms that have been successful at gaining the client's trust have an easier time uncovering the next project, gathering the information necessary to prepare a winning proposal, and gaining the attention of the decision makers in order to present that proposal and win the deal.

Of course, the trust factor is a two-way street, and this points out another advantage of working within existing relationships. Many clients, especially the large global enterprises that are being courted by every firm, have learned the art of "vendor management." They've figured out how to squeeze the profit out of every deal for the vendor and to ensure that they're buying services at the absolute rock-bottom price. Clients with whom we've developed trust, and whom we've served well in the past, are often more focused on the level of quality and the cultural fit, and so will actually allow us to make some money on the work we do. This is a definite plus! This two-way trust also positions the firm to move up the value chain within the organization, transitioning from lower-value commodity-type services like hardware maintenance or help-desk services to more strategic and influential engagements. These strategic engagements can then be referenced to open the door for higher value work with other clients.

Marketing to existing clients requires a research and analysis effort within the firm. It's not enough to know that we should be devoting a large proportion of our time marketing to our client base. We need to know which clients we should focus on, based on their potential for new work, for profit, and for possible referral to other prospects. The relationship element of our marketing campaign, therefore, starts with an audit of our existing client relationships. As I emphasize throughout the book, this should be a participatory exercise involving the entire firm, not a bunch of managers going off in a room together. Everyone, from the sales team to the delivery team to the receptionist, has some insight and knowledge into the clients the firm serves and can contribute to this conversation.

What do we want to understand about our current clients? Let's make a list of the information that can guide our strategy:

- Revenue generated with this client.
- Percent of total firm revenues this represents.
- Profitability of this client.
- Competitive positioning within the client. Are we working with the client's executive management team or with its procurement department? Do we have to bid on every deal, or do we have first crack at new projects, or are we somewhere in between?
- Who are our sponsors or advocates within the client? Do we have executive sponsorship?
- Do we have any resisters within the client? Any advocates for our competitors?

This is the minimum analysis that every responsible firm should do; yet, in my work advising IT firms I find that very few do a consistent job of gathering even this limited list of data. Most firms that I engage with go from RFP to RFP or send their teams in to work on the same engagements every day, and never step back to ask themselves which clients have the most value, with which they have the deepest relationships, and which are actually profitable. Understanding this fundamental information is a critical first step. I don't think you'd find a successful manufacturing or retail company that didn't have clear, current information on its best and worst sellers, its top and bottom customers, and its most profitable accounts. IT services firms must get a handle on this basic firm hygiene before they can develop a meaningful marketing program. Once this basic analysis is done, the firm can create a relationship leverage program. Firms that rate in the upper quadrant in revenue, profitability, and especially in strength of relationship, should be targeted for development, cross-selling, and further penetration.

For those existing clients we select for development, there are three main activities that the firm should undertake,[6] as follows:

- Deepen the relationship;
- Serve the client better; and
- Uncover additional opportunities.

Deepening the client relationship requires a commitment from all functions within the firm. The management team must reach out to the client, developing personal and business relationships and making sure that they are engaged at the top level of the client's organization. Firm managers must make this a priority, as this is an area that gets a lot of lip service but is put on the back burner in the crush of everyday business. Firm managers visiting clients and keeping the relationship fresh is analogous to project managers doing "management by walking around." It ensures that the firm is at the top of the client's mind, and it sends the message that we don't take the relationship for granted and that we want to be perceived as a partner rather than a vendor.

Sales teams also must participate in this process. It's their responsibility to do the basic groundwork of relationship building, getting to know the client's organization, culture, and personalities. They must set up the meetings and must explore new opportunities. They have the responsibility for the daily tasks of relationship maintenance, such as remembering birthdays, sending get-well cards, and organizing social events. Delivery teams must also work on the relationship. This is an area that needs much development in the IT firms I advise. Too many technical consultants are still immature at relationship skills, such as communication, facilitation, and advice. Firm managers need to remember that the delivery team is the first line of contact for the firm and that the impression they create can enhance or undermine the firm's efforts in this area. IT services firms must take the development of the "soft skills" in their consultants seriously, and they must invest the time and budget required to help consultants become better presenters, communicators, and advisors.

Serving the client better is a matter of enhancing the firm's business context skills. We need to inculcate in our teams the basic disciplines of research and curiosity, so that they'll do the homework required to contribute to the client's internal debates and discussions. Sales teams who don't know how the client makes a profit, or who can't identify the client's customers and suppliers, are doing the firm and the client a disservice. Again, consultants can add a lot of value to this activity by ensuring that they avoid "technical tunnel vision." By broadening their research and interest beyond the purely technical to the uses of technology for business benefit, especially within the client's industry, they become a far more valuable resource to both the client at hand and the universe of potential clients. From the technical trade papers to the industry magazines for each vertical industry the firm serves, the current uses of technology are written about daily and are there to be found on the web or at the library. The best situation possible for a professional services firm is for the client to see you as a font of knowledge and insight, as an informed resource that they can call on for intelligent and unbiased advice and information.

Uncovering new opportunities is a bit of a tightrope walk. I've seen many firms use the current project as a wedge to get into the client's house and try to expand their presence from the first day. These types of transparent expansion tactics not only alienate the client, but they detract from our professional responsibility to deliver the highest quality results on the current project. Coach your sales and delivery teams to keep their eyes and ears open for potential areas where the firm could assist the client, but also advise your team that you're focused on the best interests of the client, not your own interests, in every engagement. The central message here is that, if we do the right things and deliver quality, we'll set up the environment in which the next opportunity will naturally be presented to us.

One other element of relationships needs to be explored, the relationship with strategic partners, such as hardware and software vendors. Companies like Microsoft or Cisco are keen to partner with IT services firms, and many offer vendor partnership designations like the Microsoft Certified Solution Provider program. These programs can be good sources of leads, but I'd caution IT services executives on a couple of points. First, the leads that come in under these programs are often highly unqualified, sometimes consisting of a raw list of names based on responses to a direct mail piece or advertisement. Firms can spend a lot of time chasing down these leads for little result, so choose and qualify wisely. More importantly, the very notion of consulting implies some level of independence, and it's not inappropriate for your clients to expect you to be neutral and unbiased when recommending one solution over another. Therefore, it's critical that, in developing your relationship with vendors, you make it clear that you will make recommendations in the best interest of the client, not in the interests of the partner or of higher profitability. This seems obvious, yet many vendors, in my experience, can be quite arrogant and demanding in this regard, expecting you to "push" their products as part of the price of the partner designation. There is a bit of nuance to this as well, because if we partner with a vendor and grow to know their product well, we may end up recommending it because we're so familiar with it and know how to implement it successfully. This is a fine line, and each manager has to decide his or her own comfort level within the spectrum of neutrality. One thing is clear, however: When you become more focused on your interests or the interests of your partners than on the best solution for the client, you've stepped over that fine line into unprofessional behavior.

Finally, we must be sure that compensation and assessments are in line with the behaviors we want to encourage. I often find that compensation programs are designed to reward the courting of new clients and that the development of new business within existing clients is perceived as business as usual. It's a proven fact that employees do the things that they are encouraged to do by compensation and assessments. Be sure that your incentive package reflects the actions you want to promote.

Referrals and References

Referrals and references are based on one simple element: quality of service. Most clients are glad to refer you to their network of associates and to become a reference site for you to help you generate new business if your services delivery is outstanding. Every client knows from painful experience the difficulty of finding a good partner or provider, especially in the IT services arena, and they're happy to help their associates avoid this pain by referring you. This is only likely, however, when there's no risk of embarrassment or, worse, liability for them. Quality delivery, besides being a professional imperative, is absolutely essential both to the retention of existing clients and to encouraging those clients to refer you.

Referral activity is part of the effort that is often generally alluded to as *networking*. Building relationships with your client's circle of associates, including their lawyers, bankers, and other advisors, can often be as effective as a direct referral to another firm needing IT services. These networks of advisors will often present opportunities for partnering, for joint marketing or seminar efforts, or for collaboration on a specific project. I've been lucky enough, through my writing and consulting activities, to create a wide network of experts and advisors in disciplines from law through accountancy, and across the technical specialties from network design to application development. This network has been my most important asset in generating new business, as we all refer or engage one another whenever we uncover the appropriate need. We understand each other's strengths and weaknesses, know each other's specialties and competencies, and, most importantly, are comfortable with one another's commitment to quality and client satisfaction.

Both references and referrals are made easier by building them into your engagement process from the beginning. I tell my clients at the time our engagement begins that I'm hoping to use them as a reference site. This has a double benefit. It prepares them for the moment when I ask them to be a reference for me or to connect me with their circle of advisors. It also sends them a message that I intend to deliver outstanding service from the beginning, that I'm prepared to do whatever is necessary to make them *want* to refer me to their associates. Like offering a money-back guarantee, this is a client assurance factor that helps overcome the natural skepticism that is an unavoidable part of the IT services sales cycle.

Building referrals and references into your process requires that your entire organization, from the sales reps to the delivery team, understand that references are a key deliverable for the firm from every project. On the consulting teams that I've managed in my career, the creation of a case study and a success story was a required deliverable at the end of every engagement. By my definition, a *case study* is a technical exploration of the project and the technical solution provided to the client, and a *success story* is a marketing-oriented description of the business goals and objectives of the project and how our delivery helped the client achieve those goals. Every project doesn't call for both of these, but one or the other is absolutely a necessity. Getting the team in the habit of preparing these documents not only generates a wealth of marketing material, but it reinforces the discipline of focusing on the business results and of documenting the solutions they deliver.

The goal is to deliver services so extraordinary that the client *offers* to be a reference for your firm. The best referrals and references are those that you don't need to request, because the client is so thrilled with your service that he or she volunteers to refer you and to be a reference site for your firm!

SELLING THE INTANGIBLE

Marketing is the attractor. If it works as expected, if it helps build the firm's visibility and credibility, it pulls new prospects into your orbit. This, of course, is only the start of the campaign. Once your marketing program creates an opportunity for you to court a specific prospect, you must still research, discover, qualify, and contract with that prospect to convert him or her into a client. The skill of your salesforce is obviously the key success factor here, but there are other factors as well. The participation of your consultants in the sales process is, I've found, a key determinant of the firm's sales success. Firms that have a deep "everyone sells" ethic ingrained into the culture seem to have a much higher hit ratio than those that rely on the salesforce alone to close deals. Those firms that take this ethic a notch higher and offer their consultants training and mentoring in sales techniques have the best success of all.

While it's a cliché that consultants and technicians typically don't have the extroverted and competitive nature that often characterizes the best salespeople, this can actually be an advantage. Most clients are accosted by salespeople all day and have built a veneer of sales resistance. They're often quite skilled at going into "ignore" mode or at scaling down all claims by a factor of ten whenever a salesperson is pitching a deal. Consultants, however, can often receive a much more open hearing, with less internal editing and discounting going on in the prospect's mind. Consultants who carry an extra aura of credibility due to their position as an accepted expert or because of a history of successful delivery can be a firm's best asset in the sales cycle. To be effective, however, they must respect the sales process, must have some knowledge of how to participate in it, and must be motivated and encouraged to do so by the firm.

It's not just consultants who need training and mentoring in sales techniques. While there are many highly skilled and very successful salespeople in the IT services world, many of them are successful based on great sales instincts or because of their personal ability to develop rapport with clients. While these are obviously great attributes to have, it's probably not prudent for the firm to rely entirely on individual instincts and personalities for its sales success. Individuals come and go, and personal charm and instinct work in some situations and not in others. The best firms have a consistent firm-wide set of sales techniques that ensure that, no matter which sales rep is assigned to a prospect or account, the firm can be confident that a disciplined approach to qualifying and closing the deal has been applied.

This is especially important in the IT services world. We discussed earlier some of the stereotypes that consultants hold about sales professionals. Like all clichés they are based on a kernel of truth. It is true that some sales reps are more interested in closing the deal than in honestly assessing the project's suitability for the firm. It's true that some sales pros will tell the client what she wants to hear, rather than exploring the client's expectations and setting reasonable boundaries around what can be achieved. It's also true that some sales reps will "throw projects over the wall," closing deals based on unrealistic budgets, schedules, or deliverables, and then in essence tell the delivery team, "Good luck. It's your problem now!" I know that these conditions exist because I encounter them over and over in teams I manage or mentor. These situations are terribly destructive to the organization, creating resentment and hostility between the sales and delivery teams. These dysfunctional sales reps often commit the organization to low-value engagements that turn into either "death-march" projects due to unrealistic schedules or rework/free-work projects because the client's expectations are never set appropriately.

Clearly, it's not enough to just send strong "closers" out to pound out projects with every prospect we can uncover. If that's the case, how should IT services firms manage their sales function? What are the basic disciplines that firms must apply to avoid the errors we described? How do we prepare consultants to participate effectively in the sales process?

The sales function within the IT services firm must be managed actively from the top. The executive team of the firm, if they've followed the planning processes we've described throughout this book, should have a good idea of the firm's target client. They should agree on the size, number, and type of engagements they're pursuing for a given period. They should have reached a consensus on the firm's capacity to deliver quality services and on the firm's goals for growth over the coming period. All of these factors should influence the prospects that the firm selects to pursue. Marketing efforts such as seminars may bring in a thick packet of business cards, but managers must prioritize and focus the efforts of the sales team on the prospects that fit the firm's strategic goals. This prioritization and focusing has to be effected through one-on-one management, as well as through the incentive, reward, review, and compensation programs of the firm.

One of the disappointments of my career as a manager and mentor of consulting firms is the lack of discipline in the sales approach of many firms. Things that I view as absolute foundation exercises, such as researching the client's company and industry, assessing the competition, evaluating the firm's relationship with the prospect (or lack thereof), and developing a pursuit plan, are uniformly neglected. It's also apparent to me that those firms that do apply these disciplines are invariably more successful, and it's no surprise. If faced with the choice as a prospect of working with a firm that's taken the time to research and understand my company and the industry we work in, or one that hasn't, the decision is obvious. If faced with the choice of going into a client meeting understanding what competitors I'm up against, their strengths, weaknesses, and history, or not knowing, the choice is obvious. If choosing between pursuing a deal based on a well-thought-out plan of attack, with each player on my team knowing his or her role and being prepared, or not, . . . well, you get it. Many successful salespeople will chafe at the rigors of these disciplines, and the more successful will resist the most. It's management's responsibility to the future of the firm to educate their teams, to build consensus around these exercises, and then to enforce them.

I mentioned in the first paragraph of this section the activities of *researching, discovering, qualifying,* and *contracting.* These actions constitute a path through the sales process, and so I'll use them to frame our discussion of the approach I believe IT services teams must take while selling.

Research

If I, as an IT services manager, have just come back from a trade show with my team with a big stack of business cards in our hands, how do we determine our next step? If I've just run a successful seminar in-house and brought back a stack of seminar survey forms filled out by the attendees, how do I turn those prospects into clients? What criteria do I use to prioritize and focus my efforts on the high-potential prospects, and not become bogged down in pursuit of projects that are a poor fit for us? How do I avoid wasting time giving free advice to "tire kickers" or "brain suckers"?

The first thing I want to do is understand a bit about the companies whose representatives I've been chatting with. I want my sales team to take the business cards or seminar survey forms and do a bit of homework. Are these large, successful enterprises or little mom-and-pop shops? I'm not suggesting one is better than the other, but one is certainly a better fit for the firm's strategy than the other. If your strategy is to go after the Global 500, then spending time with Joe's Pizzeria is probably not a productive enterprise. On the other hand, if you've decided that every other firm in town is courting the big guys so you're going to "hit 'em where they ain't," then maybe the little manufacturing firm or startup is exactly the right target for you. You can't know this without research. Sales reps should get used to the fact that you'll be assigning them homework out of each marketing activity. They should be comfortable using the web or the library and consulting resources such as Dun & Bradstreet's "Million Dollar Directory" or Hoovers.com to uncover information about the prospects at hand. Above all, they must understand that unstructured and untargeted prospect chasing is not acceptable and will not be rewarded, even if they are lucky and catch one.

What information about the prospect are we seeking? We want to understand the following:

- Their size and scope of operations;
- Their industry;
- Their competitors;
- Their financial position;
- Their strengths, weaknesses, threats, and opportunities;
- Their use of IT; and
- Their relationships with our competitors.

This is the minimum. While I'll concede that it's not always easy to uncover this data, especially their IT program and their vendor relationships, I'm often surprised by what a little digging can do. Someone on the delivery team knows someone who works in their help desk, or one of the salesman's kids plays hockey with their CIO's kids. I'm not advocating industrial espionage, but a bit of judicious probing within ethical boundaries can still turn up some interesting information. I'll often pull together my sales and technical teams and have a discussion about a particular prospect I'm thinking of pursuing, and I'll almost always come up with some key insight through this informal "friend of a friend" sort of networking.

This sort of research pays off in myriad ways during the pursuit and selling process. Clients of professional services are naturally skeptical, and IT buyers are probably the most skeptical of all. When we walk into a meeting with a prospective client and can articulate our understanding of the client's industry, their business, their challenges, and the ways that technology is being utilized across their segment for competitive advantage, we differentiate ourselves from the crowd and make it much easier for the prospect to invite us to advance to the next level of conversation.

Discovery

When the client invites us to move to the next step, that step should be viewed by the firm as a mutual discovery. This is the chance for us to dig a little deeper into the client's circumstances and challenges and to get an inkling of their culture, organizational structure, and personalities. In this part of the sales cycle, the sales team's consultative skills come to the fore. Sales professionals must be able to use the tools of a consultant to interview, facilitate, and investigate within the client organization, to understand as much as possible, so that the firm is best prepared to propose the right set of offerings and to win the client's trust. It's important to make sure that sales teams are engaging at the right level within the client organization and not becoming stuck at the commodity purchasing agent level. This is an area where firm management can add value, as it's often easier for an executive to gain executive access. Technical people should also be engaged in this process, as technicians will often talk more freely to other technicians.

I always aim for a workshop or facilitated session as a beginning step in any relationship. By gathering our best folks in a room with the client's team, we can demonstrate our knowledge, maturity, and technique as we gather intelligence about both the substance and atmosphere within the client's world. The facilitation team typically includes representatives of sales, consulting, and technical subject-matter expertise. I've found it best to perform these sessions in a concentrated format with limited interruptions, which requires setting some ground rules. It's your responsibility to ensure that the right people from the client's side are at the table, that there's a clear understanding of the topics at hand, and that both the client's team and your team understand that this is a targeted session requiring focus and discipline. It's especially important to manage these to a result, so they don't become free-ranging bull sessions or gripe-fests, as this will surely defeat the purpose.

Many firms use the offer of a facilitated work session as a differentiator, often offering it at no cost or at a break-even cost. I'm not an advocate of no-cost sessions, as they set a bad precedent and dilute the value in the client's perception. I do think that offering a first workshop at a break-even price, and then bringing your top team to the table and demonstrating your understanding of the client's industry and company and your ability to uncover issues in an efficient, diplomatic, and thorough manner, can be a deal cincher. It's worked for me throughout my career both as a consulting team manager and an independent.

Workshop discovery can then be augmented by interviews, surveys, and onsite process reviews. You'll only have the opportunity to do these if you convince the client that you are a valuable partner and can bring real expertise and quality to their challenges. The keys to accomplishing that task during the discovery process are *research, focus,* and *professionalism.* Research, as we discussed, prepares you and your team to impress during the initial "courtship" phase by displaying knowledge and understanding of the business issues. Focus is the discipline that ensures that, as you go through the discovery process, you're not turning over rocks in every part of the client's world, but instead are gathering information that will allow you to assist in solving the very specific problem that the client has laid on your desk. This is an area where many firms err. As we discussed, clients don't let you into their house to uncover their dirty laundry, especially in new, untested relationships, so it's absolutely critical that you not allow the discovery process to turn into a fishing expedition. Always stay focused on the client's best interest, rather than on the potential for more business. Professionalism is the central skill on which all these other elements rely. Unprofessional probing, jumping to conclusions, taking sides, pushing too fast for the relationship, pursuing a technical agenda—I've seen all these sins committed during discovery sessions by immature consultants and sales reps, and they're counterproductive to the goal of building trust. Consultants and salespeople must understand that every move they make during this phase is under scrutiny by a skeptical and nervous client, and they must be sure that their presence is seen as positive, stabilizing, and non-threatening, not as a muckraking investigation stirring up issues. Again, this discovery process is mutual. Make sure that, as you are understanding the client, the client is also drawing positive conclusions about you and your team.

Qualification

The discovery process should lead to an open and vigorous debate within the firm. Is this a client who fits our strategy? Is this a project we can deliver with quality? Does the client have realistic, attainable expectations? Does the client have an appreciation of their role and responsibility for delivering this project? Are the risks inordinate for the possible reward? And, of course, does the client actually have a budget for this project, or are they just testing the waters or doing a "brain-suck" to find out what we know? This part of the sales process is often short-circuited by sales teams in their quest for commissions, by engineers in their desire to get their hands on a particular technology, or by managers clutching at every opportunity that comes in the door. Yet this is a key decision point. Most rework and free work projects I've experienced have been due to a weak qualification process.

Clients with unrealistic expectations at the beginning are likely to have unrealistic expectations throughout the engagement, unless you have a strategy for educating them and resetting their expectations and can do so successfully. Clients who think it's ethically kosher to call in consultants and glean their knowledge, only to go out—once you've educated them on your time—and award the project to their regular cronies or to the low bidder, may be ethically challenged throughout the relationship. Projects that aren't in your area of expertise, or for which you have to scramble to find the right resources, may not rebound to your everlasting credit, either within this client or in the marketplace. Clients who don't accept the fact that they have a communication, motivational, and change-readiness role to play within their own organizations in order to prepare for success may be prone to the blame game when the project doesn't deliver as expected. In short, firms that bypass the qualification process in their rush to close deals may find themselves in a purgatory of misunderstandings, unfulfilled hopes, and expensive debate and rework. Relationships that begin with clear goals, objectives, and understanding and that are a good fit on both sides are the only ones we should consider.

Contracting

Once the discovery and qualification processes are completed successfully and the results point to the possibility of a mutually beneficial relationship, it's time to attempt to negotiate a contract with the client. I purposely stay far away from the concept of "closing" in a traditional sales sense here. This is not about overcoming objections or persuading the client to say yes; it's about ensuring that the roles, responsibilities, expectations, outcomes, and measurements are firmly in place. It's about reassuring the client that you are the right firm to help them, and that you'll be as attentive and easy to work with once you're engaged as you were in the pursuit of the deal. Whether you're preparing a proposal to try to convince the client that you're the right partner, delivering a scope of work document for the client's review, or meeting with a selection committee to sign a formal contract, it's your responsibility to ensure that you've clearly and unequivocally covered all the pertinent elements, such as the following:

- Detailed scope of work;
- Detailed set of deliverables;
- Approach to solution development;
- Project management approach and disciplines;
- Schedule;
- Budget, including subsidiary costs like hardware, software, contractors, materials, consumables, travel, and expenses;
- Roles and responsibilities of all parties;
- Goals and objectives;
- Measurements;
- Risks, constraints, and assumptions;
- Fees and your fee structure; and
- Escalation procedures in case of issues.

I'm not going to go into these contract elements in detail. I've listed many works in the bibliography that cover the essentials of contracting for consultants. The point here is that, in order to ensure that the projects we take on will lead us to success, both in the individual engagement and in the marketplace, we must ensure that we go forward under a clear and measurable mandate with no room for misunderstanding or debate. Once we move into the delivery of our services, we'll find that even the most stringent contract leaves plenty of room for disagreement and miscommunication. That fact, rather than absolving us from contracting clearly, should point out again the absolute importance of a firm and stable foundation for the relationship.

Consultants Sell Consulting

The IT consulting firms I advise often ask me the one thing they should do to improve their sales results. I advise them to "break down the walls!" There is an unfortunate misconception in many IT firms that selling projects is the responsibility of sales teams and that delivering them is the job of engineers and consultants, and never the twain shall meet. This is an error that you'll very rarely find in the other professions. Lawyers, architects, and investment bankers, in my experience, know that, wherever they sit, their job is a little bit relationship and a little bit delivery. Many law firms have a rainmaker model, in which some partners, because of their natural talents and desires, gravitate to a heavier focus on networking, building relationships, and keeping clients satisfied and loyal, while others focus on delivering legal services. Every lawyer, however, except perhaps the most junior who is in "grunt mode" while learning the basics, understands that building and cementing relationships is part of the job. Even the rainmakers usually spend some proportion of their time delivering services, even if just to keep their hands in the game. Yet in IT services, we often have a very sharp dividing line, and, worse, we often have mutual disdain or distrust between the factions for some of the reasons we've discussed.

Whatever the background of relations, however, one thing has become clear to me through experience: No single action has the salutary effect on sales success that the simple act of encouraging collaboration between sales and delivery teams does. Sales professionals who move beyond the "drive-by selling" mode of salesmanship, who remain engaged even after the sale is closed, acting as a permanent relationship ambassador, have much greater success at delighting and retaining clients. Delivery teams who work with their sales counterparts on a daily basis to discuss the status of their projects, the issues and opportunities they've uncovered, and the personality and cultural issues they've observed add an incalculable benefit to the sales and relationship process. In short, collaboration is essential.

One of the simplest ways to effect this collaboration is to simply join the teams in a regular scheduled meeting. Most IT services firms hold a weekly sales meeting in which salespeople discuss their pipelines and forecasts. There's also usually a weekly delivery team meeting in which project status and issues are reviewed. Why not combine these two meetings so that consultants can see the sales pipeline and sales pros can gain a deeper understanding of the challenges and successes of their firm's delivery efforts? Firms may not want to always hold joint meetings, as consultants obviously need to be out billing rather than listening to hours of forecasts and other sales predictions, but even doing this once a month can have a tremendous impact. In firms I've worked with that have taken this approach, some amazing things happen. Consultants hear about a deal in the pipeline and immediately jump up to say,

"I know those guys—my best friend works in their IT department!" or "I just learned that technology—let me go on the sales call with you!" Likewise, sales teams who start to understand the challenges facing consultants are likely to say, "I have a great relationship with that manager—let me meet with her and see why she's resisting this project." Of course, all of this joint activity has a grander benefit as well. Mutual understanding breeds mutual respect, and learning the trials their comrades face gives each side a new perspective on the importance of the other's role.

For this to be successful, one major hurdle has to be cleared. Consultants may be very glad to participate in the sales process once they understand that they can actually add value. Sales pros may be glad to take them on calls once they feel confident that consultants can help them close deals. There's the rub, however. Many consultants, even if they overcome their negativity about selling, just don't know how to participate fruitfully. They don't understand what their role would be on a client call, and they often lack the presentation and diplomacy skills required. I've experienced situations with consultants who'll walk into a client meeting and, after reviewing the network diagram, ask disdainfully, "Who designed this mess?" Of course, invariably someone at the client's table will raise a hand and say, "That would be me." Not exactly a recipe for a cooperative relationship. I've also seen too many consultants who believe that their job in life is to be an advocate for a particular technology, rather than a neutral advisor. Many consultants struggle with jargon-free conversation and with targeting their contribution to the audience at hand. Too many consultants will have the same conversation with the CEO that they'll have with a data center techie, using the latest buzzwords and acronyms and never translating their technical ideas into business benefits.

All of these difficulties can be overcome. One of the surest ways to help consultants be successful in a sales situation is to offer them training and development in skills beyond technology. Consultants can benefit from training in facilitation, presentation, and active listening, not just for the sales process but for all of their work. Consultants also benefit from watching how its done. In fact, at one of my previous consulting companies, we had a motto: "Let them watch, let them try, let them do." Let consultants start their development as sales resources by watching how its done, being invited to client meetings as subject-matter experts, but not called on except in a very scripted way. This allows them to get over the jitters and unfamiliarity of the sales situation. Then let them try to add value in a sales call by giving them a prepared role to play, perhaps a short presentation on a technical topic. When the sales team begins to feel comfortable with a consultant's ability to participate in a sales call, they'll be more willing to let them participate in a more spontaneous manner. I've found this three-step process (which usually takes more than three meetings) works wonders in developing great consulting sales resources.

As in law firms, not every consultant will become a rainmaker. Some, however, will find that they like the human interaction and competitive give-and-take of the selling process and will turn into formidable sales assets. Whatever the case with individual consultants, the simple act of offering this opportunity and the associated "soft skill" development to consultants sends them a crucial message: We believe that you're more than a technical pair of hands. In my experience, collaborative sales teams who do their homework together, prepare a pursuit plan together, and go in as a unified team tend to "wow" the client and close the deal. From the proposal stage all the way through to the final presentation and on to the delivery of services, consultants and salespeople each have something to add throughout the engagement, and both need to be engaged from the start.

Interview with Andrew Bibby

Razorfish has been more decisively at the center of the Internet boom and bust cycle than any of the eConsulting firms. During the height of the Internet era, you couldn't pick up an IT trade magazine without seeing the Razorfish founding team of Jeff Dachis and Craig Kanarick on the cover. Their "anti-agency" approach to client engagement was first touted as innovative and revolutionary; then, as the bubble began to burst, it was excoriated as pompous, arrogant, and spendthrift. Their 1999 all-expenses-paid junket to Las Vegas for 1,200 employees stands as an archetype of the indulgences of the Internet era. From its bubble-era high of over $50 a share, RAZF now trades at about a dime.

Through it all, Razorfish has never lost its reputation among web cognoscenti as an imaginative, inventive, and original developer of web-based properties. The company has made a heroic effort to shed the baggage of the past and reinvent itself as a robust, stable, and accessible partner to companies seeking to deliver value through creative use of the Internet. Part of the renewal effort has been the appointment of Andrew Bibby as director of client services in North America. I recently chatted with Andrew about Razorfish's approach to client engagement.

Rick: Before we start, help me understand your role at Razorfish.

Andrew: I'm head of client services in North America. So the delivery side of what we do, as well as a lot of the sales side, comes under my watchful eye. It's not a direct line of report. It's a responsibility around establishing and enforcing best practices and making sure that we are looking after our clients appropriately.

Rick: So is your personal client an internal group, or is it also the external client as well?

Andrew: It's both. Internally, I clearly have a role to play in making sure that people are following process, but then externally I have a responsibility to our clients—if they are not satisfied for any reason, they can turn to me and I can help them resolve any issues that they may have with the organization.

Rick: To start at the top, how would you describe your target market? Who is a likely prospect for Razorfish services?

Andrew: We go after a number of targets. However, I would say that the Fortune 500 companies have really been where we have excelled for quite a while, and many of our long-term relationships are with bigger companies. I think that twelve to eighteen months ago we also would have counted the dot.com community in our portfolio. However, even back then we recognized that they were a much higher risk for us than were traditional organizations. Although the press wrote about the dot.com crash really affecting us badly, the core of our business has always been larger companies looking to leverage digital technologies in their business. So that's where we target.

Rick: What is your outreach program like? I'd guess that there are also folks in your target market who reach out to you based on your reputation.

Andrew: That's right. I think the dynamics have changed as the economy has tightened up, or at least the spending from those major players has tightened up. We've certainly seen a shift back into more of a classic model for generating sales and generating leads, rather than where we had been, where the majority of our business came to us. There is still a lot of word of mouth around what we are, and that will drive contacts to us. We do get contacts through our website. We do a lot of direct marketing and some indirect marketing, like holding conferences around a particular topic within a particular industry. For example, we did a conference on mobile solutions for financial services companies. We did a session in Boston and a session in New York. We reach out to those financial services clients we think may be interested in what we have to say. That generates some thought leadership.

Rick: For my audience of consultants, talk to me about this concept of conference selling or seminar selling. How do you make it work? It has to be a big expense to put together a series of seminars and to put together the presentation material and target the list.

Andrew: If you go in with the approach that "I want this conference to generate immediate leads," I think you open yourself up for failure. People don't want to sit in a room for eight hours and be pitched at. It's very important to bring in partners who will augment your message and to bring some relevant thought to the table that they can discuss among themselves. The objective for us has to be, "We know many of the questions that you face, we believe that we have some very compelling answers, and we would like to discuss those with you." Also, we'll bring in our partners, who can add some thought to the process. Conferences are more about generating buzz or interest around the particular topic that you've chosen. For example, in wireless we partnered with some of the strategic consulting companies, as well as some of the hardware providers, so that there was plenty going on during the day that would allow people to discuss their issues. That's more effective than asking them all to come into a room and then giving them a presentation on what Razorfish can produce. If people feel that that's what you're there to do, you're not going to have good attendance. People will leave at lunchtime. They'll find some excuse to go. Clients want to hear what other people are doing and what's actually working, so they can mull that over, think about it, and then hopefully decide that it's the right thing for their organization. Then, because they know Razorfish has a very strong offering, they want to partner with us. That's better than just wandering around the room trying to collect as many business cards as you can, which I don't think is the right approach.

Rick: So conference and seminar selling is an opportunity to position yourself as a thought leader and to develop some credibility, rather than a real face-to-face selling opportunity.

Andrew: Absolutely. We can do the face-to-face selling later on, once we've actually identified that there may be an opportunity.

Of course, existing clients are also an important source, particularly when the market tightens. Nobody knows you better than your existing clients. *If* you're doing a good job, which obviously you should be if you're going to stay in business. We've been able to gain some stability and revenue from our existing clients. They know us, we're less risky, they know the quality of our work, and they're prepared to work with us. Also you can have much more of a relationship conversation with them around what their constraints are. You've already built a rapport, and you gain a lot of opportunities for extension of revenue.

Rick: So you have an opportunity to build breadth or depth within a specific client, rather than shooting for total breadth within the marketplace.

Andrew: Right. I always think it's very important to define the success of a relationship, and the success of a relationship is not about building a bigger and bigger and bigger revenue stream. That's a nice thing to do, and obviously that's how professional services companies make money, but at the end of the day, what you want is a very predictable revenue stream. I think if you have a predictable revenue stream and you can work with your clients throughout their own cycles, sometimes they're spending money, and you know the reality of life is sometimes they're not. And to keep that relationship going, you need to really understand the challenges of the people who are sitting across the desk from you, helping them in their own organization to make the right business decision. We only win if our clients win, and we have to make sure that we keep that in focus. People will come to me and say, "I don't think I can sustain this revenue stream from this particular client over the long term," and my question is always "Is that the right thing for the client?" not the right thing for us. If it's the right thing for the client and if they really need to see some return on the investments they just made, then that's a good thing. Because I want them to see the kind of quality of work that we've implemented. I can certainly go down to a more comfortable run rate for them, and when they start to spend again, hopefully they'll come back and spend with me.

Rick: So you're building a relationship rather than looking at this as a transactional kind of business.

Andrew: I have a four-phase approach to relationship management, and the overriding factor is that, once a client, always a client. You know, you need to acquire the client up-front. A lot of us steer away from the "S" word, the "sales" word, but the reality is that we need to be able to show value for what we do. This needs to be a professional relationship and they need to see that you work in a professional manner. But you can go through the contract side of things and just make sure that everybody's protected. And then you're really into the mainstay of the relationship, which is running the relationship, which will last a number of years if you're doing it right. There are a number of things that you can do within that. And then there is the final stage, which I call transition, and it may mean transitioning to a non-revenue-producing model in the short term, which is realistic. But the relationship has not ended; we've just transitioned to a slightly different financial model. We're doing the best thing for our client. And when the client is good and ready and when their business is ready, then the relationship still exists, and I'm still working with that client. I'm sending them interesting articles; I may very well be doing some workshops with them; I'll certainly be talking to them about what's happening in their space. Now I'm probably not charging them for that at that time, but I know that when they come back, when they have something that's more meaningful, then they come back to me to advise them.

Rick: You know Andrew, I think you've hit on a really important concept here because too many consulting companies get into this mode of the client drops off the radar if there's no budget for a project, rather than keeping an ongoing relationship without the expectation that it's going to be immediately revenue-producing.

Andrew: Absolutely right. And something I encourage everybody to do is, after a few months, go back and talk to the client and say, "It's been three months since we launched your website or we launched your Internet portal, so how is that working out?" Even for those clients who for whatever reason may have moved on to another agency or may have decided to take that work internally, I want to know how my solutions worked. I want to know: "Are you still using it? Did you find a value out of that?" It gives me very strong and positive feedback, and it says that I care; as a relationship organization, actually if we don't care, then we're missing a trick.

Rick: So let me spin a scenario for you. You've given a conference on mobile. I'm the CIO of a Fortune 500 company, and I come to you and say, "You know this sounds interesting to me and I can see some application for it in my world. I'd like to engage with you and explore how this technology could be meaningful in my universe." What happens then? How do you begin to engage?

Andrew: We have a five-phase approach to the sales cycle before we go into a revenue-generating mode. First is client qualification. I qualify the client: Is this actually a client who has budget or is it a dot.com startup still looking for revenue and therefore I need to engage in a slightly different way. Then I qualify the opportunity: Is there really an opportunity that's a good fit for my organization and the talents that we bring to the table? That's a fairly straightforward and fairly simple conversation.

Rick: Is that a formal process? Do you have a qualification checklist or is it more of a conversation?

Andrew: We don't ask our clients to fill in a checklist or anything like that. However, internally we certainly have a process, and if we're looking at building our pipeline, we have 20, 40, 60, 80, 90 percent probability of close and we have criteria associated with each so that we can effectively manage our business. We know that if a salesman comes to me and says, "Hey, Andy, I've got this great opportunity that's 60 percent," we know what 60 percent means. Is it just that the client said, "Hey, I really loved your presentation" and you said, "I feel really great about this, so I might as well stick it in at 60"? That's not going to allow us to manage our business very effectively. So we have criteria attached. It's a formal process internally. I don't take that formal process outside. I prefer to sit with my clients and talk to them about what the opportunity is and then use my experience to measure against my internal criteria, so when I go into my customer management system, I can say, "This client meets all of the criteria laid down for a 40 percent, and therefore I'll put them in at 40 percent to define our revenue stream."

Rick: This is an important point. Many IT services use a very informal criteria. Like you said, the salesman feels good about it at 90 percent. So everything is posted at 90 percent and then when the pipeline dries up everybody is wondering: "How could this have happened?"

Andrew: Right. I shouldn't be seeing very many things drop down in percentage. I either see them close or move up the pipeline or I see them drop down to zero because perhaps we lost the pitch. I also like to see it, obviously, as a nice funnel effect, so I can see that we're moving things up the pipeline nicely. We stick to very rigid criteria and we view the prospects on a weekly basis. We look at everything in the pipeline, and then we look the guy in the eye and say, "OK, you're at 60 percent. Do we have a resource plan? Do we know what the time criteria is for this? Do we know what the budget is, and have we confirmed that that's available?" If the answer is no to any of those, then I'm going to move it down. And even if it's yes to all of them, I'm going to ask the client partner to say, "Is this really right?" and I allow them to move it down if they wish, never up.

Rick: So if somebody is posting something at a high probability of close but is not doing the other subsidiary tasks that would indicate that he really has a high degree of confidence, then that's going to generate some skepticism about the reality of that rating.

Andrew: Yes. I'm going to ask questions, and then I will probably take it down in the percentage to make sure that I'm doing the right thing for the company. I want to make sure that my stakeholders, the CFO, the CEO, know exactly what my organization is going to deliver.

Rick: Do you think that having this type of qualification process helped you when the economy slowed down? A lot of people were saying business dropped off a cliff, and that always leads me to ask the question, "How are you gaining visibility into your future expectations?"

Andrew: I think business did tighten more significantly than I've ever seen it before. I spoke to some of my friends who work at different IT services firms, just to find out what they were experiencing, and we did see a number of things disappear. Once I have verbal agreement that I have the job, I'm in my 80 percent bracket, and I saw a number of those drop off very quickly as CEOs suddenly put a hold on IT spending. So having a process like this certainly did help us, but we did have to lower our predicted earnings. Things were just very difficult to predict.

Rick: Let's say that internally we all agree that there's a real project here. Now what?

Andrew: Now we go into what we call a design and develop phase. I really like to engage in some kind of workshop. I want to be able to explore what we're actually trying to achieve, and I always bring that back to the business benefits. I'm looking at some hook that says, "I need to understand what your ROI model is going to be." Razorfish has stated that it wants to be the highest ROI service provider in its space, so we focus very carefully on understanding the business drivers. Workshops give me an opportunity to strut my stuff and to allow my colleagues to really show their capability, in a very risk-free environment for my client.

Rick: Also in an environment that's actually adding real value for the client.

Andrew: That's right. One of the things that I would warn about is throwing them around for free. People will take something for free, but how seriously are they going to take my advice? If it's for free, then they see no harm if they throw it away. Then there's nothing in the game for them. So how much are they going to focus on the workshop? For us it's a one-to-two-week deal. We need to do our research, make sure we have the right people in place and freed up, and provide a solid experience to our clients. Even if I'm just asking them to pay expenses, which may be just $1,000, then at least I feel that they have something in the game. Where we *do* give away workshops is to existing clients, where that trust has already been built up. For existing clients, it's an investment in the relationship and I'm much more happy to give that away for free. Other than that I'm going to ask for at least a nominal payment. I'm not looking to make a profit. I'm just making sure they're as serious as I am about the partnership.

Rick: That makes sense. One of the important things about this business is to always gauge the level of commitment on the other side. So what are these workshops like for the client?

Andrew: That starts to get into the way in which Razorfish organizes itself. We organize ourselves around four key disciplines, which we call "networks." We have a *strategy* network or specialty, which is fairly clear. We have a *technology* network, again very clear. We have our *experience* network, which is the creative side of what we do. So information architecture fits in there. Development, content, writing, graphical design, all of those things fit into experience.

Then the fourth is the *value* network, which encompasses our relationship and project management. We bring in the appropriate individual from each of the four networks so that we can understand what it's going to take to deliver a solution to the client. And we may find during the workshop that, in fact, this client is looking for a makeover of their website and the technology is already in place. Therefore I don't need my technology team to be involved going forward. Or we may find that the strategy has already been developed and it's fairly focused and very solid and therefore the strategy side of what we deliver is not needed. But I would rather make a conscious decision to remove something than to miss something. Also, the input of those individuals, particularly in a workshop, will give a comfortable feeling to the client.

Rick: They may bring completely new insight that the client had not considered.

Andrew: Absolutely right. And one of the huge advantages of using a professional services company is gaining the perspectives of individuals across many industry sectors, so they might be able to do a little bit of thinking out of the box. We bring that to the table in terms of what we do, and creativity is throughout all of our networks. We may use specific creativity tools in our workshops as well to try to bring out some different thinking and really explore what the client wishes to do. Again, that's one side of a workshop. We can, of course, do some very targeted workshops if the client has something very specific in mind. I don't want to blow the whole thing open if that's not what they're looking for. If they're looking for a very targeted type of workshop, then that's what I do. I consider that there are many companies that made the best-practice type of solutions, that say, "We know what the best practices are and we will help you implement best practices." I think that that's old-school thinking. That's when we were talking about business process reengineering and efficiencies. What Razorfish is in the business of doing is *creating* best practice. The very fact that someone is implementing a best practice means that somebody has been there before to establish that best practice. The background of our company has always been looking forward and putting together a number of things through convergence. We try to create best practice. We believe that that's what's going to give our clients the edge.

Rick: How do you determine who needs to be in that room from the client's side? Do you ever have problems with the client not bringing the right people along?

Andrew: That's a tough one. We really want the decision makers in the room so that they can at least hear the story first-hand. That often presents logistical problems; these people are often very busy. But it also gives us an indication of how important the initiative is within the organization. Generally, we can run our workshops in two or three hours or we can run them over two days, depending on the kind of depth that we want to go into and what kind of investment we wish to make in landing this particular client. We don't have any kind of formula. We're really setting expectations very clearly around what the workshop is about and the value we expect the client to take away from the workshop. Often one of the values of having a workshop is stakeholder alignment within our prospect. Therefore we work hard to get the appropriate people in the room. It might be the very first time that those people on the client side have ever met to discuss the particular issue. It's important for us to facilitate that. Then even if we walk away, I feel good because I gave something to my client.

Rick: That's the beauty of workshops or facilitated sessions. Whether they engage you or not, if you've done a good job, they come away with something actionable.

Andrew: To give you an idea of how successful our workshops have been, we've had somewhere above an 80 percent conversion rate from workshop participant to client, which means, I think, that we bring a lot to the table and people can see what we can do. It's been very positive. I'm not saying they all turn into our greatest clients, but they will at least engage with something, even if it's just a short study.

Rick: Let's move forward. You had a workshop and uncovered some really great opportunities to bring some business value to the client. And the client, with your guidance, has selected the top two projects that they want to proceed on over the next six to twelve months. What happens next? Do you engage a project manager, how does the engagement look, and how do you manage its quality?

Andrew: The next stage is developing the contract. We go into the negotiation process to determine exactly what this contract is going to look like, exactly what is in scope and out of scope. We look at our approach to the project. Are we doing prototyping? Do we want to do some kind of classic waterfall? How set is the functionality and the requirement? Where are the main points of risk and opportunity? We pull the team together and make sure that the client is happy with the individuals who are actually going to go forward. So at the 80 percent level, which is where we develop the contract, we're really starting to pull our resources together. Who are we going to assign to work on the account? That doesn't mean it's not the people who did the workshop, but we can't always guarantee that because of the time lag and, obviously, the needs of a professional services organization. We will use people in the workshop whenever we can who are going to take the project forward, and if not, we augment the team at this time, putting resumes together and working the contract.

Rick: After you come to agreement contractually and you're actually delivering services, do you use a standard project manager and subject-matter expert team? How do you manage the client's responsibility in that engagement, to make sure that they are collaborating and making a commitment to the project?

Andrew: This goes back to our networked approach. For example, for a true end-to-end project, we have a relationship manager in place, whom we call the "client partner," and we have a core management team from the delivery side. But I also have a strategy network lead, an experience network lead, and a technology network lead in place. They're not management overhead; they're physically doing things on the project. They're generally senior people who have knowledge of their own specialties, and they look at where the engagement is heading. I say to our project managers, "It's OK not to know everything about what's going on with your project." I may have somebody with a psychology degree who's working through the information architecture working with somebody who likes to sit in his bedroom and whack out loads of code in his spare time, because that's what they enjoy doing. And those people actually never socialize together, but they are working in the same environment. I have to make sure that they actually understand each other and understand the goal for the project—and that they have to work together to make that goal happen and they have to understand each other. They understand the business well enough that they can also talk then to the project manager, to the technical leader, and can work out any issues. I want to make sure that I'm setting myself up for success, so we have resourcing managers in place. We work through our resourcing managers, and say, "Hey, I need somebody very strong on the experience side of things and there's not a whole lot of technology here, so give me somebody who knows her way around but she's not going to be challenged too much." Or maybe it's the reverse.

Rick: How do you troubleshoot the relationship when things get dicey?

Andrew: On the internal side, there are a number of routes open to the project manager who feels that perhaps the development is not going to plan. We have network leads in place in the office, the most senior people within their discipline in that office, and the project manager can talk to one of them and say, "I'm feeling a little bit uncomfortable about this part of the project." And we have formal project reviews, either within the network or cross-network. We could do an experience audit, for example, if we felt that was warranted. We bring in people from the network to look at how things are going and to look at the process and the quality of the deliverables that we are producing. At that point, we would decide whether we wanted to replace someone or whether we needed to augment the team. That type of process is available across all of our networks. If anything is going to affect the quality of the deliverable, then the client partner sure wants to know about it because it's going to affect the relationship, and the relationship is what the client partner is measured on. It just depends on which route the person feels most comfortable with, and that's often around the personal relationships that they have. So that's on the internal side.

On the external side, we always partner our clients with a member of our executive team. We have what we call an executive partner, who's really there as a red telephone. They're able to get things done. I may pick up the phone to my client and say, "Hey, how's it going? How are you feeling? Are there any issues with my client partner? Do you think that everything is on track?" If I feel, either through what they're saying or what I'm hearing through intonation, that there may be an issue, I meet with them, or maybe meet with the project team, or I may ask to do some kind of project social event, where I might be able to put my ear to the ground to find out what's going on. If the client has issues over the delivery, but they're very happy to talk to me about them, then I'm certainly going to talk. I'm going to draw the client partner in as appropriate to make sure that we address the issues. If I decide to swap personnel or if I want to look at the negotiation of the contract again, then I'm prepared to do that. It's a very client-focused organization, and if my client is not happy, then I'm not happy.

Rick: It sounds like Razorfish has put together a pretty robust methodology and engagement approach. As an independent consultant working out of my basement, how would I take the lessons that you have learned and apply them to my business?

Andrew: It's about having an approach that you're comfortable with. As an independent contractor, which I once was, I would want to make sure that I had an approach to my clients. What is my personal value-added? Am I a great listener? Well, all consultants must be listeners. But what's my approach? Am I offering a service, or am I offering a relationship? Am I offering some kind of advice? What am I truly offering, and how do I make sure that there are checkpoints along the way that say that I'm delivering what I said that I would deliver? How do I tie that back into what the client is trying to achieve from a benefits point of view? We're a relationship company. That's what we sell. Relationships are our company's greatest asset and we've worked with our clients to maximize the return on that asset. If I believe that, then the relationship that I have with you, my client, is very, very important to me, and I live and breathe that every day. I absolutely believe that. So I would say to find something that you believe in, no matter how big you are, and stick with that. Think through what that means and what your key messages are. And if you go through the engagement process always bearing them in mind, be true to the promises you made when you engaged with this client. Seek out the moments of truth and build them into a very strong relationship and you'll have relationships that turn into two- or three-year relationships and see you through the lean times. I think that professional services is about relationships.

End Notes

1. Ogilvy, D. *Ogilvy on Advertising.* New York: Vintage Books, 1987.
2. Beckwith, H. *The Invisible Touch.* New York: Warner Books, 2000.
3. www.gartner.com.
4. www.techrepublic.com.
5. Maister, D. *Managing the Professional Service Firm.* New York: The Free Press, 1993.
6. This section is adapted from original material from D. Maister, *Managing the Professional Services Firm.* New York: The Free Press, 1993.

Organizational Culture

chapter **SEVEN**

Is organizational culture something that grows organically, based on the personalities and experiences of the entire team, or is it built consciously to serve a particular purpose? Is it an internal matter, affecting only the firm's relationship with its staff, or is it external as well, contributing to the firm's ability to attract and retain clients? Is it about the style of dress and the type of office banter we allow, or is it a strategic element of our total business model? The answer to these questions is yes. Organizational culture is all of these things, and more. It evolves based on the unique characteristics of every individual who makes up the firm, but it also needs guidance and strategic intent to become a truly integrated part of the business. It's a critical element of our relationship with our team, but it also becomes evident to our clients by the attitudes and ethics displayed by our professionals during every engagement. It's concerned with the decisions we make about everyday issues, such as dress, flexible hours, telecommuting, benefits, and recognition, but it adds the most value to the firm when it's managed as a strategic component of the firm's complete portfolio of differentiating techniques.

Many firms make the mistake of taking a narrow view of culture. I've met managers who think that, because they bring in a keg of beer on Friday or allow their programmers to wear sandals to work, they've made their contribution to creating an energizing, motivating, and healthy culture. Some managers take a laissez faire approach to culture, assuming it's the staff's role to build the culture they want, ignoring their responsibility to guide and shape culture as a strategic part of their business model. Others will try to graft elements of culture onto their firms, free soda this week and "Hawaiian Shirt Day" the next, based on the fad of the hour. The Internet foosball table is a classic example of this type of cultural thinking. These is no such thing as instant culture, and all the free cappuccino in the world does not translate into a healthy, vibrant, motivational, and customer-friendly culture. Culture can only be effective if it's guided strategically, if it is a true reflection of the beliefs and personalities of the leaders and their team, and if it is a consistent, integrated part of who the firm is and how they approach clients and one another.

Recent events illustrate again that organizational culture is more than a mere dress code. Many of the eConsultancies that exploded during the Internet bubble have since deflated or disappeared, and some of them were their own worst enemies. One of the consistent observations by journalists and analysts was that these firms were arrogant, with their often-quoted expressions of superiority and exclusivity. "The other guys just don't get it" was their competitive battle cry, and "We'll decide whether your firm is hip enough to engage us" was their target-market strategy. The foosball tables and espresso machines may have made them a great place to work for consultants, but their culture of customer service and client relationship was so warped and corrupted by their newfound ascendancy that they poisoned their well of client goodwill and gloated themselves out of business.

The recent Enron debacle is another example of a culture gone astray. Arthur Anderson may have had a formal, disciplined, and structured methodology that made its clients feel comfortable, but it also had a dangerous proclivity toward focusing on scope expansion at the expense of objectivity. Their unfortunate cultural obsession with owning every possible engagement within their clients, from consulting to accounting, led them to "go native," to forget their responsibility as protectors of the investing public and focus solely on getting deeper into bed with their clients. This error may cost them their corporate lives, and the repercussions have already begun to ripple through the laws and practices of the professional services world. The critical nature of culture to the firm has also been validated by the work of researchers and analysts. *Practice What You Preach* by David Maister, *The Service Profit Chain* by Heskitt, Sasser, and Schlesinger, and *Corporate Culture and Performance* by Heskitt and Kotter, cited earlier, validate through research and statistical analysis the suggestion that culture drives success. Through surveys and investigation, these important works have shown incontrovertibly that a positive, supportive, developmental culture that prizes mentoring and openness is the best recipe for success.

Research and history have clearly indicated that culture is more than an atmosphere; it's a strategic advantage. With that understood, let's examine the concept of organizational culture as it relates to the IT services firm and examine the choices and decisions that service firm managers must make in order to encourage a healthy culture. The cultural components that managers and entrepreneurs must consider are as follows:

- Recruiting for attitude and motivation;
- Ethics and professional responsibility;
- Accountability;
- Open book management;
- Coaching and mentoring; and
- Atmosphere.

RECRUITING FOR ATTITUDE AND MOTIVATION

In professional services, your asset is human. We've discussed this throughout the book as a central distinguishing feature of any services business. Therefore, the importance of the well-known rule that states "Hire for attitude, train for skills" should be clear. Every service employee is a business of one, representing the firm through every deliverable, action, comment, and interaction. Every consultant paints a picture of the firm's competence, maturity, and professionalism in every presentation, meeting, or facilitated session he or she attends. Surprisingly, however, there are still many IT services firms that search, recruit, and hire on purely technical grounds, writing job descriptions and placing help-wanted notices totally focused on the technical skills. The interview and selection process is also often solely focused on technical skills, rather than the consulting and personality attributes that contribute to good client relations and results.

Every job description for every position within the firm should reflect the firm's focus on customer service, professionalism, and collaboration. From the receptionist and accounts payable manager through the consulting staff, attributes such as teamwork, dedication, maturity (not in age but in behavior and attitude), and even simple friendliness and respect should be explicitly noted in job descriptions and explored during the recruiting process. Every team member who participates in the recruitment and interview process must be coached on the importance of these attributes. This coaching is especially critical for the technical staff, who will often become enamored of a particularly skilled technical candidate and overlook his or her gaps in personality or attitude. Technically focused hiring, in my experience, is one of the leading causes of personnel problems in our industry. Once hired, staffers with poor attitudes can sap the time and spirit of a firm. I've seen many managers make the mistake of disregarding attitude problems in the recruitment process, only to find themselves in a quagmire of endless coaching, team healing, and customer cleanup due to inappropriate consultant behaviors.

Another important element in staffing is the management of expectations for new recruits. The professional life is demanding, and IT is especially time-consuming and stressful, and the best team members are aware of this from the beginning. IT services managers should deliver a clear message regarding the demands of the firm and the profession. IT services work requires long hours, constant re-education, and relentless delivery pressures, plus the diplomatic skills of an ambassador. Recruiting managers who make the error of painting a rosy picture during the hiring process face the same challenges as project managers who allow clients to persist in unrealistic expectations: dissatisfaction and poor retention. They may be able to convince candidates to sign on, but signing the wrong players is far more dangerous than waiting for the well-suited few. Too few consultants on staff can limit the number of engagements and billable hours the firm can generate, but errors in hiring can debilitate the firm, sap the time and patience of managers, destroy the team, poison the atmosphere, and alienate clients. The choice seems obvious.

One final error that many firms make is "just-in-time" recruiting. They wait until they close a deal or sign a contract and then rush out and hire the technical skills called for by that particular deal. Rather than unearthing the best possible team members, this approach stumbles on whoever happens to be in the market at that particular moment. Often, those candidates are between jobs for a reason. This approach also tends to encourage the technically focused recruiting practices described earlier. Even if qualified candidates are miraculously discovered through this process, they lack the acculturation, loyalty, and team allegiance that can only be developed over time. Dropping them headfirst into a project with no time to learn and understand the culture, methods, and personality of the firm is a recipe for disaster. Hiring for the project-of-the-moment often results in a revolving door policy, in which consultants are hired and fired depending on the staff needs of the day. Nothing is worse for morale, motivation, and retention than the fear that, when their project is over, consultants will be on the street. This also can lead to a vicious cycle in which the firm stops investing in development of consultants because they'll just take those new skills to a competitor, a self-fulfilling prophecy.

I advocate instead a constant recruiting approach, in which the firm is always in the market for qualified candidates and persistently interviews and evaluates aspiring team members, ruthlessly eliminating those who fail to meet the attitude, maturity, and professionalism requirements and relentlessly pursuing those select few who fit the firm's strict guidelines. Some IT service managers I've worked with complain that this approach can saddle them with a bench full of unutilized professionals. I find the opposite to be true. Consultants who display the full range of professional skills can sell themselves, and they often come with existing relationships and reputations. They often bring the added advantages of being able to mentor their teammates and serve as examples to every member of the firm. This approach requires a bit of an investment, both in time to evaluate candidates and in possible salary costs while new recruits become productive, but the benefits far outweigh the investment. Excellent candidates are rare, and their contribution to the firm can be immeasurable. Investing in their selection and acculturation is the wisest outlay a services firm can make.

ETHICS AND PROFESSIONAL RESPONSIBILITY

Part of the culture of a firm revolves around the shared set of ethical and moral standards that the firm promotes. From simple personal integrity all the way through to professional behavior such as retention of records and honest timekeeping, the firm has a professional and legal responsibility to define and communicate a set of standards for consultants to follow. It's not enough to rely on the personal ethics of your team. IT services managers must explicitly define a code of ethics that guides the decisions and conduct of the firm and every practitioner. The recent scandals in the accountancy profession illustrate again that the actions of one professional, whether sanctioned or not, can destroy the brand equity and reputation of a lifetime. Policies outlining the firm's intolerance of gender, age, or race discrimination, sexual harassment, and substance abuse must also be codified and conveyed so that there is no room for confusion or misinterpretation.

Organizations such as the Independent Computer Consultants Association[1] and the Institute of Management Consultants have excellent code of ethics documents that can be found on their websites and used in your own practice. The Institute of Management Consultants, for example, requires that members and their firms agree:

- To safeguard confidential information;
- To render impartial, independent advice;
- To accept only those client engagements they are qualified to perform;
- To agree with the client in advance on the basis for professional charges; and
- To develop realistic and practical solutions to client problems.[2]

These guidelines represent the bare minimum of professional responsibilities, yet many IT consultants and services firms struggle to adhere to even these basic standards. Is it OK to take a job in a technical field in which the firm has no experience and then scramble to learn the technology on the client's time and money? Is it fair to use the client as a forum for touting your favorite technology or vendor, rather than rendering impartial advice in the client's best interest? Is it ethical to create solutions that are not supportable by the client's current IT staff or that are delivered with no documentation and no training? I'll leave the answers to you, but I've seen enough questionable behavior in my career as a consultant and an advisor to IT services firms to convince me that there are plenty of service firms that still honor the dollar over their reputations. I've also learned that time reveals all ethical lapses and that, in our business, reputation trumps every other consideration.

Simple written codes, although necessary to avoid even the appearance of ambiguity, are not enough. Every one of the firms that has been embroiled in the recent accounting scandals has a strongly worded set of ethical guidelines. Consultants, especially rookies and new recruits, will look to managers and seniors for cues to appropriate behavior. Through every action, every firm member must exemplify the highest standards of conduct. Only through consistent and unmistakable fidelity to impeccable ethics can managers coach their teams in acceptable boundaries of professional behavior.

ACCOUNTABILITY

When the discussion turns to motivating IT specialists, much of the talk revolves around reward and recognition. Watts Humphrey, the well-known former IBM Fellow and authority on managing technicians, makes the point in his book *Managing Technical People*[3] that, while it is critical for excellent engineering and technical work to be recognized by management, it's more important that it be recognized by the team. Technicians and engineers look to their peers for status, for recognition, and for acceptance. The smart manager of IT consultants uses the team as the instrument of recognition. Every professional enjoys the recognition of the management or the partners, as it is a critical element in achieving the rewards of promotion, preferred assignments, and enhanced compensation. The special personality traits that drive individuals to become IT professionals often seem to drive them to crave status and esteem within their teams above any other reward. The best IT service managers use an integrated recognition program that includes formal management recognition, in the form of awards, promotions, positive evaluations, and raises, and informal, team-based recognition that sends the message that the professional is valued and revered by his or her colleagues for technical achievements.

Unfortunately, most conversations about motivation revolve solely around recognition and reward and ignore the critical element of accountability. In my travels around the world mentoring IT services teams, I've observed what I would term a crisis of accountability. Over and over, I'm approached by managers or consultants with the same sad tale—someone on the team is not performing. The consultant in question was so promising at first, seemed so technically sound, and yet he (pick one):

- Can't get along with the team;
- Is consistently late with deliverables;
- Disregards the established methodology and process;
- Is secretive and incommunicative about his status and methods; or
- Is simply rude, disruptive, and antisocial.

What, I'm asked, can we do about this person? When I probe further, I typically find that the method of resolving the issue to date has been one of avoidance. Has anyone had a chat with this individual? Well, no, because he's so prickly that any criticism sends him around the bend. Has management stepped in? Well, we didn't want to get management involved because we don't want to get him in trouble and we're not tattletales. Has the team confronted him? Well, no, because we're afraid he'll just stop coming to meetings if we gang up on him. While these are all valid concerns, and this sort of situation does require subtlety, it's clear to me that the avoidance of accountability creates far more problems than its enforcement. The very fact that the entire team is agonizing over the issue demonstrates its ability to distract, debilitate, and ultimately destroy the team. The impact on the firm in terms of missed deliverables, plus the possibility of inappropriate onsite behavior, can be devastating. The effect on the morale of those team members who are achieving their goals is incalculable. In short, accountability must be enforced, no matter how attractive avoidance may seem.

As we said above, recognition from the team is the most powerful reward. The same is true for accountability. Individuals should be accountable to the team first, and the team should be the mechanism of first resort for encouraging and enforcing accountable professional behavior. Using the team as the standard bearer of accountability serves a number of purposes. If teamwork is really prized in the firm, and if projects are staffed and managed on a team basis, then loyalties will naturally be focused on the team. When the star hitter in baseball strikes out in the big game, he rarely says, "I let down the league" or "I let down the owners." The typical first response is "I let down my team." Holding the project manager or team leader solely responsible for enforcing accountability is a mistake. It relies on the individual problem-solving and conflict-resolution skills of one person, and it also sets up the possibility of a one-on-one clash, with the offender often claiming, "This isn't about the work, you just don't like me." It's usually easier for all involved to work as a team to strategize about the issue and develop a plan for encouraging, and if necessary enforcing, accountable behavior. I counsel my clients who come to me with this sort of issue to bring the team together, minus the miscreant, and have a facilitated session in which they discuss the problem at hand, the impact on the project, and the possible approaches they could take, all the way from a simple conversation through to the possible need to dismiss the individual from either the project or the firm. By thinking through all the angles and implications, the team often alleviates much of the tension and fear, just by realizing that they indeed have a range of options. The team must also address the contingency aspects of the situation. In other words, what will they do if they lose the services of this individual? How can they protect the project, the client, the team, and the firm from any negative consequences of enforcing accountability?

Finally, they must confront the malefactor—but perhaps confront is not the best word in this situation. The best teams approach these issues from a position of support, coaching, mentoring, and understanding. Perhaps there is a personal issue at home that's distracting the team member. Maybe she really wants to contribute but is over her head and can't admit it. My experience is that many teams become emotionally overwrought over these scenarios and begin to assume bad intent, but bad intent in fact is rare. Usually there is some personal, skill set, or training issue at the heart of the matter. Whatever the case, bad intent or not, the team must be the vehicle for delivering and enforcing the message that unaccountable behavior cheats the client, disrupts the team, has the potential of damaging the firm, and will not be tolerated.

While the team is the messenger in cases of individual accountability, the atmosphere created by firm management must also clearly reinforce this message. I've seen firms that would never tolerate an underachiever in the ranks let senior partners become professional golfers on the company's dime. This is hypocrisy of the highest order, and it destroys any attempts to enforce accountability in the rank and file. I'm not referring to the "rainmaker," who may use golf as a networking opportunity in order to build relationships, but the "no-show" or "special-projects" partner or manager who displays a poor example for the rest of the team. Accountability must be visibly enforced up and down the chain for it to have any credibility.

The other mechanism for enforcing accountability is the performance evaluation. The evaluation process, when used judiciously, can act as a tool of both coaching and discipline. Some organizations err on the side of informality, doing evaluations every once in a while and focusing mostly on the obvious metrics such as utilization and billable revenue. Others err on the side of bureaucracy, going through a very formal MBO (management by objectives) process, but never customizing the consultant's objectives based on that particular consultant's desires, ambitions, and talents. The best evaluation processes are a collaborative effort in which consultants are given the opportunity to set their own objectives, which are then discussed and refined with their managers. Consultants then periodically rate their own achievement against those objectives and set new ones for the next evaluation period. From enforcing this discipline myself in consulting teams I've managed, I've learned a number of interesting lessons. First, consultants have a better understanding of their gaps and developmental challenges than many managers give them credit for. I've been amazed at how often the very issue I've been experiencing with a consultant, whether it's the ability to present to senior managers or write documentation, shows up as a developmental goal in that consultant's self-evaluation. Also, consultants often rate themselves more honestly (and harshly) than we would rate them ourselves. IT consultants have selected a challenging and difficult profession, and they are typically self-motivated and ambitious. They'll often recognize and target their areas for improvement with more insight and candor than their managers will, if we just give them the opportunity.

OPEN BOOK MANAGEMENT

In my training presentations targeted at rookie IT consultants, I advise new recruits that as consultants each of them is a business of one. Each of them, I stress, represents the firm's brand, image, and reputation in every client contact and with every deliverable. To be a true business of one requires more than just the consciousness of oneself as the bearer of the firm's brand, however. It also requires a basic understanding of the fundamental business issues that drive the firm. No consultant can act like a true businessperson without an understanding of basic financial metrics such as utilization, billing rate, and profitability. Consultants, in order to contribute not just as billable bodies but as real associates, need to be brought into the inner circle on decisions regarding client matters and firm development issues. They need open and honest access to the questions and concerns that their management team is confronting. In short, they need to be trusted.

In my recent training engagements, I've done an informal survey by asking my students a simple question: "What is the one thing that annoys you most about the way you're treated at your firm?" The answers have been surprising in terms of the responses and also in the vehemence and consistency of their delivery. If this informal investigation has any validity, then managers of IT consulting firms have a far way to go in openness and in motivation. The answer I hear every time is not about compensation, or training, or assignments. It's about information. Actual responses I've received recently are as follows:

- "They manage us like we're cogs in a machine."
- "They manage us task-by-task and never give us the big picture."

- "They don't think we're smart enough to understand the business issues."
- "They tell us what to do, but never why we're doing it. Why did we take this project over that one, or pursue this client instead of that?"

Over and over again, the folks I'm mentoring tell me that they want more than just a set of technical tasks—*they want to understand the context of the project.* This desire for understanding, for an open-book style of management, is universal in the IT consulting world. On the engagement level, consultants want to understand the firm's strategic intent with each particular client, as well as the business result we're aiming for, both for each client and for the firm. They want to know, out of the mound of RFPs that come in, why the firm selects one to respond to while another is ignored. And it's not just on the engagement level. Team members want, at the very least, to understand the company's direction and strategy, how it's doing, and what the challenges and issues are.

More than that, they want to participate. One of the comments that I consistently hear from consultants is that they can't be creative or express their talents if they're not in the loop. If the firm is struggling financially, not meeting utilization targets, or striving to deepen the relationship with a particular client, team members want to know how they can participate in solving the problem. Most consultants understand that they are the product and that they can have an impact on the firm's prospects through their personal behavior. More importantly, they want to help, and their sense of connection and loyalty to the firm grows in proportion to their efforts, their "skin in the game." I believe that IT services firms can solve a lot of their motivation, retention, and recruiting problems by developing a culture of openness and participation, and then by promoting that as one of their cardinal virtues in the recruiting cycle.

There's been a lot written about open-book organizations, and there are a lot of great references for managers about implementing an open style of management. Consultants, however, are not born understanding the business issues; apart from openness, managers need to mentor and coach their teams so that the information they share has meaning and context. We've discussed in earlier chapters the central metrics by which IT service managers measure the performance of their firms. Consultants, however, are not often versed in the nuances of utilization, rate structures, bench balance, opportunity close rate, or the other fundamental elements of firm performance. The best managers not only coach their teams on appropriate consultative behaviors, but they also train them to understand the inner workings of the firm. Not only does this enrich their connection and loyalty to the firm, but it prepares them to be better firm citizens—and perhaps to take on management roles themselves someday.

Good IT services managers also grant their consultants insight into their target market strategy, helping them understand why one prospect may be a better fit for the firm than another. Technical consultants will often look at prospective projects through a technical lens, wondering (and grousing) about why they're leaving on the table a great opportunity to experience a new technology. It's the responsibility of firm managers to broaden their team's horizons so they understand that there's more to targeting and selecting new prospects than technical "coolness." Once engagements are accepted, managers need to work hard to communicate the business as well as technical goals, so consultants can add value across the board rather than as simply technical hands. They must also help consultants understand the relationship goals for the firm so that they can participate in networking within the client enterprise, representing the firm in a mature and professional manner and reporting back to the firm not only technical but also human and relationship insights into the client company. As we've said before, it's all about trust, and trust is built through confidence given and taken, both outside the firm and within.

COACHING AND MENTORING

We'll talk about consultant development strategies in the next chapter. I want to include coaching and mentoring in this discussion about organizational culture, however, because I see it as a cornerstone of the firm's values. After a long career as a professional, the jobs can sometimes run together and the thrill of a new engagement can seem muted. Partners and managers typically have had careers as practitioners, and they have seen lots of engagements come and go. They often have difficulty getting a charge out of the next project. For senior consultants for whom the thrill is gone, one thing keeps them motivated: the opportunity to groom and develop young talent. While the hundredth data center design may lose its luster, the chance to challenge, coach, and mentor outstanding rookies can be the redeeming factor, and the legacy, of a career. The partners, managers, and "elder statesmen" of the firm often have enormous demands on their time, from networking and selling to speaking and writing, but the responsibility to develop the firm's next generation must be a central element of their duties. Only they have the necessary background and experience to teach their teams the real-world lessons. Only they have the wide range of exposure to every type of client and every type of engagement required to prepare their teams for the challenges they'll face. Senior practitioners who shift their focus from billable hours and endless networking to team mentorship, I've found, often discover a new lease on their professional lives and a new commitment to the firm.

Team members also must take responsibility for coaching and mentoring. Many organizations talk the talk of teamwork, but actually reward and evaluate their staff based solely on individual contribution. This dichotomy often creates a competitive, rather than a cooperative, atmosphere, in which team members keep their best practices and key learnings hidden because they might benefit their competitors in the promotion sweepstakes. The best firms don't just talk about teamwork; they encourage it by evaluating team members not only on their contribution to revenue and sales, but on their development and coaching of their colleagues. Some firms go even further and develop formal mentoring programs that partner experienced practitioners with rookies and then measure the mentor's contribution to the newbie's growth and development. Firms that take coaching and mentoring seriously enough to shake loose a history of internal competitive behavior and focus instead on collaborative team development discover an infinite resource of education and training right under their noses.

ATMOSPHERE

The most amorphous of the cultural elements is atmosphere. From the dress code to the style of celebrating victories, every business develops its own atmosphere that is a reflection of the cumulative sensibility of the entire firm and all its members. While some elements of atmosphere can be permitted to grow organically based on the personalities of the team members, even atmosphere must have some guidance to remain positive and appropriate. Informality of relationships within the firm must never be allowed to degenerate into informality with the process and methodology, for example. Familiarity and banter within the group must never slip into a hostile or sexually charged atmosphere. Most importantly, pride and confidence must never be permitted to deteriorate into an ambiance of arrogance or superiority, as it did in many of the Internet consultancies I discussed earlier.

The best thing an IT services firm manager can do is create a team spirit that embodies excellence, achievement, and mutual support, while at the same time acknowledging that we're in a tough, competitive, and dynamic business that requires constant growth and development. Only by remembering that there's always more to learn and that someone is always sneaking up behind us can we dispel the complacency that has meant death to many promising firms. The firm atmosphere we create is often the clearest and least ambiguous indicator of our own character, personality, and aspirations.

End Notes

1. www.icca.org.
2. www.imc.org. *IMC Code of Ethics.*
3. Humphrey, W. *Managing Technical People.* Englewood Cliffs, NJ: Prentice Hall, 1983.

Consultant Development

chapter EIGHT

When clients ask us to install a new network or develop an application, our mission is clear. When they ask us to help them create an Internet strategy, the end result may be hidden in the fog, but the process of getting from here to there is well-known. But when they ask us to apply "thought leadership," many of us are baffled. What is thought leadership, how do you apply it, and how do you recognize it when it is applied? How do you develop it in your team, and how are you compensated for displaying it to the client? These are common questions I hear from my students and clients all over the world. Their customers, although certain they want and need their consultants to demonstrate thought leadership, are often just as hard-pressed as consultants to characterize it. Like art, they can't define it, but they know it when they see it.

When asked by my students or clients to define thought leadership, I ask them to visualize a doctor who graduated from medical school in 1972. "Whatever they taught me in 1972," says this fictional doctor to her patients, "is what I know. I'm too busy treating patients to read all the medical journals and papers with all the new developments. My field changes too fast! I'll just keep on practicing what I learned in 1972. After all, it was state of the art back then!" "How many of you want this doctor to treat you?" I ask. Not many volunteer. This doctor is displaying the opposite of thought leadership. Rather than taking responsibility for keeping up with all the developments in her field, she's relying on the knowledge she gained decades ago. Rather than scouring the scientific and medical journals for new and innovative developments that could benefit her patients, she's allowed complacency to dull her curiosity and professional development. Unfortunately, many IT consultants and professionals fall into this same trap. They become deep specialists in a current technology, taking courses and obtaining certifications. They go out and build a business around that competency. Then they stop learning. They view their certification or degree as a one-time investment, assuming that it's a meal ticket for eternity, rather than the beginning of a lifetime process.

Professionalism implies professional responsibilities. To command the professional fees we expect and to develop the professional relationships and respect we require to build our IT consulting businesses, we must accept responsibility for continuous professional development, both as individual consultants and as practice leaders. Consultants have a responsibility to take ownership of their own career development, to deepen and refresh their knowledge of their areas of expertise. They also must reach outside the technical disciplines. The core competencies of consultants must include more than technology.

Every consultant, even the most technically adept, should come to the client prepared to apply the latest in management, strategic, and organizational theory in order to present the best possible solutions. He or she must incorporate project skills, business skills, communication skills, and advisory skills. Consultants who remain mired in the intricacies of technology and never wonder how that technology can create business value remain mere technologists and limit their potential and growth, not to mention their billable rates. Those who don't understand the use of project disciplines are doomed to dream up exciting technical solutions that they can never successfully deliver. Those who ignore the importance of communication are destined for a career fraught with missed expectations and misunderstandings. And those who dismiss the importance of advisory skills will never see their careers reach the heights of trust and respect that true counselors and advisors achieve. The capability to disagree constructively with the client, to diplomatically but firmly tell the client that he's going down the wrong path, to firmly uphold the disciplines and methodologies of the firm against the pressures of schedule and budget imposed by clients, all are skills that have nothing to do with technical expertise but everything to do with successful consulting.

Practice managers have continuing education responsibilities as well, in that they have to keep informed of the latest developments in practice management and methodology. Professional services, until recently an underappreciated and understudied branch of business, is now one of the most studied and analyzed sectors of the economy. New works and research are published weekly. Good practice managers also stay current on developments in information technology, as they are often called on to act as the senior member of a sales team or to be the "tie breaker" in a project dispute or conflict. The best practice managers do something more. They act as developmental coaches and mentors to their consultants. They build into their motivational and compensation programs both the time and the incentive for consultants to keep on growing. They build mentoring into their own schedules, and they encourage senior teammates to train and develop their teams. They understand that building a legacy is about more than building the financial equity of a practice: It's about building a cadre of professionals with skills and careers of which they can be proud. On a personal note, I look back with pride at the talented consultants to whose development I've contributed more than the deals I've won or the IT systems I've built. Mentoring a rookie, watching her grow from a technologist to a consultant, and from a consultant to an advisor, is for me the most exhilarating experience in IT practice management.

Practice managers, then, must have a theory of development to guide them and must apply it in a disciplined and caring manner. We must remember that the talented individuals who have chosen to become consultants often do so chiefly because they crave the excitement of continual new challenges. We must remain true to the promises we make in the recruiting cycle of training and development. We must keep on growing our asset base, not just by hiring new consultants but by upgrading and improving the skills of those we've brought onboard. In short, we must make training and development a core competency of the firm. This is the true competitive advantage in professional services, not some slick brochure or some fancy marketing campaign.

What are the elements of a consultant development program? Every practice manager should have a plan for his or her team that includes the following elements:

- Technical training;
- Project skills development;
- Communication and advisory skills development;
- Business skills development;
- Project assignments; and
- Mentoring.

Each of these elements is critical for the development of well-rounded and confident professionals. They aren't meaningful in isolation, however. The most important part of consultant development is that it be viewed as a complete program, rather than simply as isolated training activities. The best practice managers use the review and evaluation process as a chance to understand the developmental needs of every consultant on staff and to create an individual program that fits both the consultant's needs and those of the firm. Consultants may be interested in a particular technology, but curiosity does not make a business model. Practice managers have a responsibility to the firm to ensure that the areas of interest that consultants pursue not only develop them personally but contribute to the growth of the firm and its billable potential. Consultants also are typically drawn to technical areas only and must be coached by their leaders to grow their skills in the non-technical areas outlined above. Finally, programs must be individualized to suit the needs and talents of each consultant. Some consultants will display great potential in the sales area and may be excellent candidates for advanced strategic sales training as well as for presentation and facilitation training. Others may show promise as strategic advisors and may be good candidates for advanced management and organizational development. Practice managers must create a program for each individual that balances his or her desires, strengths, and gaps with the needs of the firm to create a program that grows each teammate while building the practice.

TECHNICAL TRAINING

We don't want to fall into the trap that our fictional doctor has fallen into, of expecting a dose of learning to last a lifetime. Technology changes in our field as fast or faster than in any other, and clients are less likely to be satisfied with yesterday's knowledge. Clients often have technical teams on staff that keep up with the latest in technical advances, and they expect their consultants to be one step ahead. Whether we utilize the technical training and certification programs offered by vendors such as Microsoft and Cisco or the facilities offered by many colleges and universities, technical training is available and easy to find around the world. The challenge to most firms is not availability or consultant interest. Nor is it the cost of the training and associated expenses themselves. It's the opportunity cost.

Taking a team of billable consultants out of the field to attend training means a loss of immediate revenue that many practice managers find difficult to swallow. We know theoretically that we need to keep our teams' skills fresh and current, but every time the right course comes up, we're in the middle of a critical project phase or need to make our quarterly revenue numbers. How do good practice managers balance the needs to deliver on client commitments and to meet financial goals with the necessity of ongoing consultant development? First of all, we do it with planning and scheduling. Scheduling courses and other development opportunities well in advance and incorporating those dates into project schedules and plans is an obvious first step in assuring that client commitments don't derail learning. A strong connection between the sales forecast and the delivery scheduling process is also key, so managers can know in advance when packed schedules might preclude training and when lulls in billable activity might provide opportunities for developmental activities. Finally, discipline is key. Practice managers must be prepared to bite the bullet and take the financial "hit" at the moment, with the faith and understanding that consultant development will pay off in the long run, not only in revenues but in team satisfaction, motivation, and retention.

The IT training field is so rich and full of opportunities that it has even developed its own periodicals. *Certification* magazine, published by Media Tec and available for free to qualified subscribers, is a compendium of the latest offerings in technical training that can be useful to any IT practice manager in planning the technical development program for every team member.

PROJECT SKILLS DEVELOPMENT

Project skills development is also widely available and often is suitable not only for consultants but for managers and practice leaders as well. In my work as an advisor to IT practices, I often find a significant gap in understanding of current project theory among the top echelons as well as in the rank and file. From the intensity of Project Management Institute (PMI) training all the way to the frequent one-day "Project Management for IT" courses that proliferate at the college level, there are lots of opportunities for both managers and consultants to develop those delivery skills that turn their solutions into systems. While PMI certification is not necessary—or even desirable for every consultant—the theories and knowledge that come out of organizations like the PMI and the Software Engineering Institute are a good way to create a solid foundation of project skills.

COMMUNICATION AND ADVISORY SKILLS DEVELOPMENT

There is a common misconception among many technical leaders that communication is an inherent skill, that consultants either are comfortable with communication, presentation, facilitation, and other interactive skills or they are not. Others believe that IT attracts introverts and science-club nerds who will never be able to present themselves as professional advisors. Nothing could be further from the truth. Extroversion is not a necessary attribute in order to become a trusted advisor. In fact, Ford Harding, in his influential book, *Creating Rainmakers,* discovered through a course of interviews and conversations with professionals that most of the best marketers of professional services would categorize themselves as introverts![1] Communication and advisory skills, which include the abilities to influence and persuade clients and to market the benefits of solutions, are skills that can be enhanced both through training and through mentorship and observation. I've known many consultants who started their careers as back-room technicians, awkward and shy in presentations and meetings, who have made the conscious decision and effort to expand their career potential by developing these skills. Everyone I've known who created a comprehensive program, and then followed it with discipline, made tremendous progress in overcoming any doubts, in building self-confidence and fluency, and ultimately in changing his or her career. I also know because I did it myself. Formerly a shy and uncomfortable presenter, I trained myself through reading, research, and practice to the point where I make a living as a professional speaker, trainer, and facilitator.

Communication skills can be taught and learned. Again, there are "soft skills" courses available both in colleges and business schools that aid in the understanding of basic facilitation and presentation techniques. More important than training, however, are mentorship and observation. Experienced presenters and facilitators in your firm must make coaching and mentoring an integral part of their practice and must select and include teammates, not just on their current ability to contribute, but also on their need for opportunities to watch and learn. One day in the facilitation room with a master facilitator, or a seat in the back of the auditorium during a speech or presentation, can be worth weeks in a classroom. I'm not suggesting that classroom work has no value. I'm merely emphasizing the importance of coupling that with real-world experience. Consultants must see master practitioners plying their craft, have a chance to peek behind the scenes and watch them prepare, and then practice their own skills in a supportive setting. Every meeting within the firm can be a chance to develop these skills. The best practice leaders create numerous opportunities for rookies to practice their communication skills, from journal clubs in which members report on their readings in the trade papers to project walkthroughs in which consultants update their teams on engagement status. Supportive and constructive criticism and mentoring can help turn even the shyest technician into a persuasive presenter and communicator, aiding the firm, the individual, and the client immeasurably.

BUSINESS SKILLS DEVELOPMENT

In the previous chapter I discussed the importance of open-book management and of coaching consultants in the fundamentals of the IT services business. This not only aids motivation and retention, but it has a developmental purpose as well. Understanding the fundamentals of our business is, for many consultants, the first step toward an appreciation of larger business issues. Involvement in the struggles and challenges of running the business of which they are a part can provide an impetus toward strategic business thinking for those interested. One of my clients, owner of a small consulting firm, advised his team to think about ways to expand the business into new areas and offered team members the opportunity to start new ventures if they'd present him with a business plan. The response was overwhelming! Many of the consultants, formerly thought of as purely technical resources, displayed an amazing talent for identifying and justifying new business ventures that were complementary to the existing business and that built on the skills and talents of the existing staff to extend the service line. In areas from the creation of new ventures to the application of innovative ideas and strategies to the existing practice, I've seen consultants rise to the challenge of strategic thinking time and again. Practice leaders owe it to the business and to their teams to offer them the chance to sharpen their business skills and contribute in more ways than simply as billable resources.

Again, the courses are out there for everything from management fundamentals to eBusiness strategies, and practice leaders should encourage their teams to make the investment in time to select and attend some of these courses. The simple act of subscribing to some general purpose business magazines in the office and distributing them to the team, or discussing articles you read with the technical team and challenging people to keep up with general business developments, is a meaningful mentoring strategy.

PROJECT ASSIGNMENTS

Many IT services managers take a purely functional view of project scheduling, looking at a list of projects and a list of resources and matching skills and availabilities against assignment openings. This approach disregards one of the most powerful and effective consultant development opportunities in the practice, the chance for consultants to gain on-the-job training by watching, listening, and learning from the best and by solving real client problems under the watchful eye of a veteran. In order to use this technique of consultant development successfully, service managers must balance the needs of the firm, the client, and the team. Clients obviously deserve skilled, experienced professionals to manage their engagements and provide services, while the firm needs a "bullpen" of up-and-coming specialists and advisors to follow in the footsteps of the veterans as they move up or move on. Consultants have to experience the techniques, methods, and personal problem-solving styles of firm veterans so they can understand that there are many ways to solve a problem and add value for clients and so that they can gain insight into the personal "best practices" of a range of experienced practitioners.

In the consulting teams I've run, I review every client engagement with an eye toward the developmental opportunities it presents. Of course, I apply the most experienced and appropriate specialists available to every project, but I also review the scope of work and consider the prospects for giving rookies the chance to, for instance, run a small facilitated session or make a short presentation to a client group. I think about the problems and challenges that might come up and consider assigning a promising junior consultant to deal with those issues. In short, I attempt to turn every engagement into an opportunity for real-world experience and growth.

This approach to development requires some finesse. Clients have to be assured that we're not pulling a "bait-and-switch" routine on them, showing them the veterans in the sales cycle and then loading them up with inexperienced rookies once the meter starts running. This is an area of high sensitivity for many clients, who have experienced this tactic from some of the larger firms for years. My approach to this is a clear and honest recital of my intent from the beginning. I explain to the client that the engagement will be staffed with a mix of veterans and young talent, that they will be billed appropriately based on the experience level of the resource, and that all work will be reviewed and approved by a senior practitioner. More importantly, I sell them on the value of developing a cadre of professionals who are familiar with their account and their industry. It's the practice manager's responsibility to help clients understand the benefits to them, as well as to the firm, of building a bench of strong specialists that can advise them from a foundation of knowledge, organizational awareness, and relationship experience.

For many firms, the scheduling system is the centerpiece of their team development efforts. In his fundamental work, *Managing the Professional Service Firm,* David Maister states, "Many firms have no formal training and development program. Often, the pattern of work assignments is the program—no other formal administrative procedures exist to influence the development of human capital."[2] Maister goes on to describe the importance of developing a complete and tightly integrated scheduling system that considers the client's need for experience and effective service, the firm's need for profitability and staff satisfaction and growth, and the individual consultant's need for hands-on learning and mentoring. As noted before, Maister's work is required reading for any IT services manager, and his material on scheduling provides a foundation of techniques for turning the mundane task of resource scheduling into a stellar opportunity for growth and motivation.

MENTORING

All of the developmental techniques described above center on one key philosophy—a philosophy of mentoring. While there are schools and courses with offerings in all of these knowledge areas, only mentoring can develop a firm-wide set of behaviors, ethics, and cultural norms that combine to create a culture of client service. Only the dedication of the firm's managers, practice leaders, and senior practitioners to coaching and development, and the commitment of the time and resources required, can create an environment that attracts and retains the best and the brightest. While it's often said that there is only one asset in the professional services firm—the human asset—actually there is one other. It's the shared experience of the firm. The lessons learned, the lore and anecdotes, the client relationships, the practices and methodologies that identify the firm to itself make every team member feel a part of something unique and special. This communal history is the central element of culture and team spirit. The strongest firms, just like the strongest sports teams, have an indefinable bond that is the result of pride and common values. These feelings cannot be taught in school. They only come from the experience of working through challenges together, of facing difficult odds and overcoming them together, of coaching, mentoring, and supporting one another and so building a reservoir of fidelity and trust.

Managers, practice leaders, and senior practitioners must lead the way by building mentorship into the formal evaluation program and by incorporating it in their daily lives. Rather than remaining focused solely on their administrative, sales, and billable client activities, practice leaders must lead by example. They must demonstrate to the rest of the firm that coaching is the highest form of service by setting aside some of their valuable time for personal, one-on-one mentoring and development. By passing on not just the practices and methodologies, but the tales, anecdotes, and legends of the firm, they create a common history that binds every new recruit to the firm. From Goldman Sachs to IBM to Microsoft, the high performing firms have more in common than a set of procedures. They have a history and mythology that engenders pride and performance.

Many firms assign a mentor to every new recruit and evaluate that assigned individual partly on his or her success and dedication to the mentoring responsibilities. This arrangement works best when the assigned mentor is totally outside the new recruit's chain of command, so that pressures of review, evaluation, and promotion do not color or inhibit the coaching process. Rookies should be able to approach their mentors with any issue, from the professional to the personal (as it relates to job performance), and should have no concern that those conversations will impact their standing in the firm in any way. Other firms will assign utilization ratios to senior consultants that target some percentage of their time to mentoring and staff development activities, such as internal training. Utilization targets that include both time for self-development, such as formal training or self-learning, as well as time for mentoring and coaching, send the message that billability is not the only goal. The power of this message can't be overestimated. Over and over I have consultants approach me and complain that, to their managers, they are just billing machines. This "cash-cow" approach to utilization may generate the most revenue in the short term, but in the long run it does not build the firm, but tears it down by provoking endless attrition, recruiting, and repair activities.

These formal mentoring activities are an important part of the puzzle, but they are only one piece. More influential by far are the informal elements, often known by the acronym "MBWA" (management by walking around), the practice manager's greatest tool in the coaching process. Informal visits, in which the senior practitioner or manager drops by a consultant's desk and inquires about the latest project, are the most effective way of getting to know individual consultants and of offering developmental guidance in an unthreatening and supportive manner. By gently leading consultants to conclusions, rather than giving them directions, coaches can influence the behavior and development of rookies and at the same time send a message of caring and personal interest. By subtly focusing novices on effective tools and techniques, leaders can enhance the skills of individuals and benefit the firm and the client at the same time. By relating anecdotes and personal stories, coaches reassure neophytes that we all have gone through the same struggles and that success is possible even when the going is tough. A little firmness can also be an important element of a personal coaching session, refocusing beginning consultants on the need for discipline and efficiency when providing professional services to demanding (and cost-conscious) clients.

Every consultant lucky enough to have a good coaching experience remembers it throughout his or her career. Just like that chance encounter with a great teacher that changes your life, the appearance of a true coach can invigorate and energize. Talented practitioners perform best with guidance, and experienced veterans are the best source of that guidance. Simply put, that's what leadership is about.

End Notes

1. Harding, F. *Creating Rainmakers.* Holbrook, MA: Adams Media, 1998.
2. Maister, D. *Managing the Professional Service Firm.* New York: The Free Press, 1993.

Growing and Improving the Firm

chapter **NINE**

GROWING THE FIRM

Is growth an imperative? National economies that stop growing slip into recession and risk plunging into insolvency and decline. Is it so with firms as well? Or can firms find an ideal size and maintain that level indefinitely, continuing to provide excellent service to a select group of clients with a select team of consultants? As with most of the questions we've tried to resolve in this book, the answer is, "It depends." It depends on the ambitions and aspirations of the firm's founders, managers, and leaders. It depends on the desires of the team. It depends on the strategies and markets the firm has decided to pursue. And, of course, it depends on the external economic and competitive environment.

Growth has its advantages. Founders wish to build equity and wealth by expanding into new geographic markets and industries. Professionals crave new challenges and new opportunities. New segments, markets, and technologies beckon every day, summoning us to try new approaches and to claim our piece of the pie. As we reach maturity in our processes and methodologies and gain confidence in our ability to sell and deliver projects, the temptation to reach out to new markets is enticing. IT services firms sometimes open satellite offices in order to provide local services to their multi-location clients and end up with a worldwide presence. The examples of successful growth in professional services firms abound, from the Cinderella stories of Ross Perot's EDS and Perot Systems to the hundreds of small boutique shops that have become regional powers, leaving no question that, despite the challenges, successful expansion is possible and profitable.

Yet growth has its downside as well. Many firms have overextended themselves out of business. The eConsultancies of the Internet era are exemplars of the strains and difficulties of broadening scale in the flush of competitive success. The challenges of managing a far-flung empire, especially in a downturn, can quickly overwhelm the most adept managers (never mind a bunch of "whiz kids" with limited practical experience). The eConsultants aren't the only ones who've discovered the trials of expansion. From the resellers-turned-consultants to the major IT firms, there are stories galore of cultural missteps, management span-of-control issues, and simple recruiting and retention problems that have caused many firms to expand and then contract in rapid order, causing loss of focus and wasted time and money. Compaq's problems absorbing Digital Equipment, outlined earlier, illustrate that even a policy of growth by acquisition has its challenges. Anyone who watches the events on Wall Street knows that expansion is often seen by analysts as a negative, depressing the stock price and triggering analyst downgrades. Analysts know from experience that expansion, whether by acquisition or internal hyper-growth, presents tests and trials that only the most adroit and practiced managers can navigate.

I've seen many single-location IT service shops experience a similar growth scenario. The single shop has grown to the maximum size that its local sales capabilities and client base can support, yet the founders and practice leaders believe there is market potential for its specialty or approach in other markets. The firm opens another shop across town or across the country, applying its existing methodologies and practices to the new location. The new office does well at first, picking up some plum accounts based on its reputation in the original location or on its specialized capabilities. Then some issues begin to emerge. The industry segments that the firm was comfortable doing business with at the original site don't exist in the new location. The vertical market expertise that the firm counted on for competitive advantage doesn't work when the local industrial mix is different. The sales tactics and techniques that were so successful at home don't seem to resonate as well in the new geography. The local managers, who had unlimited confidence in their ability to lead and motivate, are finding the challenges of long-distance management daunting. The competitors in the new location seem to be intent on driving the interloper out, underbidding on every deal even at the cost of their profitability just to retain their existing market share. The economies of scale that the founders envisioned, in which existing methods and practices would not need to be reinvented, are not necessarily being realized as the local team must modify methods and practices on the fly as they attempt to adapt to local conditions, thus introducing inconsistencies and quality control problems. In short, expansion turns out not to be as easy as it looked.

Managing Growth

How do practice managers prudently weigh the pros and cons of growth, and what are the formulas for successful growth of the practice? What can we learn from the successful growth strategies of other professional services firms, and what mistakes can we avoid? How do we know when we've reached the right size for the firm, whether that means we remain a small local shop or open offices around the world? Let's explore the options and see how other firms manage their growth paths.

Expansion must be driven strategically rather than tactically. Assuming that because the offerings in the original office gained some traction in the local marketplace another office will do the same is shallow thinking that invites failure. Like the opening of any new business, expansion must be based on a solid foundation of research and must be entered into after a careful risk analysis and market study. Firms that expand into new territories and find that the business climate or industrial base doesn't support their offerings are victims of their own lack of planning. As we discussed earlier, the tools for analysis, from the U.S. Economic Census to the local business newspapers, are there for those who seek them. Firms that blindly rush into new ventures without the proper preparation shouldn't be surprised to find that conditions vary. Competitive analysis must also be a central element of any expansion program. As obvious as this seems, I've encountered many firms that will find, for instance, that their focus on methodology, which worked so well competitively in Peoria, grants no competitive advantage in Chicago, where every firm has a strong set of processes. New entrants into any market must also prepare for the fact that existing competitors will fight hard to maintain their dominance and must prepare a sufficient war chest to survive the initial onslaught until their message picks up steam. Again, this should be apparent, but I've seen many growing firms surprised by the tenacity of incumbents. They often are forced to turn and run, losing their investment in a new territory because they don't have the capital to stick it out when competitors fight to maintain their positions.

The issue of remote management and of gaining efficiencies of scale are more complex. There is an inherent tension between the drive to expand and the need for local control. Expanding firms seek to gain efficiencies by reapplying the methodologies and techniques that they have painstakingly (and expensively) developed over time. On the other hand, local branches need the freedom to adapt to local conditions. David Maister refers to this dilemma as the "local value" issue.[1] I have experienced this quandary first-hand as a consulting services manager for a national network integration firm. After spending years migrating from selling PC hardware in a so-called "value-added reseller" model, the firm decided to become an IT services firm and spent millions developing service standards, methodologies, and practices. When we opened new regional offices across the United States, we found that the first thing they did was discard our hard-earned processes and reinvent their own methods and techniques from scratch. Frustrated at first, we learned that only by allowing the local practitioners to participate in the development of their approach could we create consensus and consent. We also learned again that stakeholders actually do have inside knowledge and that by allowing our local teams to adapt practices to conform to the reality on the ground, we developed stronger and more appropriate methodologies.

Acknowledging this, however, doesn't solve the problems it creates. Inconsistent methodologies across the multi-location firm create management and quality issues. The dream of one consistent national presence disintegrates when every local branch acts as its own business, disregarding the established knowledge and recreating every offering. The marketing appeal of global coverage, which many firms use to appeal to their multi-location clients, turns out to be much harder to implement than it is to advertise. Why should the manager in Chicago apply his best resources to my Miami-based customer, when he has his own clients to worry about? Why should the manager in New York assign her top project manager to my project based in Kansas City, at Kansas City rates, when she can get New York rates, typically 30 to 50 percent higher, for the same resource with her New York clientele? These issues, seemingly trivial, in fact conspire to explode the myth of the "one-stop shop" and confirm Maister's contention that multi-location professional service firms are often just local businesses that share a brand name.

Firm managers must decide whether they are creating a centralized firm with dependent branches, to be managed and controlled by the central office, or they are creating a consortium of independent entities with a common brand. The former enforces discipline and consistency at the expense of local autonomy and adaptability, while the later permits local variations but imposes real challenges to uniformity and quality control. Firms need to take a look at their strategic thrust and determine which model suits their business and which challenges their team is up to handling. There's no blanket answer to this—only the choice of which set of problems the firm can navigate successfully.

The preceding discussion may make it seem as if growth is always difficult or impossible. In fact, growth presents firms with a creative challenge. Many firms, rather than expanding geographically, have decided to add new offerings or practice areas. One firm I know went from installing accounting systems to assisting clients in recovering unpaid accounts, based on the insight they gained into deficiencies of their clients' financial systems. A hospital IT firm I advise added a medical records scanning service to its offerings after noticing that its clients were drowning in patient paperwork. Another firm saw so many clients with undocumented IT systems that it developed a practice to perform system studies and create network maps and schematics. IT firms have seized opportunities to add value for their clients and add revenue to the firm, with offerings ranging from security consulting to contingency planning to outsourcing, without the need to expand into different geographies. This type of growth is often more organic and natural than geographic expansion, as it occurs incrementally and is based on real needs observed by consultants during actual engagements. It's often easier to get off the ground, as it is connected to current engagements and relationships, and it can often be sold as expansion work on existing contracts.

Another organic approach to growth is common in partner-based practices like law and accountancy. Promising practitioners, as they mature and display leadership capabilities, are given the chance to grow a small practice "cell" around their competency. For instance, a lawyer who has displayed the ability to sell and manage merger and acquisition work may be given the chance to build a small practice around that specialty, hiring or recruiting internally and growing the cell until it becomes too large for her to manage, at which time it spawns another cell managed by her most promising teammate. This cell-based growth model has significant advantages, as it provides not only a natural revenue expansion opportunity, but the chance for meaningful personal growth and development for the most promising members of the firm. This cell-based growth structure, often called a "principal-led" model, applies a sort of natural selection to the growth program, growing only as fast as talented and promising leaders and practice areas emerge.

Finally, for many firms the best approach is no growth at all. There is nothing inherent in the business model of professional service firms that requires growth to survive, as evidenced by the thousands of small doctor's offices and dental clinics that go on for decades with the same small team of practitioners happily providing service to the same neighborhood. The no-growth option is in fact being embraced by many of my clients, especially some who had previously jumped at the chance to expand only to find that the challenges and headaches were not worth the cost. Limited growth can be a powerful impetus to continued internal improvement and development and can be a great way to conserve energy that can be applied to perfecting client services and building mature consulting professionals. The client and team intimacy and camaraderie that limited growth firms achieve often makes them more fun, more comfortable, and ultimately more rewarding than their high-growth colleagues. The promise of expanding equity and wealth may not be as great, but the personal growth and development often compensate managers and team members more deeply than money.

IMPROVING THE FIRM

Every well-designed system is a loop. Not only do systems need to be planned, designed, and implemented, but they also must have monitoring functions built in. And the results of that monitoring must be analyzed and used to improve the system. This is the essence of quality control in a manufacturing environment. Whether it's random sampling or constant operational monitoring, manufacturers that value excellence have built measurement, analysis, and improvement into their processes, and as a result the quality of everyday products has increased enormously in the last twenty years.

The same feedback loop should be utilized in the IT services business. Clients should have an opportunity to review our performance and express their level of satisfaction and their recommendations for improvement. Our methodologies must also have feedback mechanisms so that we can gauge our level of compliance with the structures and processes we've put in place and continue to refine and improve them so they deliver the best results for our clients and our teams. From the client satisfaction meeting to the post-project review, feedback must be an integral part of our approach. It should test not only the technical elements of our delivery, but the perceptual components as well, from both the external and internal perspectives. Most importantly of all, we must be ready to receive criticism in an open and constructive manner, and we must be prepared to act on the results.

Client Feedback

Many of my clients use customer satisfaction surveys as a regular component of their engagement strategies. Unfortunately, however, in many cases they are cosmetic only, designed to give the customer the impression that the firm cares about the client experience. Frequently they are seen as an element of a marketing program, rather than as a crucial part of the services delivery function. In many cases, the feedback gathered from clients goes to the sales or marketing department, never making its way to the team that delivers services and enforces the firm's methodologies. Rather than reviewing client comments and deciding to improve areas requiring repair, these firms use customer comments to refine their marketing message. In other words, if clients tell them they value good status reporting, these firms change their marketing message to say they provide great status reporting, rather than actually improving their reporting processes. This is dishonest in multiple dimensions. Clients fill out survey forms and give honest feedback thinking that the firm will take those remarks seriously and act on them. They don't take their valuable time to respond to questionnaires in order to be marketed to more efficiently. Of course, the firms that take this approach also rob themselves of one of their most important assets, the real-world experience of their clients and its potential to perfect their processes and methodologies. As W. Edwards Deming and Joseph Juran, leaders of the quality movement, taught us, defects are diamonds, giving us the priceless opportunity to improve and perfect our systems. Wasting them by either ignoring them or using them as marketing ploys is counterproductive and foolish.

Client feedback is usually collected by the sales organization, and that is as it should be. The sales team is the primary owner of the customer relationship in most firms and can usually get the attention and cooperation of the client sponsors by helping them understand the mutual value of a feedback process. Importantly, the assigned sales representative is slightly removed from the delivery team, thus providing the client with the ability to criticize and suggest improvements without having to confront the actual provider of services, avoiding a potentially uncomfortable and inhibiting experience. Firm managers or practice leaders are sometimes the gatherers of this information rather than sales, and this is also appropriate in some circumstances. In some firms, sales reps are more intimately involved in the delivery process, often helping the technical team navigate through difficult political or organizational issues, and their involvement in the feedback process may hamper the client's frankness. In these cases the involvement of a partner, manager, or practice leader can send a positive message to the client, stating that the firm is interested in honest feedback on all elements and all players in the engagement.

There are a wealth of excellent customer survey tools available. David Maister offers an excellent example in his book, *Managing the Professional Service Firm*, and a quick review of it presents us with some important insights. Not a single one of the questions he presents is technical. The questions he provides—such as "Are we accessible?" and "Are our communications free of jargon?"—are all about the customer experience. They deal with process issues, querying the client's perception of the firm's ability to keep them informed, educated, and involved. This is simply another illustration of the fact that technical superiority is only one small component of a first-class client experience.

There are also many commercial firms that specialize in customer feedback systems. These firms concentrate on creating customized client feedback systems that are highly targeted and specific to each firm's core business and target market and that are often specifically designed to query different individuals within the client firm. For IT services firms, this approach can be meaningful, as the CEO may have a completely different set of measurement criteria than the IT manager or the department head, and each of their perspectives on our performance can help us improve. The key point is that it's incumbent on IT service managers to develop a feedback process that actually effects the firm's delivery system and brings every complaint, compliment, and criticism into the loop, where it can highlight our failings and trigger improvement.

Process Review

Client feedback is critical, but it isn't the only element of a good feedback system. The experiences and comments of our delivery team are also crucial elements of a continuous improvement program. Post-project reviews often degenerate into blame-fests when projects go badly, or become beer blasts when things go well. They are, however, rarely mined for their valuable insights into the strengths and weaknesses of the firm's processes. Good practice managers, of course, should encourage celebration and recognition and discourage blame and recrimination, but they must do more. They must facilitate the unearthing of flaws and defects in the methodology and ruthlessly improve the process at every opportunity. Every methodology should be a dynamic and evolving thing, absorbing the lessons of every engagement in a constant progression toward perfection. Only by debriefing the team, including subcontractors, vendors, and other members of the delivery squad, and by digging out the problems and issues can practice managers keep building their competitive advantage by developing a precision delivery mechanism. The issues log, the change control record, and the history of emails and other communications can also be valuable sources of insight into issues and challenges that should be discussed. The process of examination also encourages ownership of the methodology by the team, an important psychological benefit. Rather than needing to be bludgeoned into complying with the processes and procedures, teams that feel ownership comply with the processes because they believe in them, they developed them, and they lived through the problems that process flaws can create.

What Not to Do

Finally, I'll recount a negative experience I had in the feedback process to demonstrate an important point. As a young consultant, I was assigned to an important account by a new manager for my firm. After I had served in a demanding and politically sensitive role for about six months, my manager asked me to set up a meeting with my client sponsor for a feedback session. My manager, as inexperienced and green in his management responsibilities as I was in my consulting role, went through the prepared questionnaire with the client, with me sitting in the room. My presence was clearly coloring the client's response, so I offered to step out for a moment, an offer the client graciously accepted, asking me to give him ten minutes alone with my manager. After the time was up, I stepped back in, and my manager greeted me with a smile and informed me that my sponsor had given me a glowing review. My manager then turned to the sponsor and said, "Since you agree that Rick has provided great value for your firm, I'd like to chat with you about an increase in his billing rate." The client's face froze, and the tone in the room changed immediately. Within one minute the audience was over, with my manager slinking toward the door. I never wanted to become invisible more ardently than I did at that moment.

By introducing the sales process into the feedback system, my manager had violated every rule of appropriate client interaction. The client felt as if he'd been hoodwinked into a feedback session, only to be solicited for more money. His honest appraisal became a weapon to be used against him to extract more dollars. It took me weeks to regain the client's trust, as he saw me as an accomplice in setting him up for an awkward and inappropriate use of his time.

The point of this story should be clear. The feedback process is not an excuse to jack up rates and it must be completely separate from any sales or marketing activity in order to be sincere. Any attempt to tie results of the feedback system to selling, marketing, or rate enhancement is a corruption of the system and is guaranteed to backfire.

Firms that grow judiciously, that scrupulously apply a feedback and improvement mechanism, and that allow their teams and clients to impact their methodologies in a positive manner have a terrific opportunity to build a practice that grows better all the time and that deepens its relationships with its customers and its staff.

End Note

1. Maister, D. *Mastering the Professional Service Firm.* New York: The Free Press, 1992.

Conclusion

chapter **TEN**

The creation of a successful IT services firm requires drive, discipline, determination, and talent. Recent experience has demonstrated that, while opportunities to succeed emerge daily, so also do opportunities to fail spectacularly and publicly. Good IT services managers combine an entrepreneurial zeal with a strategic sense, a desire to build a legacy of strong relationships and successful engagements, and an ambition to be the vehicle for growing and developing superior consultants and advisors. The advice and comments in this book are based on the errors, mistakes, and missteps I've made over my career and the lessons I've learned by righting those wrongs and repairing those faults. Many of the practices I describe here have proven themselves, both in the practices I've personally built and managed and in the companies I've advised and coached. Their disciplined application, and the application of the techniques advocated by other masters of the professional service practice such as David Maister, Elaine Biech, and Andrew Sobel, will prepare IT service managers and entrepreneurs to fulfill their dreams and create firms of lasting value. The rest is up to you.

BIBLIOGRAPHY

Ackoff, R. (1981). *Creating the corporate future.* New York: John Wiley & Sons.

Ashford, M. (1998). *Con tricks: The shadowy world of management consultancy.* London: Simon & Schuster.

Beckwith, H. (2000). *The invisible touch.* New York: Warner Books.

Bens, I. (2000). *Facilitating with ease.* San Francisco, CA: Jossey-Bass/Pfeiffer.

Biech, E. (1999). *The business of consulting.* San Francisco, CA: Jossey Bass/Pfeiffer.

Biech, E., & Swindling, L.B. (2000). *The consultant's legal guide.* San Francisco, CA: Jossey-Bass/Pfeiffer.

Boehm, B. (2000). Software engineering cost models and estimation techniques: A comparative study, in Volume 9: Comparative studies of engineering approaches for software engineering, *Annals of Software Engineering.* Amsterdam: The Netherlands: Baltzer Science Publishers.

Boslet, M. (2001, June 4). Big Blue after Lou. *The Industry Standard.*

Brooks, F. (1995, July). *The mythical man-month* (2nd ed.). Reading, MA: Addison-Wesley.

Burlton, R. (1992, December) Managing a RAD project: Critical factors for success. *American Programmer.*

Cherry Tree & Company. (1998, May). *IT services.*

Cherry Tree & Company. (2000, September). *2nd generation ASPs*

Constantine, L. (1967). *Concepts in program design.* Cambridge, MA: Information and Systems Press.

Curtis, B., Hefley, W.E., & Miller, S. *The people capability maturity model.* Pittsburgh, PA: Software Engineering Institute of Carnegie Mellon University. Available: www.sei.cmu.edu/cmm-p/.

DeMarco, T. (1999, February). *Peopleware: Productive projects and teams* (2nd ed.) New York: Dorset House.

Eptish, J. (2001). *Book business: Publishing, past, present, and future.* New York: W.W. Norton.

Freedman, R. (2001, July 17). Has the ASP market gone vertical? Available: www.techrepublic.com.

Freedman, R. (2001, February 6). Listen more and talk less. Available: techrepublic.com.

Freedman, R. (2001, June 18). Quality is key to ongoing relationships. Available: techrepublic.com.

Goodstein, L.D., Nolan, T.M., & Pfeiffer, J.W. (1993). *Applied strategic planning.* New York: McGraw-Hill.

Gratch, A. (1985, February 10). Tamed rebels make good managers. *The New York Times.*

Hamel, G. (2000). *Leading the revolution.* Cambridge, MA: Harvard Business School Press.

Heskett, J., Sasser, W., & Schlesinger, L. (1997). *The service profit chain.* New York: The Free Press.

Hetzel, B. (1993). *Making software measurement work: Building an effective measurement program.* New York: John Wiley & Sons.

Humphrey, W. (1987). *Managing for innovation: Leading technical people.* Reading, MA: Addison-Wesley.

Humphrey, W. (1997). *Managing technical people.* Reading, MA: Addison-Wesley.

Johnson, J., Boucher, K.D., Connors, K., & Robinson, J. (2001, February/March). Collaborating on project success. *Software Magazine.*

Jones, C. (1994, June). Revitalizing software project management. *American Programmer.*

Kotter, J., & Heskett, J. (1992). *Corporate culture and performance.* New York: The Free Press.

Lacity, M., & Hirscheim, R. (1993). *Information systems outsourcing: Myths, metaphors, and realities.* Chichester, England: John Wiley & Sons.

Maister, D. (1993). *Managing the professional service firm.* New York: The Free Press.

Maister, D. (2001). *Practice what you preach.* New York: The Free Press.

McDougall, P. (2001, July 2). One on one with Capellas. *Information Week.*

Metzger, P. (1981). *Managing a programming project.* Englewood Cliffs, NJ: Prentice Hall.

Ogilvy, D. (1987). *Ogilvy on advertising.* New York: Vintage Books.

O'Shea, J., & Madigan, C. (1997). *Dangerous company: The consulting powerhouses and the business they save and ruin.* New York: Times Business.

Peters, T. (1999). *The professional service firm 50.* New York: Borzoi Books.

Rees, F. (1998). *The facilitator excellence handbook.* San Francisco, CA: Jossey-Bass/Pfeiffer.

Rokeach, M. (1973). *The nature of human values.* New York: The Free Press.

Ruhl, J. (1997). *The computer consultant's guide.* New York: John Wiley & Sons.

Scott, M.C. (1998). *The intellect industry.* New York: John Wiley & Sons.

Scully, J. (1987). *Odyssey: Pepsi to Apple, a journey of adventure, ideas, and the future.* New York: Harper & Row.

Sobel, A., & Sheth, J. (2000). *Clients for life.* New York: Simon & Schuster.

The greatest CEOs in history. (1999, December). *Fortune.*

The Standish Group. (1995). *Chaos study.* Available: www.standish.com.

The Standish Group. (2001). *CHAOS 2001.* Available: www.standish.com.

The Outsourcing Institute and Dun & Bradstreet. (2000). *The 2000 Outsourcing Index.* Available: www.outsourcing.com.

Troy, L. (2001). *Almanac of business and industrial financial ratios.* Englewood Cliffs, NJ: Prentice Hall.

Weber, J. (2001, May 28). The fall and rise of IBM. *The Industry Standard.*

Weiss, A. (1997). *Million dollar consulting.* New York: McGraw-Hill.

Winthrop, P., & Hoffman, C.J. (2000, March). *IDC's IT services segmentation: Definitions and methodology.*

Wirth, N. (1971, April). Program development by stepwise refinement. *Communications of the ACM.*

Yourden, E. (1975). *Techniques of program structure and design.* Englewood Cliffs, NJ: Prentice Hall.

ABOUT THE AUTHOR

Rick Freedman is an author, journalist, consultant, and trainer. His previous books—*The IT Consultant* and *The eConsultant*—have achieved worldwide readership. Rick writes the "Consultant Master Class" column for TechRepublic.com, the IT professional web community, and the "Minding Your Business" column for *IT Contractor* magazine. He teaches IT project management, IT consulting, and telecommunications technology courses at the college level at various institutions in the United States. Rick is the founder and CEO of Consulting Strategies, Inc., and in the last year has trained and consulted for global IT firms across the United States and in the United Kingdom, Germany, India, Japan, and China.

Reach Rick at Rick@Consulting-Strategies.com.

INDEX

A

B

C

D

E

F

J

K

L

M

N

O

P

Q

R

S

T

U

V

W

Y

CPSIA information can be obtained at www.ICGtesting.com
Printed in the USA
266418BV00003B/17/A

9 780787 955151